W9-BVK-327

RETURNING TO SILENCE

Zen Practice in Daily Life

Dainin Katagiri

EDITED BY
YŪKŌ CONNIFF & WILLA HATHAWAY

SHAMBHALA
Boston & London
1988

SHAMBHALA PUBLICATIONS, INC.
HORTICULTURAL HALL
300 MASSACHUSETTS AVENUE
BOSTON, MASSACHUSETTS 02115

9 8 7 6 5 4 3 2 1

FIRST EDITION

Printed in the United States of America

Distributed in the United States by Random House and in Canada by Random House of Canada Ltd.

Library of Congress Cataloging-in-Publication Data
Katagiri, Dainin, 1928-
  Returning to silence.
  Bibliography: p.
  1. Religious life—Zen Buddhism.   2. Sōtōshū—Doctrines.   I. Conniff, Yūkō.   II. Hathaway, Willa.
III. Title.
BQ9286.K37 1988   294.3'4448   87-28844
ISBN 0-87773-431-3 (pbk.)

The quotation on pp. 69–70 is from Irving Babbitt, trans., *The Dhammapada*. Copyright 1936 by Edward S. Babbitt and Esther B. Howe. Reprinted by permission of New Directions Publishing Corporation.

Contents

FOREWORD   ix

ACKNOWLEDGMENTS   xiii

Zen in Daily Life

Silence   *1*

Buddha Is Your Daily Life   *9*

Buddha-Nature Is Impermanence   *9*

Serenity and Tranquillity   *13*

Peace   *15*

Singsapa Leaves   *18*

Casting a Pebble into the Ocean   *24*

Burning the Flame of Life   *27*

Nonthinking   *27*

Mindfulness As the Middle Way   *28*

Thirsting Desire   *30*

One Finger   *34*

Returning to Silence   *39*

Sanzen Is Zazen   *44*

Emptiness   *49*

Buddha-Life   *54*

Knowing   *57*

Intimacy   *59*

Touching the Heart Strings   *62*

Breeze in the Sumi Painting   *63*

Entrance to the Buddha Way

All Beings Are Buddha   *67*

Repentance   *71*

The Triple Treasure   *78*
The Three Collective Pure Precepts   *88*
The Ten Prohibitory Precepts   *91*

Buddhist Faith and Practice

Right Zazen   *97*
Right Faith   *100*
Right Teacher   *108*
To Live Is Just to Live   *115*
Clarity and Purity   *129*
Understanding Life and Death   *132*
The Ten Steps of Faith   *138*

Commentary on "The Bodhisattva's Four Methods of Guidance"

Giving   *145*
Kind Speech   *159*
Beneficial Action   *164*
Identity Action   *170*

Notes   *175*
Glossary   *179*
Index   *189*

Foreword

Dainin Katagiri Roshi "returns to silence," and he speaks. He is one of America's great Zen masters, and he dares to begin his beautiful work, "When we think . . ."

Katagiri Roshi is my friend. He likes me. I like him. We look at each other and feel rested, each seeing how tired the other is, sharing determination. We must always try to "accept all sentient beings as the contents of our life."

When I am with Katagiri, I feel as I used to when I was with my late Dharma father, great Geshe Wangyal (whom I mention for a purpose, for the sake of fullness, to hold nothing back), and as I do when I am with some lama friends. Cheerful and content, but a bit on edge, as if many more people were there with us.

When I am with His Holiness the Dalai Lama, I feel as if at least the six million Tibetans were with us in the room, and around them inconceivable multitudes of feeling beings. When I am with Katagiri Roshi, I feel the hundreds of millions of Japan—not just Japan of this moment, but Japan as it has grown over a millennium. The people of Basho's green leaf floating, the delicate people teeming on the broad green leaf in the bright sun of Vairocana's mirror of form.

And woven between us all are so many peoples in between, especially peoples of the snowy northlands—Yakut, Buryat, Inuit, Tlingit, down to the earthy Winnebago and Ojibwa of Katagiri's Minnesota woods. All sentient beings. All feeling beings. Feelings are inconceivable.

I am honored to introduce Katagiri's deep and beautiful *shakuhachi* speech. It took me too long to read it. I still have not read every word. It is not a book to "get through." It is a book to live in. Many books are read in pausing from life, when you take some time off, when you escape, put everything on hold. This book is such; when you live in it you are more outside it, more in life. Read it a little and keep it near your places. Let it be a friend. Let it help you to keep the trivia in perspective.

From the very beginning, the book corners you. Katagiri Roshi plainly tells us: "The opportunity to experience real silence occurs when we have been driven into a corner and simply cannot move an inch." And he advises wisely that it only takes transcending desire to turn despair at being cornered into real silence, Buddha silence, the "total manifestation of our whole personality."

What a book. What a great gift. To open to us our corner. To show us how being absolutely trapped is the total freedom of being with all beings. Katagiri Roshi can do this because he speaks without budging from such a corner, he speaks in the totality of such silence. He and the corner and his words and the silence are among the dimensions of the book. Its cover opens and its inconceivability is accessed in our eye and brain and heart, and our mind and the book and Katagiri Roshi and boundless crying and laughing Buddhas are all together in the bliss dimensions.

Of course, not one specific detail is obliterated. The bliss dimension is undiluted clarity and exquisite sensitivity. We are gripped when we share that dimension with an American pilot of the great Pacific War, parachuting into Japan and injuring himself. We become the Japanese medic Senri Uyeno who sought to help him, against orders, but ultimately was falsely accused of killing him, and was executed for this deed he did not commit. We become the poem he wrote before his death. When he says ". . . putting myself in another's place without flinching, no matter how hard and heart rending it is to live," we are gratefully cornered.

"Let's find happiness by ourselves. / Within silver tears like pearls and laughter as the sun, / let's keep walking ahead each day." Katagiri Roshi is generous, too; he lets us all be with this awesome poet, find this stunning poetry in the mouth of a supposed war criminal of the grisly past. A man whose death was a wound between us, America and Japan. Even on the outermost level of this completeness, there is a shining resurrection from that death.

While it could be ordered any way, every word and phrase in the jewel dimension, the book is artfully arranged. It begins at the ultimate end, the truth body dharmakaya of Buddha silence where we all connect with Katagiri Roshi. It calls that first section "daily life," and we live a rich daily life together for a hundred pages.

Katagiri's description of "supreme knowledge" meets the realm of peerless Shantideva; "with supreme knowledge we can see one beautiful picture where two things are constantly interchanging. This is the place in which we have to stand up. . . . I cannot survive without all of you. I can help because others are not other; others are the contents of my life, others are completely embraced by my life, my life can be found with others' lives. At that time I can do something with full commitment. . . ." And he connects it with the sublime earthiness of the matchless Dogen. "We can help in many ways. Using toilet paper carefully is helping others. Don't expect helping to be a big deal. In our everyday life, we can help someone or something all the time."

Katagiri makes his biggest statement when he unfurls Dogen Zenji's banner of zazen, the sitting-as-Buddha that is the goal of all Buddhism, the goal of all life, the true entrance, foundation and ultimate goal of all religion. He initiates us in Dogen's seamless monument mandala of perfect religious security—just sitting zen is eternal peak experience, the realm of end-in-itself. Katagiri Roshi offers it to us all, whether we be Buddhist or Christian or Jew, atheist or hedonist. "Zazen penetrates and is available to all circles of human life: skiing, basketball, dancing, whatever you do. . . . This is basic universal practice, because we create life anew, day after day." This is the peak of the book as well. This is where we are allowed to sit when we read it. This reminds us there is nothing more important. It reminds us it is not only a "just sitting," it is an "exclusive sitting," an initiated, sacred sitting that excludes all egotistic ordinariness of means and ends, a sitting that is "just," that is "exact," exactly balancing absolute and relative, exactly here and everywhere, that is "total," totally embracing life and death, sterility and fertility, good and evil, love and hate, and all ordinary opposites in harmony.

Katagiri Roshi ends with some of the best advice for Buddhist social action I have yet seen, talking in comment on Dogen's essay on the "Four Methods of Guidance" (which can also be "four social graces," or even "four political practices"). These four are giving, kind speech, beneficial action, and "identity action." This section touches the beginning of a bodhisattva movement to save the world, the untiring messianic action to free all beings from suffering. It is why Buddhists love America and will make America finally come to life. Those who would be these new age bodhisattvas should read this good advice with eager hearts, until "it penetrates their skin, muscle, and bone."

"Identity action means there is no difference between the object of our devotion and us—we are completely one. . . . 'Action,' in this case, means behavior that is characterized by courtesy and sharpness, that keeps people naturally in awe and that has a sort of majesty or dignity coming from the bottom of human life. . . . [The] relationship between I and nature involves not only the "I" we can see, but the huge "I" that is extending into the present, the past and the future, to heaven and hell, in all directions. . . . [It] is an endless relationship, constant and dynamic."

I pray that these new age bodhisattvas will rise up out of this land of great silence like grass growing on the Minnesota prairie. Let them act and speak like this last chapter. Let them learn the power and responsibility of oneness, and the competence of precise awareness. Smiling, let them arrest the nuclear launches with gentle fingers. Sweating, let them find "gold sufficient to all nations"—and let them make food to share with all peoples. Giving, kind speech, beneficial action, and identity action. They should study this book. And enjoy it. Savor it slowly and repeatedly. Thank you, Dogen Zenji. Thank you, Katagiri Roshi.

ROBERT TENZIN THURMAN
Amherst, Massachusetts
December 1987

Acknowledgments

WE EXTEND our deep appreciation and gratitude to all those who helped in producing this work. It has been the effort of many people in a number of ways.

The text came from Katagiri Roshi's Dharma talks, which were carefully listened to on tape and transcribed. This took many hours of work on the part of many people, and we thank them for their patient effort.

We also thank those who previously edited some of these Dharma talks that were printed in past issues of the Minnesota Zen Center newsletters and in the Minnesota Zen Center journal, *Udumbara*. Without that initial effort our task would have been much more difficult.

We are grateful to all those who gave us their encouragement, advice, and support over the last two years. It helped us continue the day-to-day routine of making this work a reality.

Finally, we offer our deepest gratitude and respect to our teacher, whose clear and wholehearted expression of life as it really is, of Buddha's practice as it really is, inspired us to attempt and complete this work.

YŪKŌ CONNIFF
WILLA HATHAWAY

Zen in Daily Life

Silence

WHEN WE THINK ABOUT what real silence is, we have to look at it from two angles; the first is to see silence through human eyes and the second is to see silence through Buddha's eyes or the universal eye. The opportunity to experience real silence occurs when we have been driven into a corner and simply cannot move an inch. This seems like a situation of complete despair, but this silence is quite different from despair, because in the area of despair, the conscious flame of human desire is still burning. But real silence is the state of human existence that passes through this despair. How can we experience this silence? Without everyday life, it is impossible to experience silence.

In terms of the human perspective, silence has at least three flavors: pessimistic, optimistic and mystical. They work together and cannot be separated. That is why it is very difficult to know what is going on when silence is seen from the human perspective. There is an interesting poem by a World War II war criminal that shows these mixed feelings of pessimism, optimism and mysticism. His story was very sad. He was accused of killing an American pilot, but the accusation was not true. After his death the true story, which he had recorded in his diary, was found.

An American pilot had parachuted from his airplane and was injured in the fall. The writer of the poem, Senri Uyeno, started operating on him, but during the operation he was ordered by a senior officer to kill him. He did not obey the order and continued to operate. In the middle of the operation, the place was bombed and he had to leave. When he returned, the American pilot had been stabbed to death by somebody else. Nobody knew who did it, so the person who wrote this poem took all the blame for the crime and was executed. He wrote this poem a week before he died.

> Thanks to lamenting over the pain in the world,
> I am able to become laughter when my life is happy.

Due to being struck and trampled upon and biting
my lips to control my temper, I fully realize how
precious it is to be born. Even if I am intentionally
tired of an ugly world, look! What a blue sky!

Even if one laughs scornfully at my penniless life,
there is something much more beautiful,
true and worthy that everyone knows.
I don't care so much about anything else,
except love and sincerity, the sun,
and a little amount of rain from time to time.
If I have a healthy body and a little piece of bread,
I want to walk with a smile in great spirits.

I will do my best to work without complaining
about anything at all.
I always consider things by putting myself in another's
place without flinching, no matter how hard and
heartrending it is to live.
If there is someone unfortunate, I will help
him out with anything.
If I can forget myself to help out,
that will surely delight me.

In the morning the sun rises. I greet it.
I will do my best to live today.
In the evening, the sun sets.
Staring at the evening glow, I want to sit still.

With a little dream in my heart, I sleep
as quietly as a little bird.
If I have my own time, I want to spend it
reading an old collection of poems, meditating
on them alone, quietly.

Let's find happiness by ourselves.
Within silver tears like pearls and laughter like the sun,
let's keep walking ahead each day.
Certainly some day, as I look back over my past,
I will quietly see my life with a smile.

[Translated by Dainin Katagiri]

The first lines say, "Thanks to lamenting over the pain in the world, /
I am able to become laughter when my life is happy. / Due to being
struck and trampled upon and biting / my lips to control my temper, I
fully realize how / precious it is to be born." By passing through pessi-

mism and optimism, or affirmation and negation in his life, he found something more than them. He found something mystical—how sublime and precious human life is. It is really something great, like a glowing sunrise.

Next he says, "Even if I am intentionally / tired of an ugly world, look! What a blue sky!" Everyone feels how ugly the human world is, how ugly we are. But still there is an optimistic world. It's a mixed world. The two worlds of pessimism and optimism are working together.

Next he says, "Even if one laughs scornfully at my penniless life." Look at your life. If you don't have anything, no position or material wealth, people laugh scornfully at you. And some people put us down for becoming Buddhists. Even in Japan, monks with bald heads doing *takuhatsu* (mendicant begging) on the street are laughed at scornfully. So "even if one laughs scornfully at my penniless life, / there is something much more beautiful, / true and worthy that everyone knows." This something that everybody knows is the universal life, a spiritual life. It is something beautiful, something worthy. We don't know what the spiritual life is, because it is a big issue. The first step is that we reconsider everything again from a different angle, not from our usual understanding. There is something much more beautiful and much more worthy than we usually see. This is the first step to enter the door of nonduality or the spiritual life. That is why he says, "I don't care so much about anything else, / except love and sincerity, the sun / and a little amount of rain from time to time. / If I have a healthy body and a little piece of bread, / I want to walk with a smile in great spirits." The actualization of the first step to the spiritual life must be encouraged by "love and sincerity, the sun, / and a little amount of rain from time to time." This is his everyday life. But it is pretty mystical for ordinary people. We don't understand it. How can we be happy right in the middle of a mixed sense of optimism and pessimism? We don't know. But we have to go through this. We have to taste the flavors of optimism and pessimism without being tossed away by them. Then we can find out something mystical.

Next he says, "I will do my best to work without complaining / about anything at all." It is very difficult for us to deal with pessimism and optimism without complaining about anything at all. He says he just does his best to work hard. It is very difficult for us to do just this.

But what is the mystical aspect of his life that goes beyond optimism and pessimism? This is a very simple life: "I always consider things by putting myself in another's place." He realizes how precious it is to be born, so very naturally he cannot think of his life only. His life is completely the same as another's life. He always puts himself in the other's place and then considers everything in the world. This is a very compassionate attitude. This compassion is not a sense of kindness and friendliness that occurs from time to time under certain circumstances. He is living this compassion under all circumstances; it never changes. So he says, "Without flinching, no matter how hard and / heartrending it is to live." Constantly he does this.

Still there is a little disappointment concerning how strong the ego is. It is very difficult to be free from his life. "If there is someone unfortunate, I will help / him out with anything. / If I can forget myself to help out, / that will surely delight me." In his heart, he is constantly ready to share his life with all sentient beings. That is his hope, but still there is some suffering there.

"In the morning the sun rises. I greet it. / I will do my best to live today." This is a very simple life from day to day. Today is today, tomorrow is tomorrow. "In the evening, the sun sets. / Staring at the evening glow, I want to sit still." In the morning there is enormous energy to live with all sentient beings. So he says he will do his best to live with all beings. This is his greeting with the morning sunrise. But in the evening, we don't know what the next day will bring. I was told that the time when a criminal was served with a special dish in the morning was the day he was to be executed. If they didn't have a special breakfast, they felt relief. They had one more day to live. But in the evening they didn't know what would happen the next day. That is why he said that when the evening sun set, he just wanted to be still. There was nothing for him to do. All he could do was taste many flavors: pessimism, optimism and something more than these. We cannot say that this is exactly silence, because real silence has no flavor, but it's working. When silence appeared in his life there were at least three flavors there.

"With a little dream in my heart, I sleep / as quietly as a little bird. / If I have my own time, I want to spend it / reading an old collection of poems, meditating on them alone, quietly." This is all he could do. But he always had a little dream, and with that little dream he could just sleep quietly like a little bird. In his own life he found a little bit of happiness and expressed it as appreciation to all sentient beings.

Next he says, "Let's find happiness by ourselves." This little happiness is of enormous value. No one can give us happiness; no one can give us satisfaction. Even the Buddha's teaching can never really give us any satisfaction or happiness. Let's find happiness by ourselves. By ourselves doesn't mean to show our ego. We cannot show our ego and find true happiness. He passed through many things in his life and there was no opportunity for him to show his ego, because of "being struck and trampled upon and biting my lips to control my temper." Finally what his life expressed was happiness. That is why he says, "Let's find happiness by ourselves." Let's keep walking ahead day by day. This is his resolute activity, because of no clear answer to "why" or "how."

"Within silver tears like pearls and laughter like the sun" is really a contradictory statement, both pessimistic and optimistic. Silver tears mean sadness. But within sadness we have to see the sun shining. This means we have to have great laughter. Near the beginning of the poem he says, "I don't care so much about anything else, / except love and sincerity, the sun / and a little amount of rain from time to time." The sun means great laughter or the bright aspect of human life. On the other hand, we need a little amount of rain from time to time. This rain is tears on our face. We don't need much, because if we have a lot of rain it is too sad. So he hopes for a small amount. But within silver tears like pearls, there must be the sun shining like great laughter. Then he says that if we live like this, then certainly, some day, we may quietly look back over our past and see our life with a smile. We can smile at our life, whatever it is, whatever mistakes we have made, whether we are successful or not.

This poem really shows us what silence is from the human perspective and what kinds of flavors we can taste. It is really a mixture of pessimism, optimism and mysticism. But remember, in the deepest reaches of human life, deeper than these three flavors, there is still a vague disconsolate pain or unsatisfactory feeling there. It is very difficult to be free from this pain. It is not exactly pain, but a kind of silent lamentation inside. This is always there. Remember, that is why Buddha says life is characterized by suffering. This suffering is not the usual sense of suffering. It is quite different. There is no other way to experience this really deep suffering without the three flavors of optimism, pessimism and mysticism. This is silence seen from the viewpoint of human eyes.

In terms of the universe or Buddha's eye, silence is exactly as-it-isness, or what-is-just-is-of-itself. It is very quiet. Buddha's teaching always mentions this. If we want to know who we are and touch the real, silent, deep nature of our life, we must be as we really are. How? Sit *zazen*, that is all. That is why sitting is very important for us.

When we sit, two flavors are there. One is very sharp, cutting through delusions, suffering, pain and any emotion like a sharp sword. This is called wisdom. But within wisdom there must be compassion. That compassion is to see human life for the long run. Compassion is not something we try to create; we cannot do it. Compassion comes from the measure of our practice, which we have accumulated for a long, long time. It naturally happens.

The second flavor of silence seen by the Buddha's eye is to accept all sentient beings just as they are; what is just is of itself. To see everything just as it is, is not so easy for us. We need to polish ourselves again and again. We have to refine our spiritual life with all sentient beings. Otherwise we cannot see a thing as it is.

Silence means, how do we take care of the usual aspects of human life? This is important. For instance, if zazen makes us sleepy, that is because of our attitude toward zazen. If we are lazy or have an unconscious dislike toward zazen, then very naturally we can easily sleep in zazen. The point is how we deal with this human problem. We have to taste the bitterness of sleeping in zazen, but also we can still taste something great and optimistic through sleeping in zazen. Due to having slept in zazen for a long time, some day we can wake up, some day we can have pretty good zazen. Our basic attitude is that we shouldn't be tossed away by sleeping in zazen and by the expectation of good zazen.

Our life must be rooted on earth, not in sleep. This is not a particular technique. It is silence. That's it. Silence means you have to be you as you really are—what is just is of itself. If we want to know real spiritual life, we have to taste ourselves as we really are. It is not necessary to stick to the forms and rituals. All we have to do is taste ourselves as we are.

In terms of the Buddha's eye, silence is the total manifestation of our whole personality, in which we have digested the three flavors of optimism, pessimism and mysticism. They never come up, because they are all digested. They become just energy for us. This silence is quite different from silence in terms of human eyes. According to human eyes, there is a vague disconsolate pain or pensiveness in the depths of our life that we cannot wipe out. It is very sticky and we stumble over it pretty easily. It is beyond our consciousness or unconsciousness. It is already there. But in terms of the Buddha's eye, or Zen teaching, silence is exactly the total manifestation of our whole personality. Whole personality means our individual personality is manifested with the whole universe. All other beings are the contents of our personality. So when we manifest our whole personality it is not just our individual personality, but simultaneously through this personality we can feel the whole universe. That is why we can feel magnanimity, tolerance and compassion.

If we had asked the man who wrote this poem what he felt about his death, he might have said, "I don't want to die." This "I don't want to die" is just like a greeting, in the same way that we say good morning. There is no motive behind his words, just "I don't want to die." That's it. But for us, we want to think of the meaning behind that. We always try to translate or decode what people say, what the Zen teacher says. But for him, it is just as it is. That's all. This is real silence.

In reading this poem there is always a deep disconsolate feeling or flavor there. There is another poem that shows us this same flavor. It was written by Miazawa Kenji at the age of thirty-six. He was a great poet in modern Japan and also a very serious Buddhist. This is one of his most famous poems.

> neither yielding to rain
> nor yielding to wind
> yielding neither to
> snow nor to summer heat
>   with a stout body
>   like that
> without greed
> never getting angry
> always smiling quiet-
>   ly
> eating one and a half pieces of brown rice
>   and bean paste and a bit of
>   vegetables a day
> in everything
> not taking oneself
>   into account
>   looking listening understanding well
> and not forgetting
> living in the shadow of pine trees in a field

in a small
        hut thatched with miscanthus
if in the east there's a
        sick child
going and nursing
                him
if in the west there is a tired mother
going and for her
        carrying
                bundles of rice
if in the south
    there's someone
                        dying
going
  and saying
        you don't have to be
                afraid
if in the north
            there's a quarrel
                        or a lawsuit
saying it's not worth it
                        stop it
in a drought
        shedding tears
in a cold summer
    pacing back and forth   lost
called
        a good-for-nothing
                by everyone
neither praised
nor thought a pain
        someone
                like that
is what I want
        to be[1]

This is a very mystical life, just like a stream of water. Still there is an indefinable, disconsolate flavor there. This is human suffering.

Buddhism teaches us that we have to pass at once through this deep human suffering and be touched to the heart. Then we can experience silence. But as Buddhists, we have a responsibility for doing something more than that. We have to transmute the silence seen by human eyes into the silence seen by Buddha's eye. At that time we can show our life just as we really are. When we encounter each moment of life, we face it, penetrate it and practice it. This is not egoistic. It is not a narrow view. It already accepts all sentient beings as the contents of our life.

Buddha Is Your Daily Life

If you can chant the Buddhist teachings while having a meal you are very lucky. The policeman has to have breakfast in order to chase thieves; the pickpocket gets up in the morning and has breakfast in order to steal ten-dollar bills from the pockets of others. Breakfast is breakfast, but its world is represented in different ways by different individuals. If you have breakfast to offer your body and mind to the Buddha, to the universe, how lucky you are. Offering your body and mind to the Buddha is offering your body and mind to emptiness, or in other words, to the pure sense of human action.

People misunderstand and misuse Buddhism. If you study Buddhism thinking that it will help you, that means that you use Buddhism for your ego, for selfishness. No matter how long you do this, it is egocentric practice. If you continue to practice like this you will never be satisfied, because desire is endless.

When the *Dharma* is close to you, you do not feel satisfied. When the Dharma is far from you, then you feel satisfied. This is important. If you take only one small step into the study of anything, physics, psychology, Zen, then you feel happy. But the deeper you go, the more you realize that you do not feel satisfied. Whatever you do, not only in Buddhism but in life in general, if your life is close to human life you do not feel satisfied. There is always something you have to do. As you move toward the future, studying and developing, the more deeply you enter into something the more unsatisfied you feel. This is very natural. The same is true of Buddhist practice. So do not use Buddhism for yourself. Offer your body and mind to the *Buddha-dharma*. Buddha is not divine. Buddha is your daily life.

Buddha-Nature Is Impermanence

The realization of impermanence is the first step to pass through the gate of religious life. If you study Buddhism, you can realize impermanence intellectually. You may have been motivated to study Buddhism or to sit zazen by the realization of impermanence in your life. Even if you don't study Buddhism you can get a taste of impermanence or transiency in your life.

Everyone has already experienced the meaning of transiency or impermanence, but it is very difficult for us to understand impermanence as Buddha-nature. Impermanence is the state of existence, which is constantly changing from day to day, from moment to moment. Everything exists, but according to time and conditions, everything is constantly changing. You may realize that things are changing, but you also already have preconceptions about the continuation of time. For instance, your idea of change may be that one thing changes into another thing, that yesterday becomes today, today becomes tomorrow. But in this understanding, there is an idea that something exists constantly from yesterday through today to tomorrow—that one being exists continuously behind the idea of change. This is a very common understanding. That's why you look at your practice as a way to deepen your life or to change your life. You believe that by practicing yesterday, you may be able to change your life today, or maybe you can change your life tomorrow. Within this understanding, there is always the idea of something that exists constantly, and that something is you, yourself. Consciously or unconsciously, you attach to this idea that you exist constantly.

The Buddhist understanding of change is a little different. In order to understand the meaning of change or impermanence, you have to understand the meaning of moment. The present moment is completely beyond before and after. It is completely beyond the previous moment and the following moment. Present moment is present moment. Previous moment, which has disappeared, is nothing but the previous moment. Present moment is nothing but present moment that will disappear simultaneously with the appearance of the next moment. So, to say what the present moment is—right now, right here—is to say that this moment has already disappeared. This means the present moment is completely beyond the previous moment or the following moment. It is just the present moment. The present moment, seen according to common sense, is the cause of feeling lonely, because it is completely separate from the previous moment and the following moment. But this is because we understand the moment in the time process. We should pay attention to the moment in its pure sense.

What is a moment? A moment is nothing more than a being that arises constantly. It is just arising. "Just arising" means if you focus on the true meaning of moment, moment is seen as no more than a being that you can see in time. It is nothing but the pure working of the moment. There is nothing to comment on, nothing to compare with, nothing to add to moment.

According to the Abhidharma, a moment is said to consist of sixty-five *ksanas* or instants. This is completely beyond our understanding. It means in this moment you have already missed sixty-five instants. The Abhidharma tries to explain what a moment is by using numbers, but don't worry about the numbers. A moment consists of sixty-five instants. What does this mean? It is completely beyond before and after. There is nothing to say about this. A moment is just arising, just being. The present moment is not something you can hold on to. The moment you can hold on to is already your idea of the moment. It is not the real moment. The real moment is constantly working, arising, disappearing, appearing. In Buddhism this is called emptiness. This is why, according to Buddha's teaching, all beings are impermanence. They are impermanence because of impermanence. There is nothing particular that creates impermanence. In this respect, both cause and effect are exactly impermanence in themselves. Emptiness or impermanence means there is nothing to compare, nothing to hold on to, nothing to ignore. It means just appearing, that's all. This is the basic nature of existence. It is completely beyond our speculation or judgment. No matter how long we try to hate or how long we try to love ourselves, this is the portrait of our existence.

Emptiness, Buddha-nature, impermanence exist forever. This means impermanence is immutable. Wherever you may go, only impermanence is immutable. Constant change is completely beyond your speculation. It just is. That's why impermanence is Buddha-nature. Buddha-nature is being preached constantly. It is something you can explain, you can demonstrate. For instance, if a tree wants to demonstrate what it is, the tree has to work, has to exist. How does it exist? The tree exists as impermanence, appearing and disappearing according to season. From moment to moment the tree explains itself.

All beings want to know who they are; this is the natural state of everyone's heart—to seek for the knowledge of who one is. Not only human beings, but everything wants to know this. Even the tree wants to know what it is. The tree that you understand by projecting your-self into it is just a concept of the tree that you have. The real tree is nothing but a being that is just arising. There is nothing to compare, nothing to criticize, nothing to evaluate. This is tree. If you want to know the tree as it really is, you should work with the tree. Simultane-ously, this is the best way to know who you are.

We have to know ourselves through working in the realm of imper-manence. Our body and mind are nothing but impermanence. Imper-manence is Buddha-nature. Buddha-nature was born into this world and Buddha-nature dies. This means that if you really understand the moment, then tree is really tree. A person is just a person. From this point of view, everything is continuously practicing. When you mani-fest yourself right now, right here, becoming one with zazen or with your activity, this is Buddha-nature manifested in the realm of emp-tiness or impermanence.

In the realm of emptiness, zazen appears as a bubble. But this bubble called "zazen" is not really a bubble. It is a moment in its pure sense, because this bubble appears on the surface of the moment. The mo-ment you understand is already a bubble. It is just arising. It is called emptiness, which means pure sense of existence. There is nothing to compare here. There is nothing to say, nothing to ignore. This is the portrait of your existence. Day after day we have to take care of our life. So, if you want to know who you are, you have to take care of your daily life. This is taking care of human actions, which appear and disappear in the realm of impermanence. It is not a pessimistic under-standing, because taking care of yourself in the moment is real human action.

The pure sense of emptiness means vastness. Your existence is not just in the small scale of the world—it is vast. This is the pure sense of moment. But if you see the moment from just your individual view-point it becomes limited. The pure sense of moment is vast. Imme-diately your individual existence expands to all sentient beings. This is total manifestation. It is not just an aspect of human life, it is the real portrait of existence itself. Not only human beings, but all sentient be-ings exist like this. So, just taking care of yourself is not just taking care of yourself while ignoring others. You have to take care of yourself simultaneously with all sentient beings. At that time you can really get a taste of impermanence.

This is the best way to know who you are; this is Buddha's compassion. You can get a taste of the core of existence, which is called Buddha-nature. How sublime your life is!

Serenity and Tranquillity

To live a spiritual life is to learn and to practice the Way-mind. The Way is the universal path that is complete serenity and tranquillity. It is called Mind. This Mind is not ordinary mind. Mind, as serenity and tranquillity, is the original nature of human consciousness. This path is open to all beings, animate and inanimate, not just to human beings. Regardless of whether we are conscious of it or not, our life is constantly right in the midst of this universal path, serenity and tranquillity. The Way-mind is in everything, constantly.

Serenity and tranquillity as Mind are universal consciousness. It is just like a waterfall that is flowing constantly, regardless of whether you are conscious of it or not. Although this Way-mind is serenity and tranquillity, this serenity is not our usual understanding of serenity; it is at the same time dynamic. If you see a waterfall in the distance, it appears to be quiet, but if you see it close up it is constantly moving. The original nature of human consciousness is just like a waterfall, which is serene and tranquil, and yet simultaneously dynamic.

In the study of psychology, one tries to understand the basis of consciousness, which is called the unconscious. The unconscious is vast; it is filled with many things because it is connected with times past, present and future. Psychology tries to understand this unconscious level, and to take things from it. When you try to take things from it, this is nothing but the functioning of ego-consciousness. Ego-consciousness is the source of selfishness, the source of egoistic understanding. Ego considers Way-mind something specific because it can be experienced, and then wants to know what is going on there. But whatever the ego can pick up and look at is only the surface of Way-mind.

Buddhism is to learn serenity and tranquillity directly, and to practice it. In other words, Buddhism wants to know how to be present in Way-mind, how to be one with Way-mind, not how to take things from it. That is why we have to learn and practice serenity and tranquillity. This is because when ego-consciousness understands the source of existence it immediately picks it up as though it were fixed and tries to hold on to it, calling it "I."

If we thoroughly understand ego, simultaneously we can be free from it. We must be free from it because this "I" exists with all sentient beings. Universal consciousness is dynamic and yet simultaneously serene and tranquil. We must become one with it; this is the point that Buddhism emphasizes.

When the Way is experienced by you, it is called enlightenment, or *bodhi*. Enlightenment, or the universal path, is always supporting you, whether you like it or not. Even if you try to ignore it, you can experience the universal path.

To learn and practice serenity and tranquillity is to be one with the universal path with full awareness. At that time we can appreciate serenity and tranquillity. We have to learn and practice this because we are living in the dualistic world. If we don't awaken to it, we will never have a chance to be grateful for this serenity and tranquillity.

How can you be one with serenity and tranquillity? First, let's see into the flux of arising and decaying, and recognize the transient nature of the world. This is what we call impermanence, or constant change. When the transient nature of the world is recognized, the ordinary selfish mind always fixes on something, saying, "I've got it!" But there is no chance to do this because everything is changing. All you have to do is to be there from moment to moment. When you do zazen, just do zazen. That is all you have to do. There is no particular idea by which zazen can be defined. If you define your zazen, it becomes something specific, and then it is not real zazen. Ego-consciousness defines zazen, saying, "This is *my* zazen." Then very naturally judgment follows. Judgment and evaluation are fine, because they are functions of our consciousness, but the problem is that when we judge and evaluate we grasp things and attach to them. This is ego-consciousness at work.

If you have certain ideas about zazen it is very difficult to know zazen as it is, right in the midst of transiency. There is no way to escape constant change. So, how can I be one with zazen as it is? How can I show the truth of impermanence? I must be I as I really am. This is not just a problem for human beings. A pine tree must be alive as a pine tree. That is all it has to do. Pine tree, bamboo, lake, winter, all show impermanence constantly. Pine tree must be pine tree as it is when the pine tree exists. Winter must be winter as it is when winter comes. Snow must be snow as it is. Only when the pine tree becomes the pine tree as it is, can it show impermanence, which is called nature. This is why we notice how beautiful the pine tree is. When the pine tree is the pine tree as it is, the pine tree really exists with everything else in nature—pebbles, lake, river, sky—this is really the way the pine tree becomes the pine tree as it is. This is the practical aspect of impermanence.

Impermanence leaves no chance of bringing your selfish consciousness into it. All you have to do is be you as you are. Zazen must be zazen as it is. Very naturally then, ordinary selfish mind does not arise.

According to Buddhism, ordinary selfish mind appears in several ways: as craving, as anger and as self-delusion. Self-delusion means ignorance, arrogance and doubt. You don't trust anything. You deny everything. Finally only you are left. Then you say, "It's mine," or "This guy is most important." With fame and profit, selfish mind appears very easily. Only human beings want fame. Dogs and cats don't care about fame or profit. If you show a diamond to a cat, the cat doesn't care about it. Only human beings love profit and fame. Profit is constant grasping, not only for the material world, but for a psychological and a spiritual life as well. It's pretty busy. Even though this grasping is for the spiritual world, there is still craving. We want to gain spiritual wealth and profit from it. This is selfishness. Without profit it is very difficult for ego-consciousness to exist.

Ego-consciousness is very strong and very deep. It is present in the depths of our unconscious mind. We want, constantly; so very naturally, even in zazen we cannot just sit down. We are always seeking for profit, even from zazen. This is noisy zazen; it is not serenity and tranquillity. We can be one with serenity and tranquillity, if we ourselves are serene and tranquil right in the midst of zazen. This is most important. If we seek something extra, it is already not serene. We must be serenity and tranquillity appearing in zazen, walking, eating, whatever we do. This is to live a spiritual life.

We have to see into the transient nature of the world. If we understand this, change is very serene; there is nothing to say. Yet it is something dynamic, it is working. We have to learn this. We have to touch this. We have to be this, directly. In order to turn this into reality, zazen must be serenity itself, just a flower, blooming.

Peace

There is a beautiful story about Shākyamuni Buddha that I cannot forget. It think of this story whenever I look at the human world and see the necessity for finding a way to live in peace and harmony with all sentient beings.

There was once a time in India, long ago, when diplomatic relations were going well between the neighboring countries of Magadha and Kapilavatthu, where Shākyamuni Buddha and his people, the Shākya clan, lived. In those days it was the custom for nobility to marry only nobility, so the king of Magadha asked the king of Kapilavatthu to send a princess to marry his son. The king of Kapilavatthu sent a woman to Magadha as he had promised, but rather than a woman of noble birth, he sent a housemaid. Not knowing this, the king of Magadha went ahead and celebrated the wedding. Later, when the prince took over his father's position and became king, someone told him of this scandal and he became very angry. He wanted to attack Kapilavatthu at any cost.

When the Shākya people realized that the king of Magadha was planning to attack them, they asked Shākyamuni Buddha to stop him and he accepted the task. Even though the Buddha was an expert in using weapons and was well trained in the martial arts, he didn't fight. Instead he tried to negotiate with the king in many ways. However, there was one person near the king who persistently encouraged him to fight and to destroy the Shākya clan. So the king couldn't hear the Buddha; the inside of his mind wouldn't stop burning and finally he decided to attack.

Shākyamuni Buddha knew the king and his army were coming, so he sat in zazen under a dead tree on the side of the road leading to Kapilavatthu. As the king traveled along this road with his army he saw Shākyamuni Buddha sitting under a dead tree. Since it was very hot, he couldn't understand why the Buddha was sitting under a dead tree; usually people sit under beautiful green trees. So the king asked, "Why do you sit under the dead tree?" The Buddha calmly said to the king, "I feel cool, even under this dead tree, because it is growing near my native country." This really pierced the king's heart and he was so greatly impressed by the message of the Buddha's action that he could go no further. Instead of attacking, he returned to his country. But the king's attendant still continued to encourage him to attack and finally he did so. This time, unfortunately, Shākyamuni Buddha didn't have time to do anything. Without saying a word, he just stood and watched his country and his people being destroyed.

There are two important points to this story. The first point is that real peace is not a matter of discussion. This is why Shākyamuni Buddha sat under the dead tree, realizing real peace, moving toward real peace, merging with real peace beyond the idea of peace or no-peace. If we look at the human world, we cannot believe there is peace. If we debate peace, the world appears as "no-peace." But *originally* the world *is* real peace; trees, birds, spring, winter, autumn, and we, sitting here, are already peace. We *are* peace before we discuss whether there is peace or not. However, if someone says, "There is no peace," and then we argue this point with him, finally we will be fighting about the idea of peace itself. This is not real peace.

Working toward world peace is not just dealing with nuclear weapons. Who created nuclear weapons? We created them. We already have the embryo of nuclear weapons in each individual mind. Remember this. It is very important. When the time is ripe and conditions are appropriate, nuclear weapons are created. They are not produced by politicians or scientists. They are produced by individual human life. We should look at this. The embryo of nuclear weapons and everything else that human beings create is always rooted in human life.

How then can we achieve real peace? According to Shākyamuni Buddha, real peace is completely beyond whether there is a way to stop the king from attacking or not. Buddha knew how to use the weapons of those days, but he didn't use them. He just sat. Just sitting is peace—Buddha's peace. He didn't say anything, but his sitting was perfect peace, real peace that he could create from moment to moment. Even though Buddha didn't say anything, the king was very impressed because Shākyamuni Buddha manifested himself as real peace beyond any discussion of peace.

The second point of the story is no matter how long we emphasize the need for real peace to all beings, there are still many individuals who don't accept our peace. If people don't accept our peace, where can it be found? Peace has to be found in us. We have to digest, we have to chew real peace in our hearts by ourselves. It is pretty hard. This is why Shākyamuni Buddha just stood and watched his native country being destroyed. No one accepted his peace, so finally, real peace came back to Buddha himself. There is no other way. This is why he just tasted, chewed and digested real peace within his own life.

The more Buddha chewed real peace in his heart, the more he realized how stubborn and ignorant human beings are. Human beings are very ignorant. The nature of ignorance is to lack deep communication with nature or with the universe. It is to separate, to isolate, to create discrimination and differences, so that finally we cannot communicate as a harmonious whole. These differences we create appear as fighting, anger, hatred and war.

We are always trying to fix the surface or object-discriminating aspect of the human world. In this aspect of the world there are countless holes through which ideas are leaking—the idea of nuclear weapons, the idea of peace or no-peace, the idea of armament or disarmament. But if we want to fix some aspect of the world, if we want to have a peace movement, it is necessary to remember that armament and disarmament are the same thing in a sense; they are a principle or doctrine created by human ignorance. If we attach to the idea of disarmament we create a problem. On the other hand, if we attach to the idea of armament we create still more problems. Look at both sides. Which is better? Temporarily we use disarmament as an idea through which we can approach real peace. But this disarmament is just an idea. We cannot hold on to it as opposed to armament, because if we do, finally under the beautiful flag of disarmament we fight—about the idea of peace, we fight. What kind of peace is this? It is nothing but an idea. So why don't we see the idea of peace as just an idea that can be used temporarily in order to approach real peace. There is no other way to approach peace.

To approach real peace requires a very strong, stable, spiritual commitment, a vow. Just take a vow. Make a commitment toward real peace, just like Buddha sitting under the dead tree. But remember, even though we do make a commitment toward real peace, there will be many individuals who don't accept our way. So finally, where can real peace be found? With us. We ourselves must remain with peace. This is pretty hard, but we cannot stop. Buddha has to continue to sit under the dead tree. This is our sitting.

The more we sit like this, the more we realize the strength of human ignorance. There is no reason why we create this terrible situation, but we do, constantly. When we make a spiritual commitment toward real peace, day by day, we have to go beyond whether people accept peace or not. This is not a political matter. It is a spiritual commitment toward peace. We have to taste it and digest it, constantly. Next we have to live it. This is pretty hard, because the more we taste and chew real peace, the more we realize human ignorance. But the more we realize human ignorance, the more we cannot stop teaching real peace, living real peace.

Singsapa Leaves

The purpose of the Buddha Way is to learn the self. To learn the self means to study the problem of life and death of the individual. The Buddha Way is not a teaching that forces us to practice. We are practicing already. Everyone has the problem of life and death. To live, to die—these are great problems for human beings.

To study the problem of life and death of the individual must also be to study the problem of life and death of the universe, of all beings, not only human beings, but also trees, birds, all sentient beings. In other words, the great problem of life and death of all beings must be alive in the hearts of individuals. When this happens, practice really works.

Usually people think that to learn the self makes us selfish, that it makes us keep Buddhist practice just for ourselves or for certain people. However, Buddhist practice belongs not only to the individual, but to all beings. We have to think constantly of the problem of life and death of all beings, not of a particular race of beings. This is very important for us.

Regarding this point, we must be a little pragmatic, not idealistic. For example, in former times the Japanese could think only of the Japanese. The Japanese didn't care about Americans. But now, they cannot do this. Because of nuclear weapons, we cannot think only of our survival as a nation or as human beings. We have to think of the survival of all sentient beings. This is not idealistic. This is very practical, and it is very much an emergency situation in the world now.

Before the Buddha talked to his disciples he usually showed them something. On one occasion he gathered up a few leaves from the *singsapa* tree in his hand. Then he asked whether the monks thought there were more leaves in his hands or on the trees overhead. The monks answered that there were more on the trees, of course. And the Buddha said that just like the greater number of leaves on the trees, there were many more things that he knew than he had told them, and that there were three reasons why: because they were not concerned with profit; because they were not basic to living a holy life; and because they did not encourage dispassion, cessation, tranquillity, full comprehension, wisdom or *nirvāna*.

The first point of this story is that the Buddha has not taught those things which are not concerned with profit. This may consist of interesting theories and information but it is of no practical use, particularly in everyday life. Everyday life is just like an emergency situation. When you look back on your past life you find lots of gaps; it's pretty hard to catch up with life, which is moving ahead now. On the other hand, you cannot ignore looking back and reflecting upon your life. We have to reflect, but we cannot do this continually. It may be interesting, but after a while it is of no practical use.

How can we deal with an emergency situation? It's pretty hard. Your brain must not be numb. It must work smoothly, normally; but you cannot be stuck in the functioning of your brain. This is a pretty difficult practice for us. For example we are now really sensitive to the issue of a nuclear freeze. We are very sensitive to politics. I don't know the definition of politics exactly, because we are right in the middle of politics, but without the political aspect of human life we cannot live. For instance, our names are registered at City Hall and we always have to carry a driver's license or identification card; we have to consider other people, our neighbors; in order to complete even a little project, we have to negotiate with people. All these things are already being political. It's very complicated. Political theories may be good but sometimes they don't work in daily life. If we just continuously discuss politics, it's pretty hard to know both what is going on and what politics is. I don't mean you should keep your mouth shut. You have to think about politics, but sometimes politics doesn't help, because in reality life is very complicated. This is one reason why Buddha didn't teach more than was necessary.

The second point was that he only gave what was basic to living the holy life. In this case "holy life" means excellent practices, something more than the practice we usually understand. "Excellent practices" are the *bodhisattva* practices, the six *pāramitās*.[1] So he only taught that which was useful in understanding the excellent practices. No matter how long we discuss any aspect of Buddhism, such as emptiness, that discussion does not give us a clue as to how to start truly excellent practices. Emptiness is not a philosophical aspect of human life. No matter how long you discuss emptiness, what you are discussing is not emptiness, exactly; it is just you creating a frame of emptiness. But emptiness itself has no frame; you have to be alive in everyday life. This is emptiness. If you try to understand emptiness through discussion, you create a certain frame and become stuck there. Such discussions are not necessary to learning the basic practices of the holy life.

The third point Buddha mentioned is that the things he did not teach were not conducive to dispassion, cessation, tranquillity, full comprehension, perfect wisdom or nirvāna. In this story "dispassion" means the absence of passion, making your mind calm in order to see where you are, what you are doing. "Cessation" means to stop, to cease action. When you act, when you express some action such as having a nuclear freeze, there are always some waves of emotion, but cessation means stopping in order to realize calmness. "Tranquillity" means the state of being calm. "Full comprehension" means to embrace all things. In the case of the peace movement this means to embrace the nuclear freeze, people working in the government, people working in various companies, and others, whether for or against the peace movement. Full comprehension means to think on a broad scale. Finally, "perfect wisdom" means you can create the wisdom that leads to nirvana, but it is not created through discussion, it is created through appropriate action. For instance intellectual discussion and angry demonstrations are not conducive to perfect peace. If you constantly emphasize peace, carrying a placard and protesting angrily in front of City Hall, where is peace? If you get angry at politicans and scream, "Peace!" where is peace? Peace is completely lost. This is why Buddha did not teach that which was not conducive to nirvana.

Buddha only taught about what is suffering and about the path that leads to the cessation of suffering. "Suffering" means that human life is limited by conditions, such as economic, scientific, political, as well as by personal circumstances, such as your education, your psychological state, your past life, your *karma*, your daily life, your daily routine. All these things are conditions by which your life is limited. This is called suffering.

These conditions are not something bad. Conditions themselves are emptiness. According to Buddhism the ultimate nature of conditions is just like water. Water can be turned into any shape or color by people, by time, by place. Certain conditions called the American constitution, or the Minnesota constitution, or Zen Center rules have appeared in the past and the present that affect your life. That your life is limited by conditions is suffering. To be in the human world is suffering. Even though you do not realize it, it is suffering.

The cause of suffering is that we have an object. "Object" means conditions, your friends, parents, teachers, Zen Buddhism, Christianity, ethics, science, nuclear weapons. Suffering comes from our attachment to these conditions or objects.

Buddha taught us the way that leads to the cessation of suffering. He pointed out that we can neither ignore nor escape conditions, because without an object we cannot live as human beings. What, then, does the cessation of suffering mean? It means that as best as we can, we should create better conditions from moment to moment. Usually when you have an object, you become crazy about the object and you can be blinded pretty easily. Even though intellectually we know it is wrong, we constantly create attachments to a certain way of living. We create strong attachments instead of understanding deeply and doing our best to create wholesome conditions.

The other day on the news I saw a government official who takes care of nuclear weapons. He knows pretty well how dangerous nuclear weapons are, but he cannot stop his work, because his life is already limited by certain conditions, such as government policies and the relationship between America and the Soviet Union. We know well that this situation is dangerous, but we cannot stop it, because we have already created strong attachments, and these attachments really make us blind. Even though we know intellectually that the situation is dangerous, it is hard to create wholesome conditions day by day. So individually we have to do our best to create wholesome conditions, even though it is hard.

When you look around at the human world you say this world is terrible, but this is your imagination. The world you have imagined, that you can see, is not all there is. There is still a chance for you to create a peaceful world. For instance, while you sit zazen you are pretty peaceful, you are creating a peaceful world. No one is fighting. So there is still a chance for each one of us to create wonderful, wholesome conditions. Let's just start to create wonderful circumstances, better circumstances and conditions, individually and as a group. Of course, in the human world there are many individuals who don't care. This is why we have to make people aware of the way to make better conditions. This is our effort. It is called the way to nirvāna, or the Eightfold Path.[2] This is the cessation of suffering. Following this is what is really helpful in bringing about peace, real peace, for you and for others.

Actually, I don't know exactly how we should express our feelings for peace or our feelings against nuclear weapons, but there are a few important points to remember regarding this. If you have seen films of Nagasaki and Hiroshima after the atomic bombs exploded there, we should remember that nuclear weapons today are much more powerful, hundreds of times more powerful. This is an emergency situation. It is something more than just politics, something more than philosophy, something more than a certain category of religious activity. We have to act, I feel this, but we should not be blind toward politics and the complications of human life. When people act individually, they can be very kind and nice, but when people act as a group something happens. They are taken over by the group and become blind. For example, during the Second World War in Japan, priests, philosophers, teachers, parents were all very nice as individuals, but these same people belonged to a certain group called "Japanese"; they belonged to a certain time called "World War II"; individuals were completely negated and they became blind.

It is important for us to help in this effort toward peace, but we must be careful. When individuals come together and act as a group things can happen that you would never expect. This is why we have to consider how to help each individual's activity. But this is not to discuss or to look at the problem from a distance. We have to think of how to inform people of this emergency and how to make people aware. I don't know how, but we have to think about this.

So, one point is that this is a real emergency. It's not a situation in which we can have the kind of discussion where we decide how we feel about politics. It is completely beyond this. We should be careful, but we have to do something. So don't be too sensitive about politics, because, more or less, we are already right in the middle of politics. If politics is at a distance, you can keep away from it. But if politics is already in front of you, politics is already in your life. In other words, if a bulldog comes from a distance, you can keep away from it. But if a bulldog is right in front of you, you must be careful. You must be calm; you cannot show your fear, or fight, or show anger. The bulldog knows immediately what you feel. So you must stand up straight and still. Our situation is something like this. The bulldog, nuclear weapons, is already barking at us. What do we do?

What I can tell you is to please be judicious. It is not necessary to ignore the situation, nor do you need to be involved in it exclusively. You must act, but you must be careful and you must be thoughtful. It will not help to express your anger against nuclear weapons, because you are already right there. If you express your anger, nuclear weapons will just keep barking at you, and there will be no end. Don't express your anger or hatred toward certain people, or toward politicians, or even toward nuclear weapons themselves. Express your peace. Do research on how to set up peace. There is a big difference between angry and peaceful action. If you express anger toward nuclear weapons, even though theoretically it is useful, it is not good because at that time you are already not peaceful. If you express anger you also create a strong attachment toward "no nuclear weapons." This is the same problem as attachment to nuclear weapons. From beginning to end, we must try to express peace in order to create better conditions. So let's create wholesome conditions. This is our activity.

Casting a Pebble into the Ocean

In Sōtō Zen we pay careful attention to forms of action. Forms of action are very important in Zen practice, but not when used as a technique. If you use them as a technique, sooner or later you will become fed up with repeating the same forms day after day. In each form— walking, chanting, eating, *gassho*—you must find peace and harmony.

Some people criticize Zen practice because it is very strict. They say it is too much to pay careful attention to each form. The believe that in Zen practice there is a lack of Buddhist spirit. But what do they mean by "Buddhist spirit"? Maybe there is the belief that Buddhist spirit is to be swimming in the huge ocean called the universe. However, the ordinary universe is not good enough; it must be the "cosmic universe," which is something more than just the universe. But then the cosmic universe must be that which is free from any conceptualization of "cosmic universe," the "supreme cosmic universe." And the supreme cosmic universe must be that which is free from any conceptualization of "supreme cosmic universe." What is that? Keep your mouth shut. Just do it! This is a very simple practice for us. "Just do it" means each form is a way of life in which peace and harmony must be found.

There is a Zen teacher who uses the English term "meticulous" to describe Zen practice. Meticulous is like looking at a tiny particle of dust in the corner of a box through a microscope, and then picking it up. Zen practice is not meticulous. If you meticulously take care of each form, you will become nervous. You will never be free from your daily life. What I want to teach you is a little bit different.

When you swim in the ocean, you have to take your forms of action into the "cosmic universe." In the cosmic universe you have to take care of your daily life—washing your face, having breakfast, doing gassho, doing *kinhin*, walking, studying. This is our daily life, our daily routine. Our daily life is just like casting pebbles into an ocean that is very serene. Every form, every action is just like this. The moment when the pebble becomes one with the ocean you can immediately see the ripples. These ripples are called "form"—form of washing your face, form of having a meal, form of doing gassho, form of walking, form of zazen. Ripples are the posture you sit with now, or this *mūdra*, or this gassho. Ripples are: When you talk, just talk. Ripples are the form of action. You are always living right in the middle of form of action. You cannot get out of this. In the religious life this is ritual, or everyday life.

We always misunderstand what human life is. We always think that ripples as form are formalities; but ripples as form are not formalities. You say you don't like form. Nobody likes form. If there is lots of ritual you really hate it. I don't like it either. But ritual is important. If you handle the form of an action as a technique, without giving quality to the form, it is dead. Sooner or later you will be fed up with your daily life. You get up in the morning, wash your face, say, "Good morning," have breakfast, have dinner, go to bed, get up in the morning, repeating the same things, but there is no quality to your life. Of course, you learn lots of things about life and about Buddhism, but whatever you experience, finally the question is: Where are you going? Do you know where you are going? It should be clear. You are heading for emptiness. Simply speaking, you are heading for death. Is there anything that you can carry with you? Whatever your teacher gives you may make you happy, but we all have to die; it will not always be someone else's death. It's not anyone else's problem but mine. And when I die there is nothing I can carry with me.

Some Zen teachers tell us how helpful it is for us to do zazen. But zazen is useless. At an international yoga conference in Chicago some time ago, I was asked to talk about Zen life, so I explained Zen life and zazen. In yoga meditation, meditation must be useful physically, mentally, psychologically. But I said just the opposite: zazen is useless. No one was interested. But remember this, in the place where no one is interested, there is something that you have to be interested in, and that is life and death. In Zen monasteries there is always a verse written on a wooden gong that reminds us of how important the problem of life and death is. The person who hits this gong is always looking at this verse. This is Zen practice.

We have to come back to emptiness. How? Through form, through the form of an action. We have already cast a pebble into the ocean. This is the starting point of our presence. It is great proof, or verification, that we already exist, regardless of whether we like it or not. The problem is that we simply cannot perceive this action, because it is the activity of the pure oneness of the universe. But what we can understand is the ripple, our daily life, the form of actions. The unique way to come back to the starting point is to jump into the ocean and become one with the ocean. This is why form is important.

For example, gassho is jumping into the ocean. We cannot know the starting point of gassho in action but we can be one with it. How? Do gassho. What we can understand is the form of gassho. This form is very important because through this form we can return to the starting point, to the ripples that extend to every inch of the ocean and disappear in the immensity of the universe.

Through form we can return to the starting point of our presence and also of the presence of the universe. This is our daily life. That is why gassho is not the idea of gassho. Doing gassho, in its pure sense, is the dropping off of body and mind. Freedom! What is freedom? Freedom is not something hanging over your head, like paradise or heaven; nor is it being caught up in spiritual fascination. Freedom is something that is fully alive in your daily life. It is pure sense of practice or undefiled practice. It is precise, but not meticulous.

The form of your action must be clear. If the form of your action is blurred, you are confused. For instance, when you jump into the ocean you must first stand up physically on the cliff. Your psychological situation must be clear. You should know past and future. You have to know the proper way in which to jump, and the right spot into which you can jump. At that time you can say, "Yes, I am ready. One, two, three, jump!" That is to be precise. There is no idea or concept to insert here. After careful consideration, just do it! Next, forget it! All you have to do is to return to emptiness, which is pure activity. At that time it is called "practice in preciseness." This is Buddhist practice.

If you have never heard of this practice, it may seem a little strict. Maybe you sometimes feel tense or uncomfortable, but that's fine. What's wrong with being uncomfortable? What's wrong with being tense? You cannot always learn the way of comfort. From where does comfort come? It comes from discomfort. If you want to learn what peace is, you should learn what is not peace. Then, you should not be stuck in comfort, or peace, or nonpeace. You should be free from both sides. This means keep your mouth shut, just do it! This is zazen. You cannot expect anything from this practice of preciseness. All you have to do is just practice from day to day. Sooner or later you will understand this practice.

Burning the Flame of Life

If you start to practice zazen, very naturally thoughts come up; but when thoughts come you play with the thoughts. When you think, your frontal lobe starts to work. This is daily life. It is the cause of stress, confusion, conflict.

In Zen we let the frontal lobe rest for a while. Then very naturally there is no chance to create stress or distress by consciousness. Very naturally you become free from nervousness and stress.

In zazen, posture is very important. That is why we sit in the lotus posture. If you use this posture, your center of gravity is right in the middle of the triangle formed by your knees and your buttocks. The zazen form is really a three-dimensional triangle. It is a very stable posture.

Posture says something about you. Posture also gives you a chance to create energy. If you do not have proper posture, sooner or later your energy will dissipate. If you sit zazen, zazen is your life, whether you like it or not. When you study literature, literature is life itself. When you study science, science must be burning the flame of life. The study of science must be connected with the problem of life and death, otherwise science is something very dreary and cold. And if science doesn't pay attention to human life, it becomes dangerous.

In sitting there is already the full manifestation of your life as well as the whole universe, past, present and future. This is posture. Posture is like ripples formed by casting a pebble into the ocean. It is the unique opportunity to realize the whole universe. This is why posture is important for us.

Whatever your activity, literature, science, zazen, all you have to do is to devote yourself to taking care of life in literature, in science, in zazen. To take care of life is to burn the flame of life.

Nonthinking

A Zen master once said, "Think not-thinking." A monk asked, "What do you mean by 'Think not-thinking'?" The Zen master said, "Nonthinking."

When you are sitting in zazen, don't think. Don't use your frontal lobe. Your frontal lobe is sitting with you already, so don't use it to think. This doesn't mean to destroy thinking or to keep away from thinking. Just rest; don't meddle with thinking.

As long as you're alive, thinking will come up constantly; but don't meddle with it or fight with it. When you say "I shouldn't think," it's already thinking. All you have to do is to sit down in peace and harmony from moment to moment. Then there is no space to think. This is to "think not-thinking."

Of course, if you really think you are not-thinking, you fall into arrogance because next you may think, "I did it! I am enlightened!" Very naturally a haughty air comes up. Even though we think it's good, "good" is not so good. If you think, matters get worse. Much worse. So what should you do? Not-think. Not-thinking means please, rest your frontal lobe. Sit down. That's all we have to do.

We always measure things by our personal yardsticks. For example, if you experience a great feeling from your "not-thinking," you say, "Wow, this is great!" But this is already a measurement. Finally, neither "not-thinking" nor "thinking" hits the mark. So instead of measuring something by your yardstick, just try to be right in the middle of the world. This is called "nonthinking." It is nothing but practice; sit down there, peacefully, harmoniously. But watch out. Every day, from moment to moment, watch out, because egoistic consciousness is always coming up.

Mindfulness As the Middle Way

The Middle Way is the central teaching of the Buddha. It is not merely walking in the middle of the street. The Middle Way is the state of human body and mind working freely.

One way to understand the Middle Way is that it is the middle point, which is equal in distance from both ends of a line. This means when you get to the middle point you can see both sides, one on the left and one on the right, equally distant. In other words, you can see equally both good and bad, right and wrong. Whatever happens, if you are in the middle you can see both sides in the dualistic world equally. If you stay on the side called "good," or on the side called "evil," you cannot see either of them. In Japan, this is called *tan pan kan*, a board-carrying fellow. A man who carries a board on his shoulder can see only one side. The other side is the aspect of life he cannot see. Human life exists in the dualistic world of good and bad, right and wrong. We cannot stay on either side. But even though we cannot do this, it doesn't mean we should ignore good or bad, right or wrong. We have to understand both sides. In order to approach the destination, the beautiful, ideal image of human life that we call bodhisattva life or freedom, our mind must not be paralyzed. We don't know what freedom is, but more or less we are really seeking freedom. In order to reach freedom we have to see both sides of the dualistic world and handle both sides in equality. This is wisdom or the Middle Way.

Another way to understand the Middle Way is that it is the center of a ball. A ball is constantly changing, rolling, acting. This is human life. Human beings never stop acting. Whatever you are doing—sitting, sleeping, even standing still—you are always acting. Without action, you do not exist. It is just like a ball that is constantly going here and there or standing still according to circumstances. When a slope comes, the ball rolls down the hill. It acts, but even though it appears to be moving, the center is always still. We call this stillness *samādhi*. It is like the center of a torpedo. A torpedo is centered in front, and this center suggests which direction the torpedo should go. This means its center is always still, like the center of a ball. On the other hand, the center is not still. The center must be dynamic; it works, it acts. We call this dynamic centeredness, mindfulness.

In Theravāda and Mahāyāna Buddhism, the practice of mindfulness is very important. Mindfulness is very closely related to samādhi and wisdom. If we are without mindfulness we cannot have samādhi, which is perfect stillness.

Zazen is the basic practice that allows us to experience exactly what perfect stillness is. It is very difficult to experience this stillness without zazen. But you can experience samādhi in your daily life through mindfulness. Mindfulness has exactly the same meaning as "not to forget." "Not to forget" means to think, be mindful of something, be mindful of not forgetting. In our daily life it is pretty easy for us to be mindful of some things, for instance, playing ball, gambling at the races or at poker. It is pretty easy to be mindful and forget the time. We can be mindful of some things, but it is not always good. It is very difficult for us to be mindful of something good.

The Buddha says to be mindful of Dharma. Dharma is that which makes it possible for everything to exist. In other words, Dharma is the basic nature of existence. So, to be mindful of Dharma is to be mindful of that which maintains existence. To maintain something is a function of the dualistic world, because to act, to maintain is, generally speaking, to have an object. So, to be mindful of Dharma means when you do gassho, be mindful of gassho. When you walk on the street, be mindful of walking.

Mindfulness is to go toward the center, whatever you are doing. Usually the mind is going in many directions; instead of going out in all directions, let's go in. This means, look at the walking itself that you are doing now. This is to move toward the beautiful, ideal image of human life. It is Buddhist practice in zazen and in everyday life.

Thirsting Desire

When Shākyamuni Buddha was about to die, he talked with the people who were suffering from grief at the thought that he would soon pass away. They asked him what they should follow after his death. The Buddha said, "After my death you should see the Dharma. People who can see the Dharma can see me. People who can see me can see the Dharma."

The Buddha gave this same teaching to one of his disciples who was about to die. This disciple had practiced under the Buddha's guidance for many years, and he wanted to see his teacher before he died. When the Buddha came, the disciple said to him, "I have had a cherished desire to come and see you, but unfortunately, my strength is on the decline." The Buddha said, "Even though you have the chance to see this body, which will decompose, of what use is it? If you want to see me, see the Dharma. If you can see the Dharma, you can see me." This is the Buddha's teaching. It is a very strict teaching for most of us because we really want to receive something directly from our teacher.

This teaching is based on the four holy truths.[1] The first holy truth is suffering. This is a very important point. Suffering is not merely suffering as opposed to pleasure. Suffering is a *holy* truth; this means that it is one aspect of human life from which no one can escape. It is completely beyond what one likes or dislikes. You have to face it directly because your life is right in the midst of suffering. You cannot ignore it. If you ignore suffering, it becomes monstrous.

Human beings are apt to attach to the aspect of human life called pleasure. This is why we often say, "Enjoy life." Why, then, does Buddhism say, "Look at suffering"? Because suffering is the one aspect of human life that people don't want to see. We try to close our eyes to suffering, but we cannot do it. It is because we cannot close our eyes to suffering that the Buddha has to say, "Look at this other aspect of human life that you don't see." Suffering is a holy truth, so to say that life is characterized by suffering is not a pessimistic teaching.

Suffering is divided into three types. One is physical suffering; another is mental suffering; and a third is radical suffering, very basic suffering. Physical suffering is birth or life, sickness, old age and death. Everyone has to face physical suffering. According to Buddha's teaching, sickness is a holy truth. This means you have to accept sickness, which is completely beyond the world of your likes and dislikes. For instance, if you have cancer, how can you be free from this suffering? Buddhism tells us to accept the suffering from cancer. But it is difficult to accept it because you believe to accept the suffering from cancer is not to be free from cancer. This is why you struggle to get rid of the suffering from cancer instead of directly facing the suffering as it is. No matter how long you struggle to be free from the suffering from cancer you will never be free. Suffering from cancer is real reality, which is inescapable.

It is possible to accept the suffering from cancer as a great opportunity to touch the core of human life. This is the total acceptance of suffering. If you can totally accept the suffering from cancer, you can be free from it.

It is like trying to fall asleep. If you try to sleep, you cannot sleep. The more you want to sleep, the more your eyes are open. If you cannot sleep, then just be one with the fact that you cannot sleep. In other words, don't struggle. Suffering, as a holy truth, gives us a great opportunity to awaken to the truth of human life.

Mental suffering comes from being apart from those whom you love, or from being together with those whom you hate. Everyone experiences this. Mental suffering also comes from the fact that you cannot have what you want. Finally, mental suffering comes from the fact that you attach to the five *skandhas*, which are form, feeling, perceptions, impulses and consciousness. Again, these are aspects of life that everyone experiences.

The third kind of suffering is radical suffering, very basic or fundamental suffering. Radical suffering is the suffering produced by the transiency of phenomena. Realization of this suffering is something you can experience through deep practice or through deep understanding of the total picture of human life as it interrelates with all sentient beings. In other words, through deep practice of Buddhism you can understand and experience radical suffering. When your mind is busy and noisy it is very difficult to have this experience. Only when your practice is moving along very deeply will you experience this kind of suffering. This suffering is very calm, very still and very silent; but still it is there.

It is very difficult to be free from radical suffering. When your practice is very deep and your body and mind are very calm, you understand human feelings, you understand the feelings of the bird, the feelings of the tree; you understand everything. Still, there is suffering that is very calm and silent. It is a kind of fear, a very deep fear coming from the bottom of the human mind and body. You cannot explain it but it is always there. You have to face this suffering too.

Why do we experience radical suffering from a deep understanding of human life? According to Buddha's teaching, such suffering comes from ignorance. Ignorance is human attachment, which is tenaciously rooted in the depths of the human body and mind. It is completely beyond human control. You don't know when or how it will come up.

Ignorance is thirsting desire. Thirsting desire is the usual human desire, but very strong. Thirsting desire is of three kinds. First is the thirsting desire to please oneself continuously. It arises from our deep fear of the transiency of life.

The second kind is the thirsting desire for the continuation of one's individual existence. Through deeply practicing zazen you may say, "I am ready to die anytime, anywhere." I tell myself I am ready to die, but when I see the reality, the fact that it is I who am dying right now, my mind screams for help from zazen, from Buddha, from Avalokiteshvara Bodhisattva, but nothing happens. Finally there is nothing to do. Just sit zazen, that's all.

What is zazen? Zazen has nothing to say. Zazen lets you touch the core of your suffering. This is okay, but still delusion is going on and on, thoughts and ideas are going on and on. You may think, "What will happen after I die? Maybe my friends and relatives will remember me for many years." This is delusion. Whatever you think is delusion. We don't want to believe that the body and mind disappear immediately after death; but even though you don't want to believe, the transiency of phenomena takes you and your delusion too.

The third kind of thirsting desire is the desire to have and to maintain power and prosperity. It is a very strong desire that emerges from the discrimination of seeing things as separate beings. For instance, it is very important to us what others will say about us after our death.

This is because we really want to have some power to control others. We want to say, "Don't forget me. After my death you should remember me and put up my picture." Do you understand this? I understand pretty well because I always think, "Please don't forget me."

I knew Suzuki Roshi, the first abbot of San Francisco Zen Center, very well. After his death pictures of him were getting bigger and bigger—in the bookstores, at Zen Center, all over. And I thought, "Oh, you are a lucky guy! Look at you. But what about me?" This is really thirsting desire and it always creates suffering and fear. This is why we have to see very deeply and face this fundamental fear based on the three kinds of thirsting desire.

Thirsting desire makes you want to enjoy yourself instead of realizing what it is. In other words, it drains you and keeps you from seeing thirsting desire. This is a very common way of living. This is why there is no end to fighting and human trouble. The point is you have to face thirsting desire and realize it through your skin, muscle, bone and marrow. At that time you can be free from human suffering.

You cannot extinguish thirsting desire. Do you know why not? Thirsting desire is a holy truth. This means it is always with you. So, Buddhism doesn't ignore or try to destroy it. Buddhism knows very well what thirsting is. It knows that you cannot accept thirsting desire blindly. So, what should you do, practically, in your daily life?

According to the story from Zen Master Rinzai's life, he planted pine trees at the temple for two reasons: one was to make the scenery of the temple beautiful, and the other was so they would be there for future generations. His activity was based on human thirsting desire, but his purpose was vast, extending in the universe. If you use thirsting desire in a selfish way it is really dangerous, but if you use thirsting desire for the benefit of others, your purpose, your hope extends far. But you cannot be obsessed with your purpose and your hope because no one knows what will happen in the future. So, in this transient world, how can you use thirsting desire for future generations, for human beings, for temples, for trees, for birds, for all sentient beings? You must be free from thirsting desire. If you can be free from thirsting desire you can prosper in activity that is fully alive from moment to moment. Zen Master Rinzai taking a hoe and digging the ground to plant the pine tree is activity that is alive. He knows that thirsting desire is something to be used for all sentient beings. He doesn't ignore or try to extinguish human thirsting desire; he takes care of it.

Usually we are completely obsessed with thirsting desire. This is why we expect a lot of things. It is a big problem. For instance, your parents expect a lot from you. When you are a child, they expect you to study hard and show your capability. They want you to become rich, to get a college degree, or to get a good job. This is your parents' purpose, your parents' hope. It's beautiful. But parents must not be obsessed with their purpose or hope. They must be free from thirsting desire. This means that parents should just help their children grow from day to day. The children may study hard, get a college degree, and get a good position in human society or they may not, but that's okay. At that time, when the parents are open-minded, their hope is very broad, it's always there, working and helping. But if they expect too much from human thirsting desire, it creates trouble, because then there is no bridge that can be used to communicate with others. If Zen Master Rinzai expects too much from his act of planting the tree, there is no bridge between his hope and reality. This is because no one knows what will happen in the future.

If you want to build a bridge between your hope and reality, you must be free from that hope and from human thirsting desire. Then, just take care of reality based on the human desire to help all sentient beings. This is why Rinzai took a hoe and dug the ground.

If you study the four holy truths, you can realize that the extinction of thirsting desire, or human suffering, is not to cut off or to destroy human suffering. You cannot do this. Therefore Buddha has to say that human suffering is a holy truth beyond what you like or dislike. So, practically, what should you do? Just focus on actual human life and put the four holy truths into practice.

One Finger

If you want to learn life you must simultaneously learn death. If you try to learn only life and ignore death, your life becomes very dry. You have to learn both life *and* death. This is the Buddhist Way.

Buddha is represented as *tathāgata* in Sanskrit. Tathāgata means "looks like going, looks like coming." In Buddhism we say "no going, no coming." Buddha is not an angel, or some sort of divinity who has control over your life or who gives you spiritual power. Buddha is just going, just coming.

"Looks like going" is a wonderful term used to express the Truth.

When you want to express the total function of a thing, say a fish when it swims in the water, the function of the fish is exactly one with the function of the water. However, consciousness always sees the fish as being separate from the water. That is why you cannot see exactly the total function of the fish becoming one with the water. But real fish is no-discrimination-between-water-and-fish. They are one, but they are not one because they are two, but they are not two. They are really working together, so we can say, "Looks like a fish." "Looks like a fish" means it is not exactly a fish. If this is true is it water? No, it is not water, it's a fish, but it's not a fish. It is just oneness. This is called "looks like just going, looks like just coming."

Life and death means "looks like going, looks like coming." When you are about to die, can you say where you are going? We don't know where we are going. But just because you don't know where you are headed does not mean you are not going. So just be here, now. This is Buddha Tathāgata, just going, just coming.

If you are with a person who is about to die, regardless of whether you like it or not, just be present with this person. This is really great teaching because there is completely nothing to say, nothing to throw away, nothing to grasp. On the other hand, if there is completely nothing to do, can you just do nothing? No you cannot. Right in the middle of the road where there is completely nothing to do, to say, to grasp, to throw away, you have to do something, constantly. When breakfast comes, just have breakfast. When you want to drink a glass of water, just drink a glass of water. Whether you get up in the morning or just lie in bed, continuously you are doing something. This is just going, just coming.

Zen Master Gutei always presented one finger in answer to any question. To show one finger is Buddha's world. In Buddha's world there are two things that you have to learn. One is that there is completely nothing to say. If you say "life," life completely occupies the whole world. If you say "death," death completely occupies the whole world; you have to die with the whole world. There is nothing to say, but you have to be there and you have to act there. On the other hand, you have to know not going, not coming. This is really oneness, which is called "death," which is called "life." If you understand this life, this death, you are called buddha.

Let's see this situation according to human feelings. It's pretty hard. Human life, which includes sorrow, is nothing to say, nothing to grasp, nothing to throw away. It is very painful. You can't stand up there, but you can't escape either. In the middle of this pain you have to do something constantly, day by day. You have to get up in the morning, go to work, study, and take care of your life. This is the total picture of human life, which is called "one finger."

We offer beautiful flowers to the Buddha, but these flowers are not always grown in a beautiful garden. They may be thistles taken from the roadside in the country. No one pays attention to them because they are considered ugly. But look at a thistle. It's beautiful. If we take care of this thistle and put it in a certain place we can see that it is beautiful. So when you walk on the street from now on, pay attention even to the thistles as a buddha. Even though you don't pay attention to this thistle when it grows along the roadside, this thistle is really helping your life in many ways.

Why is this thistle beautiful? Because sooner or later it will fade away. Wherever it is, by the roadside or here helping your life, it is fading away. We don't know when life will fade away. We should remember this. When we think of life, simultaneously we should know that life is fading away. When you are very young you feel beautiful and full of life. This is true, but you should understand once more what youth is, what beauty is. You cannot understand beauty just in terms of beauty and ugliness. You have to understand it also in terms of both life and death, because beauty, like life, is fading away.

It is a dangerous situation. If we look at the human world, we don't know what will happen. This thistle is beautiful now because it is fading away. But we don't know when it will be gone. Its life is constantly going on in a dangerous situation. Nevertheless, the thistle must find its own life that is refreshing. This is beauty.

We cannot despair, we cannot be arrogant, we cannot say anything; but right in the middle of dangerous situations we have to live, we have to let our life force bloom with our best effort. At that time the flower of our life force becomes beautiful. This is why a thistle or any kind of flower is beautiful. It is fading away from moment to moment. This is very painful to human feelings. It is difficult to stand up in this situation. But even though we cannot stand up there, we cannot despair, because there are no exceptions. Look at yourself. You are fading away from moment to moment, you are marching toward the grave. You may not accept this, but it is really true, and this is why life is beautiful. We have to understand the beauty of life by understanding this situation. We cannot understand our life without thinking of fading away. At that time we can really let the flower of our life force bloom.

We have to live right in the middle of dangerous situations. If we live in that way life becomes very beautiful. This is the thistle. We accept the thistle according to our feelings, but the thistle itself is constantly accepting the Truth: life is life, one finger, no exception. Wherever it blooms there is nothing to say, nothing to throw away. Life is life.

The thistle cannot stop living its life. Wherever it is, it has to live with its best effort. At that time the thistle blooms. So when we put it in one place, it's beautiful; when it is blooming in another place, it's ugly. When we see it with ugly feelings, it becomes ugly. We don't care about the thistle's presence. But whatever happens, the thistle is the total manifestation of its life. That life has two points: there is nothing to say, but right in the middle of nothing to say, it has to take the best care of its life. This is just going, just coming, looks like going, looks like coming, which is not going, not coming.

In Japan it is customary to make lacquer bowls and china bowls. But recently, there are more plastic bowls being made. The plastic bowl looks the same as the lacquer bowl made of wood, but when it falls to the ground it doesn't break. So you can have it for a long time. When you drop a wooden bowl or a china bowl it breaks, so, according to common sense, which would you rather have? Do you want a china bowl that costs a lot of money and breaks very easily or a plastic bowl that is very reasonable and never breaks? Even though the plastic bowls are cheap and nonbreakable, people still want the breakable, expensive china bowls. The china bowl is beautiful because sooner or later it will break. If you make a mistake, or do not take good care of the china, it could break at any time; or it could last a long time if you pay careful attention and take care of it. The life of the bowl is always existing in a dangerous situation.

The same applies to human life. Usually when your life is busy you are only thinking about life. There is not enough time to think about death and besides, you don't want to think about death because you are still young. But when this is the case, your life becomes very greedy, like a hungry ghost. If you become greedy and want to have lots of money and material things because you want to be happy and healthy, that's all right. But what is real happiness? What is real health? Is it real happiness to be right in the middle of life, excluding death? Sooner or later, everyone must die. Everyone, without exception, becomes unhappy because of having to die. And when you die you are not healthy. When you die you are completely at the very bottom of unhappiness and unhealthiness. This is death. If you expect to keep living and to be happy by ignoring death, this is okay, but you won't be able to keep this up for long, because moment after moment, life is fading away, happiness is fading away. Sooner or later you have to die. Nevertheless, right in the middle of this situation we have to be refreshed constantly. This is Zen teaching. Your life must be refreshed whether you are young or you are old. It is only temporarily that we say "young" or "old." We have to see human life once more from the depths, from a different angle. You must constantly be refreshed right in the middle of sickness, suffering or despair, because this is life.

In everyday life there is no excuse. One day you like your life, the next morning you don't. But whatever you say, it doesn't hit the mark. Finally, all you have to do is just live. This is pretty hard and very painful, because, from day to day, you have to do something in this situation where you feel as though you cannot move an inch at all. You have to get up in the morning when you have to get up, wash your face when it's time to wash your face, have breakfast even though you don't like it, go to work and take care of your life. This is just going, just coming, not going, not coming. This is your life that is refreshing. This is Zen Master Gutei always showing one finger whenever any question was asked.

When Gutei was practicing in the heart of a mountain, a Buddhist nun visited his hut. She said, "Say a word of truth to me." But he couldn't say anything, so she started to leave the hut. As it was already dark Gutei said, "It is so late, why don't you stay here tonight?" Then she said, "Say one thing, then I can stay in this hut." He couldn't say anything so she left. Gutei despaired and was ashamed of himself. He decided to leave his hut and visit his teacher and practice harder. But the day before he left he had a dream, and in the dream someone told him that a great Zen teacher would come to visit him and suggested that he should wait in his hut. So in the morning he didn't leave, and the great Zen master Tenryū came. His teaching was to always show one finger, and Gutei was very impressed by this so he became a disciple of Tenryū.

Gutei like his teacher always showed one finger in answer to whatever questions were asked. But his teacher knew that Gutei's one finger was only an imitation. Just like plastic flowers, it was just a plastic one-finger. But Gutei was very proud when he showed just one finger. One day a monk asked him what Buddha-nature was and, as usual, Gutei showed just one finger. But when his teacher saw this, he immediately cut this one-finger off. Gutei screamed and ran away. Then from behind him, his teacher called, "Gutei!" Gutei turned around. Zen Master Tenryū showed one finger and then Gutei attained enlightenment, because this one-finger was not an imitation. Right in the middle of Gutei's pain, Tenryū showed one finger that was real and it really pierced Gutei's heart. From this attainment he said, "I can use this one-finger forever." This is Gutei's story.

One finger means real life. One finger of life, one finger of death, one finger of sickness, one finger of despair, these are not imitation. One finger is fading away constantly. It is always in a dangerous situation. There is no excuse. On the other hand, you cannot just be there, you have to do something there day by day. That's pretty hard. When it is something you want to do it is pretty easy, but when it is something you have to do it is very difficult.

When you do "just going, just coming," one finger becomes real one-finger, one finger becomes refreshed. Life becomes refreshed. In sickness, in despair, in hard work, in easy work, whatever it is, happy or not happy, you must be constantly refreshed. To be refreshed is to digest your life completely. This is the meaning of one finger.

Returning to Silence

Zazen is the right gate for entering the Buddha-dharma. But the Buddha-dharma is actually human life. So this zazen is not an exclusive practice; it is the most fundamental practice for all sentient beings. For instance, when you really want to know who you are or what the real significance of human life, human suffering, pleasure, Buddhist teaching is, very naturally you come back to silence. Even though you don't want to, you return to an area of no-sound. It cannot be explained, but in this silence you can realize, even if only dimly, what the real point is that you want to know. Whatever kind of question you ask or whatever you think, finally you have to return to silence. This silence is vast; you don't know what it is.

Whatever question you want to study, you cannot study it from your own shallow viewpoint. Finally, you will come to a vastness that is like spring water endlessly coming up out of the earth. The more you study something seriously, the more you will realize that everything is boundless.

From where does this spring water come? Not from anyone's small, individual territory. The water that comes from your territory is limited, not deep. The original nature of your life, or of your study, or of your personality or character is the spring water that comes up from the vastness of the earth. This is where you have to sit down.

There are many interesting things to do in the human world. To do as much as possible keeps you busy making lots of sounds. That's fine, but you have to understand that these sounds come from no-sound. If you always understand sound as coming from sound, you become confused and lose the direction in which you should go. You have to know no-sound, because no-sound is your nature. Then, very naturally, you will want to come back from no-sound and look at your own particular sound. That's wonderful. Then you can know it.

Zazen is to come back to no-sound. Come back to the sound of no-sound and see it. It's not just your limited territory, it is a vastness from which your capacity, your knowledge, your nature comes, just like spring water coming up from the earth. This is zazen, exactly; this is you.

There are many kinds of schools, many kinds of teachings. If you study these teachings you can find something excellent being handed down from generation to generation. Why, then, is zazen emphasized as being most important? All of us who are practicing Buddha's teaching in the Buddha's world, in other words, the Truth or the universe where you, trees, birds and all sentient beings exist, do not need to discuss the superiority or inferiority of the teaching. This kind of discussion is ridiculous. Eventually you will say, "This is best, this is wrong." Under the beautiful flag of religion, philosophy, psychology or whatever, we fight. This is always the human problem. We know that Buddha's teaching is deep. Some people think that Buddhism is very theoretical because modern physics is now giving us almost the exact same teaching that Buddha taught twenty-five hundred years ago. When we hear this, we say that Buddhism is wonderful. But this is not the point. The important thing is whether the practice is geninue or false. This is something you have to take care of right now, right here. How serious are you? How seriously do you practice? How thoroughly do you accept practice? How much determination do you have?

If you always discuss this practice in comparison with something else you will never find peace and spiritual security. This is not really seeing into human life.

Genuineness is right now, right here. If you do something with wholeheartedness, that is temporarily called "genuineness." In the next moment, if you do gassho with a feeling of slothfulness, it is false. Falseness and genuineness are right in the middle of the process of your practice. Remember this. It's not a matter of discussing how wonderful your teaching is or how wonderful the teaching of Buddhism is. The teaching of Buddhism, the teaching of Christianity, the teaching of modern physics, the teaching of anything is nothing but a finger pointing at the moon. If this is so, is the finger not important? The finger is secondary, but still it is important; when you deal with the finger, do your best. Without the finger it is pretty difficult to know where the truth is.

For century after century, consciously or unconsciously, human beings have depended on toys. Since birth we've all had toys to satisfy our desires. Even though we've grown up, still we have toys—cameras, tape recorders, video tapes, philosophy, psychology and even religion. Everything through which we try to satisfy our desires becomes a toy.

If we use zazen as a toy, it is not real zazen, it's just toy zazen. When zazen becomes a toy we are lost. We have lost sight of ourselves right in the middle of the human world because we are using zazen, philosophy, psychology, cameras, everything—offering ourselves to those things and then trying to get something from them in return. The important point is that we should not be a toy. If you deal with zazen as a toy, you become the toy, not zazen. Zazen doesn't care. If you become a toy, you become restless. More and more you want to get something from the toy.

We create more and more new toys endlessly. Look at all the toys we have created: video games, airplanes, guns, cars. In Japan there is a huge building thirteen stories tall devoted to video games. Imagine thirteen stories of video games. You can spend your whole life there. You can get prizes such as chocolate, tobacco, whiskey, whatever you want. That's Japan. Wonderful. And the parents are complaining that it is not a good education for the children. But the children don't care. It's lots of fun. They want to know why they should stop playing with toys when their parents are doing the same thing. Maybe they don't play with video games, but they use different things and enjoy their games very much.

This is ridiculous, but we are already in a ridiculous situation in the human world. But this is all right because through this we can find the Buddha's world, we can find what is important. To do this we have to know how ridiculous we are. This is the point. Through our skin and muscle and bone, we have to realize why we don't come back to silence and the vastness of existence. In the vastness of existence there are many sources of spring water. So come back to the silent world.

If I say this is why zazen is important, then you will compare it to other practices. You will start to discuss it. We are always curious about the teaching or philosophy of zazen instead of doing zazen. Just doing zazen, right now, right here, is endless. Finally if we continue to talk about zazen, under the beautiful flag of Zen practice or teaching we begin to fight. This is very common in the human world. We should concern ourselves with the genuineness or falseness of practice. This concern has to do with how seriously we take care of practice right now, right here. Genuineness changes very quickly; we cannot keep it for long because genuineness and falseness are sentient beings that are constantly changing. You cannot say, "I did it so I am a good person," because in the next moment you may fail. That's why from moment to moment, right now, right here, you have to act carefully. This is genuineness with wholeheartedness. This is practice.

How can zazen, just sitting and doing nothing, be depended upon for attaining enlightenment? This question is always asked. No one understands this kind of zazen because we are always looking for the zazen that can be used as a toy to satisfy ourselves. If we use zazen as a toy, even though we feel good from the toy, we can throw it away at any time pretty easily. Look at modern society. We always throw things away and then we have to create new things, new toys to replace those we have thrown away. All sentient beings are being used as toys.

Right faith is perfect trust. Perfect trust means to accept silence, and in the silence everything becomes zero. When you come back to the silent world, everything becomes "not-personal," no-person, no-sound. So come back, become a zero and there is wonderful peace. This is the silent world. Even though you say "I am," the "I" is shrinking—until it disappears. If I think, "I am good," this is making a sound. Finally, I ask, "What am I doing here?" Nothing. If I try to know who I am finally I have to come back to silence.

A famous Zen master named Sawaki Roshi always taught us that all we have to do is to just sit with the robe and the shaved head. That's all. I didn't understand this. This Zen master didn't have any education; he didn't have any temples; he didn't have any position or high social status. All he did was to go to various places to conduct *sesshin* and give lectures. He went everywhere, and he always emphasized just sitting zazen with the robe and the shaved head. Everyone loved him very much. Eventually Komazawa University invited him to teach zazen, and he said, "Finally, I am at the market." Zen Master Sawaki always emphasized real zazen, not toy zazen. But finally real zazen becomes a toy. Even though he didn't make zazen into a toy, somebody else did.

You have to keep a certain genuineness in practice. This is always the target you have to aim at, and not discussing the teaching, how deep or how shallow it is. But even though you keep this genuine practice, someone else may make it into a toy. That is human life. That's why from beginning to end we have to focus on genuineness of practice.

All we have to do is just sit, just come back to the silent world and the vastness of existence. This is just sitting. Even though you don't understand, this is zazen. Then when you come back, there is total trust, total trust because you are silent. This is called right faith. Faith does not mean belief. You cannot believe anything. Right faith means you must just be there, soaking in the silence and the vastness of existence. This faith is called trust. Then, when you really feel something through this practice, temporarily we call it faith.

To enter into this realm of faith is zazen. Zazen is not a method. If you think so then zazen becomes a toy. If you are going to use zazen as a toy, it's not necessary to do zazen; there are lots of other toys that are better.

Those who do not have faith will not accept zazen, however much they are taught. If you don't trust this silence and the vastness of existence, if you do not soak yourself in this realm, how can you trust yourself? How can you trust others? How can you deal with human life? No matter how long you try to study the *sūtras* or Zen, you will never understand. Even though you say, "I understand," that understanding is not understanding. Without this trust you don't understand. If you want to understand the sūtras or Buddha's teaching, not as toys, but as a finger pointing at the moon, with your wholehearted-ness, jump into the silence and the vastness of existence. Let the teaching really penetrate your skin and muscle and bone. Then you can get a hint of where the real moon is, of what the real moon is. Don't expect too much through scriptures and words. Don't discuss superiority or inferiority. All we have to do is to study the scriptures with wholehear-tedness and jump into the silence and the vastness of existence. At that time the scriptures become light through which you can see many things in the darkness. Whatever it is, not only zazen or Buddhist scriptures, but sports, music, or anything else, if you really devote yourself with wholeheartedness, you can learn many things. Never-theless, if you really accept those things totally on the basis of silence and the vastness of existence, the beauty of your life blooms, the beauty of existence blooms. This understanding is completely beyond human speculation.

Sanzen Is Zazen

Sanzen is zazen. Usually sanzen is translated as practice. But in En-glish, practice doesn't hit the mark of what sanzen is. Literally, sanzen means to surrender ourselves to tranquillity or simplicity in life. Sim-plicity is manifested only when our life, our circumstances, are very clear. When our life is clear it is a great opportunity for us to manifest simplicity or tranquillity in life. It's very difficult to manifest sim-plicity and tranquillity in our complicated world. Living in the compli-cated world, how can we manifest or understand simplicity? This is a difficult matter for us, but we have to do it because it is our original nature. So every day we try to practice. In order to submit to tran-quillity or simplicity in life we do zazen. Simplicity is zazen.

Zen Buddhism sees or hears or understands the world and human life as action that is constantly going on. Dōgen *Zenji* particularly men-tions that, under all circumstances, we should understand the hu-man world in terms of the flow process and not in terms of concepts. The world we usually see is already something conceptualized. But if the world is present as something other than our conceptualization, we are very confused, because there is nothing to depend on. People usually depend, consciously or unconsciously, on their conceptualiza-tions of the world. The Buddha and the ancestors tried to present the world before conceptualization. It is a little difficult to understand. But it is important that we taste it and understand it.

The world of conceptualization is kind of a blueprint for a house. Through the blueprint you can imagine what the house will be like. Or you can build the house from the blueprint. So the blueprint is important. But a blueprint is a blueprint, and you cannot live there. In the world of conceptualization people become onlookers or builders but they don't understand what the actual house will be through the blueprint. We can look at the blueprint with hopes and desires, always thinking and imagining. The carpenter knows pretty well what kind of house it will be. But even though you become a carpenter you never have a chance to live in that house. If you live in the house you find out that the world of conceptualization is not perfect. The blueprint is not perfect. You will realize many things. There are good points, weak points and a very close, deep communication between the house and the one who lives in it. But even though the world of conceptualization is not perfect, it is important for us, because without blueprints we cannot live. The point is we have to see the house in terms of the practical point of view of the person who tastes the house, through his life, every day.

Another example is the relationship between a piece of paper and fire. If you burn the paper, you may say, paper is something other than the fire in terms of the world of conceptualization. It's very clear you can see the existence of the paper as separate from the fire. But actually, what do we mean by burning the paper? In terms of active understanding, active penetration, flow process between fire and paper, in other words, in terms of true reality of fire and paper, you cannot separate them because paper is fire, fire is paper. But if I use the term "paper is fire, fire is paper," it's already dualistic. So in terms of true reality of the paper and fire, you cannot separate them. The paper is the fire, simultaneously, with no gap between them. But it's very difficult to understand it, because we get used to seeing and hearing and understanding the world in terms of concepts. No matter how often we are reminded of this point, we don't see it. But it's important to understand it.

There is a story about Gazan Zenji, who was a disciple of Zen Master Keizan, the fourth ancestor from Dōgen Zenji. One day Keizan said to Gazan, "Do you know there are two moons?" Gazan Zenji said, "No, I didn't know that there are two moons." Then Zen Master

Keizan said, "If you don't understand, you are not my successor." According to history Gazan Zenji took this very seriously and spent three years constantly contemplating this message with full concentration.

"There are two moons" means if you see the moon in the sky and say there is one moon, that is your understanding. But that is really seeing, hearing and understanding the moon in terms of the world of conceptualization because, in conceptualization, you always bring up *you* first and then you see the moon: *I* see the moon. There is always separation between you and the moon. So there is no opportunity for the moon and you to be interfused wondrously beyond your conceptualization, your speculation. True reality is something wondrous, where moon and you are interchanged and create something. This is the true reality you live in. This is your life. You don't know it. It is inconceivable. You cannot see the true reality of the moon and you, who are merged, interfused completely. This is exactly like the relationship between the fire and paper. We always see the paper and fire in terms of concepts, so, even though paper is fire, fire is paper, you don't believe it. But it is true, because in the world of the truth, something is always happening. Something is always going on.

This is the cold, true reality in which we live. Beyond whether we like it or dislike it, something is going on constantly. Whether we hate ourselves or like ourselves, it doesn't matter, actually, our life is going on. Our life is going on beyond human criticism. Our life is growing, our life is supported by something else.

The first paragraph of the Lotus Sūtra (Saddharma Puṇḍarīka) mentions the reason why Avalokiteshvara is named compassion. Avalokiteshvara means "to see the world and to be seen by the world." If I see with compassion, then all of you, because you are already seen by a compassionate being, will see me as a compassionate being. There is true reality or communication between the world and human beings. At that time there is nothing to separate or analyze like paper and fire. There is oneness, which is called compassion. True reality, which is going on between the world and Avalokiteshvara, is very compassionate, supporting, helping, sustaining, upholding the world. According to general Buddhism, it is called Dharma or the truth. The meaning of the Dharma is to support.

In the Lotus Sūtra, after mentioning the meaning of Avalokiteshvara's name, the Infinite Thought Bodhisattva asks Shākyamuni Buddha the reason why he is called Avalokiteshvara. This is a very interesting point; it is not an ordinary person who asks Buddha this question. Only one who is infinite thought can ask Buddha. If you are a person or being who lives in the usual conceptual world you cannot talk about Avalokiteshvara or true reality. You don't see Avalokiteshvara. That is why, first of all, the Lotus Sūtra introduces a being named Infinite Thought Bodhisattva to ask the reason for Avalokiteshvara's name. Then the Lotus Sūtra says there are myriad beings who suffer troubles. If they see or hear the name of Avalokiteshvara and they call upon him with wholehearted effort, simultaneously Avalokiteshvara will save them from their troubles.

This story reminds me of the meaning of zazen, that is, casting off body and mind. If you sit down, that is simultaneously casting off body and mind, dropping off body and mind, being free from body and mind. If you burn the paper, paper is simultaneously fire. In terms of conceptual thinking, we don't understand this, but actually the paper becomes fire simultaneously. If you sit down, immediately your body and mind are cast off. We don't believe it, but it is true, actually true, completely true.

The passage from the Lotus Sūtra goes on to say, "the Buddha answered the bodhisattva Infinite Thought: 'Good Son! if there be countless hundred thousand myriad *kotis* of living beings, suffering from pain and distress, who hear of this bodhisattva Regarder of the Cries of the World, and with all their mind call upon his name, the bodhisattva Regarder of the Cries of the World will instantly regard their cries and all of them will be delivered.'"[1] We don't believe it. If we believe it we call upon the bodhisattva's name, but nothing seems to change; suffering is still suffering. Suffering is still with us so we don't believe it. And then we decide that the sūtra lies, because we always see the world in terms of our concept of the world. But it is true. There is no other way to be delivered from human suffering.

If you see the world very deeply, then you can hear the sound of the world. The sound of the world is something you are always looking for. But you cannot actually find it through your experience, so finally that is suffering. It is a very direct cause of suffering. So finally you say, "Please." Please make me simple. Please make me free. The moment that you call, saying "please," is called Avalokiteshvara. There is no subject who is calling and there is no object you are calling upon.

Because the one who is calling upon something is simultaneously what one is looking for. That is Avalokiteshvara.

When you sit down in zazen, you don't know why. If you think about it, you can come up with many reasons. But the reasons don't hit the mark exactly. You cannot ignore the reasons you have thought of because they are part of truth, but not the complete truth. What you want is just to be present, right in the middle of true reality, where you and zazen exactly merge, nothing else. To sit zazen is to call upon something, and to sit zazen is exactly the something you are calling upon. You sit exactly in the middle of something you are always looking for and calling upon. We don't know what it is but it's always there. If you sit down, you feel something, you taste it. By virtue of deeply seeing the human world, of hearing the sound of the world, immediately we manifest ourself with wholeheartedness. This is the meaning of "with all their mind." Whoever we are, whatever reason we have to decide to sit down, immediately we can sit with our whole mind, our whole heart. Even for a moment, that's pretty good. Very naturally, all we can do is constantly return to the source of zazen, which means zazen based on casting off body and mind. This is the point we are always seeking. This is called faith. Philosophically, this is called emptiness. In the beginning, emptiness can be seen quickly, just like lightning and thunder. It is wonderful and it makes you excited. But if you penetrate gradually and deeply into Zen practice, again and again, it moves very slowly into your mind, into your life. It sneaks in, invades your life, very slowly, like something squeezing your neck with a jellyfish. You don't notice it but it feels suffocating. You may become confused and find it pretty hard to stay with the practice. But you have to go through this. If we go through it, in the middle of Zen Buddhism we can see many things. We can see emptiness wherever we may be. If we go through it, that something sneaking into our life turns into the effort, into great energy. It is exactly great energy coming up. Energy or human effort is just like spring water coming from the ground.

True reality is structured by emptiness. We have to live in the structure of the world even though we don't know what's going on there. But we have to be there because we are looking for that point which is the source. Usually we are always involved in intellectual understanding. It is important, but it's very difficult to taste true reality, which is going on as process, through the intellect. That's why practice is very important. And zazen is the essence of our practice.

Emptiness

The Buddhist teaching of emptiness is quite difficult to understand, but this teaching is very important for us. Emptiness is that which enables us to open our eyes to see directly what being is. If after careful consideration we decide to do something that we believe is the best way, from the beginning to the end we should do our best. We must respect our capability, our knowledge, without comparing ourselves with others, and then use our knowledge and capability and think about how to act. Very naturally a result will occur. We should take responsibility for the results of what we have done, but the final goal is that we shouldn't be obsessed with the result, whether good or evil or neutral. This is called emptiness. This is the most important meaning of emptiness.

When I became a monk I had no idea about the practical aspects of Buddhism or about life at the temple or about life as a Buddhist. My master told me very often that I was a person who was blessed with good fortune. I didn't understand exactly, but from my life at that time I could feel a little bit that I was fortunate. When the village people came to the temple and offered something to us, they didn't say, "This is a present for the teacher," they always said, "This is for Dainin Katagiri," for me.

My teacher, Daichō Hayashi Roshi, became a monk at the age of ten. He had practiced and studied very hard since his childhood under the guidance of a famous teacher of those days, at a monastery. Finally Hayashi Roshi became a very famous preacher, traveling all over Japan to preach about Buddhism to the Japanese people. And then he was given a wonderful, big temple in Nara, a very nice old city next to Kyoto.

Hayashi Roshi was very concerned about his teacher, who had been criticized and asked to leave his temple by the people he served, after he used money for his own personal needs that had been given to him to rebuild the temple after it had burned. My master found a small temple and made a place for his teacher there so he could take care of him. That is the temple of which I am now the abbot. By chance, at this same time, my teacher found his mother, whom he had not seen for many, many years. He couldn't leave her alone, because she was very old, so he brought her to this temple too. After his teacher died he was very concerned about how to care for his mother, who was now alone at the small temple. He had to decide whether to take his mother to the big temple in Nara or whether he should go to the small temple and live with her. Finally he decided to leave the big temple and he moved to the small temple and lived with his mother. It was fortunate that he did, because that big temple in Nara burned up right after he left.

At that time Hayashi Roshi was a very famous teacher and many people wanted to be his disciple. He had had six disciples, but when I became a monk under him, he had no disciples left. Actually one person was left but he was in a mental hospital, and then several months later, that disciple died. So all his disciples were gone. Some of them died, some committed suicide, some ran away from the temple, one disciple fought with the master and was put in jail. And then only I was left, but unfortunately I also went away, and came to the United States. So he died at his temple by himself.

He continued to plant good seeds, helping people, preaching about Buddhism, but his life was not lucky. In a sense it was a little bit sad and pensive, but he enjoyed himself. He said to me, "You are really a person who is blessed with good fortune. Sometimes you take my good fortune. I am jealous." Of course he said this with a smile. I asked my teacher, if he believed that he was an unlucky person, why did he practice Buddhism? Even though he did good things still he was an unlucky person, so why did he continue to practice? He said, "The karmic retribution of good and evil occurs at three different periods in time. One is the retribution experienced in one's present life, second is retribution experienced in the life following one's death, and third is retribution experienced in subsequent lives." The karmic retribution will continue from past, present, future, life after life; someday, somewhere, it occurs. This is the understanding of karmic retribution in Buddhism. He also said to me, "Dōgen Zenji says that if you discontinue practicing the Buddha Way you lose merit." I was very impressed by his answer. This was why he wanted to continue to practice the Buddha Way.

There is the law of causation and we shouldn't ignore it. If we do something good, there will be a good result. If we do something wrong, a wrong result will occur. This is the law of causation. But, actually, even though there is the law of causation, human life doesn't seem to follow this law, because, just like my master, sometimes we do good things, but we are not lucky people, and the results are not good. So apparently there are two possible results following the law of causation: a good cause will bring a good result and a good cause will not bring a good result. We have to understand both. But we are always tossed away by these two ways. If we see our life according to "good cause will not bring a good result," it is easy to allow our life to become decadent and not to care about a sense of morality. If we see people who are still lucky even though they have done something wrong in the past, we become skeptical and are unable to trust anybody. This way of looking at life is pretty hard to take care of, so it is necessary that we understand the law of causation within the overall picture of human life. It tells us to "watch out," to be cautious about our actions.

According to the law of causation, karmic retribution or results occur in the present life, or in the life following this one or in subsequent lives. My master didn't like his unfortunate life. He would have liked to be more fortunate. But he was not, he was unlucky. He did something good every day, but the results were not often good. Was there something that compelled him to be an unfortunate person? Maybe it was the result of his previous life, or his lives before his previous life. We don't know. But if we look at our life with straightforward stability, we can do something good every day. Whatever happens, all we have to do is to continue to sow good seeds. For whom? For when? For you, for all sentient beings, for this time, or that time, for the life after the next life, for future generations, all we have to do is sow good seeds. This is the practice for us.

The important point is that we shouldn't be obsessed or bogged down with the results that we see, feel and experience. All results, whether good, evil or neutral, must be completely accepted. All we have to do is sow good seeds day after day, without leaving any trace of good seeds, without creating any attachment. This is why my teacher, until his death, just continued to practice and help people. This is the meaning of emptiness. We cannot attach to either idea about the law of causation, that a good cause will bring a good result, or that a good cause will not bring a good result, because everything is changing constantly. Within this situation the point is how can we live in peace and harmony for the good of people and of future generations, life after life.

Emptiness doesn't mean to destroy our life or to ignore responsibility or a sense of morality, or our knowledge or our capability. We should use our knowledge, our capability, our career, whatever we can offer, to do our best to accomplish what we have decided to do. Results come up very naturally if we do our best. They can be a good hint, showing us what to do next, so we should completely accept them. This is emptiness. This is how to live, how to handle our daily human life.

But in daily living there are lots of distractions, both criticism and admiration. These things are distractions for us because it's pretty easy to be obsessed with them. If people admire us we are completely infatuated with that admiration. If someone gives us criticism we are completely tossed away and it's pretty hard to spring back. Always there is something that we are obsessed with, and we are stuck there. This is not emptiness. It's very hard, but this is daily living, so we cannot escape from this. The question is, how should we handle the admiration, criticism and judgment, good or bad, right or wrong? In daily living it's pretty difficult to do our best in order to accomplish what we have decided to do, because between the time we have made the decision and the time when we start to act, many things come up. Sometimes, before we start to act we are already tossed away. So it's pretty hard. This is why we have to know the overall picture of human life, which is very tangled with complications.

For this, zazen is a very simple practice. Zazen, itself, teaches us how to handle our daily living. We should think carefully about zazen, using our body and mind, using our knowledge, our perceptions, our emotions, everything. Then, after deciding to do zazen, just do it. If we do our best to accomplish this practice, according to the suggestions and information that the ancestors have given us, immediately we can see the result. Good zazen, good concentration, delusions, the beautiful face of Avalokiteshvara, angry *arhats*, many things come up. These are results in the realm of zazen. But these results are something we have to accept completely, because they are coming from our decision, our life. We are changing day after day, so whatever results come up, we have to take responsibility for them and accept them. But our zazen must be empty, so don't be obsessed with these results. All we have to do is do our best to accomplish our zazen after thinking carefully about what zazen is and then deciding to do it. Immediately results come up whether we like it or not, but these things are just within us. Nothing is given by others outside of us. These things are given by ourselves. When we realize this, it's a little easier to concentrate, to sit down without being tossed away by these results. It's a very clear human life, we can see who we are, how we have handled our life in the past, how we are handling our life now, and how we will handle our life in the future. In zazen we can see anywhere. These pictures of life in zazen are good hints for how to deal with life moving toward the future. If we see something we have to correct, we should just correct it. If we correct it and then believe we are correct, immediately we are off balance again. Then we have to correct again. Always there is something happening. This is zazen. This is why zazen is exactly life. The important thing is to accept completely those things that happen. If you see something you have to correct, correct it. If there is nothing to do, just do nothing. Whatever happens, from beginning to end, just continue to do your best to do zazen. That's all you have to do. In zazen there is regulation of mind; regulation of mind is having no sign of becoming buddha. This is emptiness.

Whatever happens, don't create attachment. "Don't create attachment" doesn't mean to ignore attachment. There is already attachment. The important point is to understand how to use attachment without creating too much trouble. If you see trouble, confine the trouble to a minimum, understanding what attachment is. Consider carefully what to do, using your knowledge and capability. This is already attachment. Without attachment, how can we do anything? Attachment is desire. Broadly speaking, without desire, how can we survive in this world? Using our knowledge, we consider carefully what to do next. And then whatever we decide to do, let's just do it, do our best to accomplish it from the beginning to the end. That's all we have to do. Immediately, see the result and accept it. Just continue to sow good seeds from moment to moment. This is zazen, which is called *shikan taza*, in which all delusions, doubts, distractions drop off. This kind of zazen is exactly Buddhist faith.

Buddhist faith is not an idea. It is practical action, something we have to actualize. Even though we can explain what Buddhist faith is, what zazen is, through and through, finally there is a little bit we cannot explain. This is the core of zazen or of faith. This is the core of being. Zazen, nose, mouth, ears, whatever it is, this is something we have to actualize in our daily living through our body and mind. Religious faith can become something dangerous that hurts people, so we have to polish our knowledge, polish our perceptions through and through. Then this is Buddhist faith, which is based on emptiness.

Buddha-Life

Buddha is always present in what-is-just-is; buddha just is. If we think we understand ourselves, this is already not exactly what-is-just-is, or thusness or as-it-isness. This what-is-just-is, or thusness, is not a state of being that we can know through our consciousness. In Zen Buddhism it is said that this is "the self prior to our parents' birth" or prior to the germination of any single thought. This is the self before something runs through our consciousness. The problem is that our consciousness is always working, going this way, that way, in every direction from moment to moment. So how can we know the state of "the self prior to our parents' birth," or thusness or what-is-just-is-of-itself? This is a big question, a big project for us to research. The best way to do this research is just to sit down and do zazen, and let the flower of life force bloom in thusness. That is all we can do. Nothing else. In other words, whatever problem we have, we have to take care of it and constantly keep walking.

This is not so easy for us, and many people give up on the way. Most people become angry with practice and many complaints come up. This is why we need to share compassion with each other, encourage each other, and walk together listening to the Buddha. This help is very important for us. If you are a very strong person you can walk by yourself. But usually it is pretty hard, so we need to practice in the *sangha*, walking hand in hand with the Buddha, Dharma and Sangha. This is buddha, or what-is-just-is-of-itself.

We can see the original principle of existence in the life of a tree, a pebble, snow, the seasons and other forms in nature. This principle is what-is-just-is-of-itself, before it runs through our consciousness. This original principle as a manifestation of buddha is not separate from the form of trees, form of pebbles, form of the seasons or the form of everyday routine. It is always manifested and completed. "Completed" means there is no excuse, because it is completed in every single form of existence. It's there, speaking. Trees are always speaking about the original principle or buddha. This is called Dharma or teaching. Everything becomes a teaching for us. We realize the Buddha in every single existence. We realize all sentient beings are buddha.

This buddha or pure nature of existence is not abstract; it is manifested and completed in every single form of existence. If so, we can practice it, we can manifest it. Even though we don't practice, we are all buddha. But if we don't practice Buddha's life, we cannot manifest buddha. So we have to practice it. In other words, if we don't take care of our life as Buddha's life, then our life doesn't make sense; it is a very shallow, very thin life, like a piece of paper. But if we take care of our everyday life, finding it within the life of the universe, then our life becomes very deep. We have to practice what-is-just-is-of-itself. Whether we understand this or not, forget it! Forget it because what-is-just-is-of-itself is exactly manifested and completed beyond our speculation or understanding. It is always with us. It is a qualification of our existence, of our presence. So all we have to do is live in the domain of this qualification of our presence. If we live within it, we can manifest it. How? This is zazen. It is a very simple practice. Without zazen, each single buddha cannot be buddha as it really is. Without zazen, we cannot be buddha. This is the authentic teaching of zazen handed down from generation to generation and open to everyone.

Sitting is zazen. This is a great opportunity wherein we encounter buddha exactly. But we cannot see, we cannot touch this with our six physical senses. All we can do is accept this reality as a whole, and then just walk within it. Using our flesh, bone, muscle and marrow, then sitting down, is not the sitting we think it is. Sometimes people say that sitting is wasting time, or that it is a great opportunity in which we can get good ideas, or that it is a way to calm ourselves down, or that it strengthens our lives. Whatever we say, it doesn't hit the mark. Whatever ideas we have about it, they are nothing but a part of impermanence. These ideas always appear and disappear. Beyond these ideas, we should pay attention to the moment itself when we sit down right now, right here, with wholeheartedness. What is this opportunity and time? What can we experience? When we sit in zazen, buddha encounters buddha. This doesn't mean we encounter another separate buddha. If there is another separate buddha, there are two; "I" encounter "buddha"; this is dualistic. Buddha encounters buddha. Winter sees winter. It doesn't run through our six senses, because buddha means what-is-just-is-of-itself. There is nothing to see through our six senses. But when we sit down, we can exactly encounter what-is-just-is. And then, within what-is-just-is, which is called buddha, we can become one with winter, trees, birds, all sentient beings, exactly.

However, consciousness always pokes its head into zazen. That is why in the next moment that teaching becomes blurred, and we don't understand it. Then that teaching is far from us, and it's pretty difficult to really taste it. Finally, what can we do? If we want to practice the Buddha Way we should believe what-is-just-is-of-itself, without confusion, perverted ideas, suffering or pleasure. There is nothing to say. All we can do is just believe. Believe means do it, practice. In Buddhism, to believe is simultaneously to practice. So, sit down. Then, belief comes up.

In Zen, the form of zazen is simultaneously the life of the Buddha. In other words, the form of zazen is something more than just a form; it is nothing but the expression, the manifestation of the whole universe or what-is-just-is-of-itself, before we can understand it, before we can know it. This is called universal life. When we sit down, immediately we can switch the form of zazen into the Buddha's life. How can we do this? Practice in motion—sit down right now. There is no space, no room for us to poke our head into this zazen. This is a pivotal opportunity to turn our zazen into Buddha's zazen. But we always *try* to do zazen. This means we try to get something, we try to see something in zazen. When we try to see, we try to know, we completely ignore the fact that we are allowed to know. Then there is no opportunity to turn the form of zazen into Buddha's zazen.

Our life is something we can know, but simultaneously something we cannot know, because it is universal. To try to know what the universe is, is like always pouring water into a bamboo basket that is small and loosely woven. How can we keep the universe in this bamboo basket? It's impossible. But this is our usual pattern. We always want to know, we want to acquire, we want to see something. But life is not exactly like this. Life is something we can know, and at the same time it is something we cannot know.

How can we know what we cannot know? We can devote ourselves to doing zazen, put ourselves right there, and then we can see both the zazen we can know and the zazen we cannot know, life we can know and life we cannot know. This is to become buddha. Regardless of whether we are conscious of it or not, there is no other way. This is the unique way to live, whether we are Christian, Buddhist, or whatever else we practice; it doesn't matter.

For instance, how can we know what real death is? There is no way to know. All we can do is surrender, completely give up right in the middle of life and death. We have to give up lots of ideas. "Give up" doesn't mean to destroy ourselves. It means to make our life alive, make our life refreshed. At that time, we can just walk from day to day toward death. That is all we can do. But we always try to know what death is. There is no way we can know. But if we put ourselves right in the middle of death we are allowed to know even though we don't want to. How can we accept this opportunity through which we are allowed to know or to see? We must be magnanimous, compassionate, tolerant and openhearted. In terms of the Buddha's eye, in terms of the universe, the whole world is really given to everyone in equality. Equality is not something we try to know. Equality appears when we put ourselves in the appropriate place and then naturally we are allowed to know. We are always trying to live in order to enjoy our life. This appears to be strength, but real strength cannot be obtained by only trying to know. We have to open ourselves, and at that time, we are allowed to know, to live. This is the pivotal opportunity where we can know oneness of Dharma and person, oneness of life that we can know and life that we cannot know.

Without exception we have to practice this way, and then we become buddha. Buddha is not something separate from us. When we use the term, buddha, it seems to us that buddha is far from us and we think we are not buddha. That is a great misunderstanding. We are buddha. Buddha means we become something more than a human being; we become a great being from whom the light of our personality as a whole is given forth. Then people are very moved by our presence, by our talk, by our silence, by whatever we do.

Knowing

The most important thing handed down from generation to generation by buddhas and ancestors is the characteristic of knowing. This is not knowing by virtue of relating to objects or encountering the external world. This knowledge is subtle and inconceivable, so strictly speaking there are no appropriate words to express it. It is not something we can experience by means of discrimination, because this knowing comes without using one's strength or power or any technique. It comes from the depths of existence. It is knowing that has no gap between subject and object. Knowing is exactly the real dynamic working of knowing. Real knowing participates in itself, becomes one with itself. It accepts the structure of its being and other things. Knowing has no doubts. It is "just exactly so"; from the bottom of our heart, we say, "Yes." This knowing or "just exactly so" means to allow oneself and other beings to be as they really are. In order to do this, we have to participate in knowing itself.

In other words, if we want to know who we are, we have to participate in ourselves. This is very difficult. We seem to participate in ourselves, but even though we say, "Yes, I know who I am," this "I" is not the real self as it is; still there is a little gap. The self has to participate in the self exactly, intimately. Real knowing must be something like wearing contact lenses. If we wear contact lenses or clear glasses sometimes we do not even realize we have glasses on, but if we are wearing colored glasses we are usually very aware of their presence.

When knowledge is completely digested in our life, that knowledge becomes illuminated. Illuminating means that knowing is working in a concrete way in every aspect of human life. Dōgen Zenji uses the term "light" and says that light means merging of the eyeball and the skin of the eye. It is just like a contact lens. Contact lenses usually don't bother the eyes, they fit exactly. The contact lens becomes one with your eyeball and it works. You don't notice its presence on your eyeball because the eyeball and the contact lens work together very smoothly. This is like knowing or illumination or light.

The first line of the Heart Sūtra is usually translated into English as "Avalokiteshvara, when practicing deeply the *prajñā* pāramitā . . ." But more literally translated it says, "Avalokiteshvara seeing and illuminating prajñā pāramitā . . ." Seeing means knowing and this knowing is completely digested until it turns into life energy. This energy appears in every aspect of human life, gassho, a cushion, a cup. Within each single form of being we can see this total dynamic life. This is seeing something with our whole body and mind. At that time we become one with our object and this is illuminating. So Avalokiteshvara practiced deeply, by seeing and illuminating.

If we attain enlightenment we can see the whole world turn bright and beautiful. We are attracted to this enlightenment. Then we tend to define enlightenment as an experience that creates a difference between us and others. But real knowing is not a technique or a way that creates a difference between us and others, nor is it something that depends on something else. Usually we want to have something to depend on, but even the slightest indication of wanting to depend on something is already a mark of the dualistic world.

Even if we don't use our own effort or power, real knowing comes up when we stand in the appropriate place. But usually we don't. First we want to understand something according to individual knowledge, prejudice, customs and habits. This means we are standing up in our individual place, not in the universal perspective. This egoistic behavior makes it very difficult to see the overall picture. But buddhas and ancestors recommend that we first stand up in the appropriate place. Just stand up, be present in the universe itself. We have to stand up in a concrete way in the universal perspective that appears in every single aspect of human life. In walking, standing, eating and talking, there is an appropriate place where we can stand. If we have nothing to depend on, we find it difficult to stand up steadfastly. But actually, in order to stand up steadfastly, we have to realize that there is nothing to depend on. At that time we can see the overall picture of existence and then we can stand up in the appropriate place. This is what we have to do.

This is an important point we have to understand in order to know the real meaning of zazen practice. Zazen is a needle that points exactly to the cause of human sickness, human suffering. Zazen is very subtle, wondrous and inconceivable; that is why it is difficult to know. Zazen is just like a bird flying in the vastness of the sky, like a fish swimming in pure water that is clear to the bottom of the ocean. But if we are trying to find something we can depend on, zazen becomes a task, or a job, or a responsibility. It becomes difficult for us. Real zazen is not like this. It is the manifestation of dynamic energy, like a leaping fish or a bird flying in the vastness of the sky whose spirit can be extended into everyday life.

Intimacy

Through a very deep intellectual sense we can see how the Truth and the phenomenal world work together. They are not separate. Through any of the religions we can experience that God is in us, the Truth is in us. This is called enlightenment. This is oneness between phenomenon and noumenon, the world and Truth, or form and emptiness. But still there is some question about how to actualize the Truth or emptiness in everyday life, in form. Emptiness and everyday life are working together, but we don't exactly understand this oneness or intimacy; that is, we don't participate directly in intimacy itself. We see intimacy at a distance.

The final goal is that we have to participate in intimacy itself. We have to live there. This means we have to live in the samsaric world.

That is why after attaining enlightenment we still have to continue to practice, and then through this continuous practice, we can know how intimately Truth and our everyday life are working together. Gradually we can see this, not with our intellectual sense, but through our body and mind. We can hear the sound and the voice of how intimately they are working together.

Form in everyday life is manifested as customs, habits, education, social structure, morality and ethics. Individual customs are completely different from one culture to another, but there has to be some organization so that people can work together in human society. This is called culture or a constitution, or laws. This is also the purpose of ritual or ceremonies in one's life such as a wedding service or a funeral. When we participate in ritual, we can feel the intimacy of individual customs and habits working together with us. This is really the quality of life.

For instance, in Japan there is a particular national day called Adults' Day. On that day, people who become twenty years old have a ceremony marking the advent of becoming an adult. Through this ceremony we can feel a sense of intimacy between adolescence and adulthood. After participating in this ceremony, we don't feel any different; one is still the same person. But there is a change. Through this ceremony one becomes an adult, someone who is completely different from before, and on the other hand there is no difference; one is the same person. We can feel two feelings: I am an adult; I am not an adult. Through the ceremony we can feel the intimacy between feeling like an adult and not feeling like an adult. We cannot analyze that intimacy, but there is a kind of steadfastness in our life, right now, right here. It is completely undefiled by the ideas of adult or not adult.

The same is true for other ceremonies or rituals. For instance when we perform a funeral service, we don't know where the dead person is going. But we can feel relief because there is a kind of intimacy between the dead person and us. Even though we don't know what it is, there is great intimacy there. When this intimacy is actualized, it is called ritual or form. Form in action is ritual. Ritual is very important for us because it is through participating in form that we can experience intimacy. The intimacy we can experience through ritual is inconceivable. It is what we call nonthinking. Nonthinking means beyond thinking and not-thinking, beyond adult or not-adult. If we are present right in the middle of intimacy, through a ceremony, what did we experience? We don't know what it was, but by participation in the ritual, we can feel something deeply, not only through the intellect but through the body and mind. We can see the working together of adult and not-adult. This is intimacy, this is form. Form is something intimate of itself. So form is not form. Form is pretty broad; it is a big world we can experience.

If, through intimacy, we see form, at that time form becomes a very serene ocean in which all sentient beings are reflected. Strictly speaking, it is not a reflection. The ocean and all phenomena are one, working together. This is samādhi. There is no gap between them. Form becomes a bright mirror where all sentient beings are working together. Form is the total functioning of all beings. It is not dead, it is always working. It is nothing but practice. If you see form as having no quality, no depth, just like a piece of paper, or in other words, if you use form as a means, then form is dead. Form is not a means to reach something. Form itself is very important because it is really deep and unfathomable.

Whether or not a particular form brings about the feeling of intimacy—as opposed to any of the other practices that people do in their daily lives—depends on individuals and how they deal with form in their lives. If form is dealt with in terms of a moral sense, or in terms of social manners, it becomes culture: rules, regulations, customs, morality, and so on. Then it is very limited. But if form is dealt with in a religious sense, it means learning the connection of life with all beings. This is the very broad sense of form; it is universal.

We perform rituals all day. We get up and brush our teeth, wash our face, get dressed, and all of these are forms through which we can experience samādhi if we bring full concentration to them. It does not have to be a religious ritual in order to experience this oneness. Buying an ice cream cone can be a very deep ritual. That is why it depends on the individual attitude, how we deal with each form, whether we do so in a deep sense or in a narrow sense. Washing the face is a form, but if we just wash our face in order to keep ourself looking nice, it is the usual sense of form. If we deal with washing our face in a religious sense, we can see the overall picture of human life. But it's very difficult because it is just routine everyday life. That is why we bring particular practices into everyday life. For instance, in Buddhism we have the six pāramitās: giving, patience, discipline, effort or zeal, concentration and wisdom. If we decide to practice one of the six pāramitās every day, then, in a deep sense, we forget how to deal with everyday form, because we are always focusing on this one practice. We don't know how to deal with the rest of the forms in our everyday life. That is why washing our face is very important. We can participate in our individual life and also in universal life in everything we do.

The experience of intimacy is not a particular practice we have to do, separate from everyday life. We have to see intimacy within the form of everyday routine. Everyday routine is the practice of intimacy. This is the basic practice that we have to carry on forever.

Touching the Heart Strings

When we have an experience that lets us touch the heart strings, at that time we feel great joy, with words or with our mind or body. Sometimes we cannot say anything, because touching the heart strings is a deep, spiritual experience. Sometimes it can be explained, and sometimes it cannot; but it really influences your life.

If you have an intellectual or emotional interpretation of this experience of "touching the heart strings," it is already your individual experience. But before your interpretation, touching the heart strings itself is vast. You cannot say anything. You can experience this through zazen or Buddha's teaching or in your daily life. You know what it is, but you cannot explain what it is. It is very effective and it influences your life directly. This experience is a great suggestion or hint of what to do, from a very deep perspective. So this experience is very important before your consciousness or even your intuition catches it. Touching the heart strings is the pure sense of experience. This is important for us. Buddhism always emphasizes this point.

Hui ch'ao asked Fa Yen, "What is buddha?" Fa Yen said, "You are, Hui ch'ao," meaning "You are buddha itself." This "You are buddha itself" is something you have to experience as touching the heart. And then when you have this experience, immediately two things are apparent: You can explain it because you can experience it directly, and although it is explainable, at the same time it is not, because you have to pay attention to the experience of touching the heart strings itself. At that time there is no way to explain anything. This is called buddha. It is you because without you, there cannot be an experience, you cannot know anything. The pure sense of experience, which is called "touching the heart strings," is, characteristically, completely beyond your explanation. But it is something active, functioning constantly; that is why you can have the experience. So, in a sense, it is explainable.

Zen practice always focuses on the pure sense of experience. Touching the heart is completely beyond individual satisfaction or dissatisfaction. All you have to do is just continually move directly toward the pure experience of touching the heart. It is just sitting, gassho, chanting. But we are not satisfied because we always evaluate with our consciousness. But something evaluated by your consciousness will never guide you to touch the core of your experience.

The important point is that touching the heart strings is something you have to experience. Otherwise you cannot understand human beings from a universal perspective. The buddhas and ancestors constantly teach us to move directly toward touching the heart. Sometimes you feel good, sometimes you do not feel good, but that's all right. Whatever you say about it, let's just go toward this. In other words, touching the heart is to rock your heart strings to their ultimate state. You do not know how much you can rock them; this is because we are already in ignorance. All we have to do is just constantly rock the heart strings to their ultimate nature. Sooner or later, ignorance opens its own door and then you can open up a straight path toward the heart strings. This is Fa Yen saying, "You are buddha."

Do you remember the story about Shākyamuni Buddha, when he was asked to help the Shākya clan, which was about to be attacked by a neighboring country? The general found Buddha sitting under the dead tree in the hot sun and asked him why he was sitting there. Buddha said very simply, "It is cool under this tree because it is near my native country." Do you understand this feeling? The general was very impressed by these words. They touched his heart, so he turned back and left. Intellectually it doesn't make sense because it is not cool under a dead tree in the hot sun, but it was cool for Shākyamuni Buddha. Touching the heart is something that is alive in the deep awareness of oneself and in illuminating others. It is not sentimental or emotional, in which condition one is easily spaced out, nor is it intellectual; it is an activity that is firmly and clearly grounded in the reality of one's being.

Breeze in the Sumi Painting

In Japan there is an art form called sumi painting. Sumi painting uses just black ink and a brush. Black ink is black ink, but black ink is not black as a single color. If you paint a pine tree with black ink, that one color creates many colors. Perhaps you have seen a sumi painting: tiny boat, fisherman in the boat, ocean. And in the corner, just one tree; that's all. Can you imagine this? Just one tiny boat, and just one little tree, and no colors, just white. White is one color, but from white, space is created, and many colors. From this you can see the huge scale of the world: sunny days, cloudy days, oceans—all this expressed in different ways. From sumi painting you can feel this; that is why in sumi painting black is not just black.

Another characteristic of sumi painting is that with sumi painting you have to listen to the rhythm of the universe, the rhythm of the world—the tree, the boat, the ocean. The ocean is white, but you have to have eyes to see, ears to listen to the rhythm of the ocean, the rhythm of the boat, the rhythm of the tree. This is very important. For instance, there is an interesting poem composed by Ikkyū Zenji, a famous Zen master. It says:

> And what is it, the heart?
> It is the sound of the pine breeze
> There in the sumi painting.[1]

According to Buddhism, mind is just like the sound of the pine breeze in the sumi painting. There, on the paper, is the pine tree, and the ocean, and the boat. And you can feel the breeze, and the sound of the breeze, from the painting.

In another poem a Zen master says:

> The breeze in the sumi painting—
> How cool it is!
> Even oneness disappears
> When culminating in not-two.[2]

Two means the dualistic world. For instance, when you want to swim, there is the ocean and there is you. It is dualistic. "Culminating in not-two" means jump into the ocean. Ocean and you become one. That is the ultimate state of becoming one. In other words, oneness is not an idea of oneness. The oneness of the ocean and you is something active, something that leaves no trace of form. Activity is constantly moving from moment to moment. We do not realize it, but mind is always picking up activity right at the moment of activity. When you pick up activity, immediately it is form or experience. But right in the midst of activity there is no form. All you have to do is just be there. This is oneness.

Oneness is the rhythm of the sameness of ocean and you. At that time it is called "to swim." To swim is constantly to swim. If something is wrong with the power of your body, you cannot swim. So your whole body and mind must be operating smoothly; that is "to swim." It is leaving no trace of any form. That is why the Zen master says, "Even oneness disappears when culminating in not-two." That is the breeze in the sumi painting. It is not something dead. It is something you have to realize. It is cool. "How cool it is" means you cannot explain, but you can feel how cool it is. That is most important. If you leave no trace of any form, experience becomes just like a breeze in the sumi painting.

In sumi painting there is something painted by a brush; but even though you paint the pine tree on paper, that pine tree is not something painted. It must be something alive, something that is exactly the same as the pine tree living in nature. At that time, people are moved by the painting. When you really understand the pine tree, the pine tree becomes alive on the paper. You can feel the breeze moving in the pine tree. You can feel the sound of the breeze and how cool it is. You cannot explain it, but it is beautiful.

Entrance to the Buddha Way

All Beings Are Buddha

THERE IS A RITUAL in Zen Buddhism for entering the Buddha Way. It consists of making formless repentance, of taking refuge in the Triple Treasure, and of vowing to practice the Three Collective Pure Precepts and the Ten Prohibitory Precepts.[1] This ritual is based on the idea of repentance, which means, in Buddhism, perfect openness of heart. If we open ourselves completely, consciously or unconsciously we are ready to listen to the voiceless voice of the universe.

First we make repentance, which allows us to listen to the voice of the universe, then we take refuge in the Triple Treasure (or three refuges). If we open our hearts, next we have to manifest our lives in the realm of the universe, because our whole bodies and minds are embraced by the universe. There is no other way. So the Triple Treasure is our goal in life. When we realize our existence in the realm of the universe, then naturally we can see this goal. The Three Collective Pure Precepts are the way to live in the profound aspiration to help all sentient beings. The Ten Prohibitory Precepts are the teachings to follow in order to throw ourselves into the universe by putting aside the assertiveness of the ego. All we have to do is carry on the continuity of this practice forever, day by day, regardless of whether we feel the voice of the universe or not.

The entrance to the Buddha Way is signified by three points: first, by the realization of the truth that all beings are buddha; second, by the profound and steadfast aspiration for living our lives with all beings in peace and harmony in the light of the Buddha; and third, by helping all beings. To enter the Buddha Way is to see and to create the opportunity by which we can realize these three important points.

The first point is to realize the truth that all beings are buddha. For twenty-five hundred years ancestors and buddhas have been showing us that we are all buddha. This is verification for us that we are great beyond human speculation. All we have to do is to realize this truth.

To realize this truth means to know and to digest this truth, and then this truth will manifest itself.

What does it mean "to know"? There are three kinds of knowledge: ordinary knowledge, knowledge beyond the ordinary, and supreme knowledge. Ordinary knowledge is the discriminating or analytical thinking that we use every day. It is seeing the world as if it were made up of fixed and separate beings. Our friends, our children, our parents, objects—all are seen to be separate from one another and from us. From this viewpoint it is very difficult to have peaceful communication or to give ourselves with full devotion, full commitment, to another's life. When you have to help your children with school work, why don't you help with full devotion; at that time, your life can be found exactly in the children's lives. It is your time, but your time doesn't appear on the surface; the children's time appears on the surface. Your time is found within the children's time. Buddhism always teaches that you should find your time within another's. This is called full commitment; this is called "help." There is no separation. You are the child; the child is you.

The second kind of knowledge is knowledge beyond the ordinary sense. It means to try to know the truth—that the world is impermanent. In the ordinary sense, we see things as fixed. If we want to know deeply what human life is, we should put our mind in the truth of impermanence. Immediately we feel something from impermanence. We may feel pensive and say, "Don't teach that the world is impermanent, because it's pessimistic." But, no matter what our experience or our feelings about impermanence may be, the world is impermanent. So we shouldn't stay with our feelings or our experience of impermanence. You should see *you* who are always disappearing, disappearing in the world of others. When you help someone, you must always be found within that person's life; the figure of your life must leave no trace of your life. This is just like the relationship of waves and water: If you recognize the existence of waves it does not mean waves exist separately from water; they are always found in the realm of water, working constantly in the larger scale of the world that is water. If you do gassho, gassho occupies the whole world. The rest of the world's beings are completely hidden behind one gassho. When you help somebody, you are just full commitment. At that time, you occupy the whole world. The other's life is hidden within you. This is called "help."

Put value on the Dharma, not on individual experience and feeling. This means to put value on the bigger scale of the world and to open our hearts; even though you feel pensive, open your heart. Then when you have to help, help; when you have to take care of your life, take care of your life. Whatever you feel, pensive or not pensive, like or dislike, open your heart, and then do what you have to do. From this way of life, you can really take care of individual feelings and experience; your life will bloom. It really helps.

The third kind of knowledge is supreme knowledge. Supreme knowledge is to know how to live in the world where we can clearly see the total picture of beings interchanging one with another. This means when you help somebody there is the same and one ground where you can see two lives constantly interchanging. They cannot be seen as separate. If I say "I," simultaneously the other's life is there. If I say "the other's life," immediately his life can be found in my life, because the contents of my life are not just my own life, but simultaneously include his life. I cannot ignore his life. Very naturally we are connected. So his life is not his life, his life is my life. With supreme knowledge we can see one beautiful picture where two things are constantly interchanging. This is the place in which we have to stand up. Buddha's world is always showing us the total picture where many things are interchanging constantly. I cannot exist, I cannot survive without all of you. I can help because others are not other; others are the contents of my life, other are completely embraced by my life, my life can be found with others' lives. At that time, I can do something with full commitment. This is called supreme knowledge.

Having understood the three kinds of knowledge and what it means to *know* the truth that all beings are buddha, we must next *accept* this truth. To accept this truth means to digest the knowledge that you already have. Digest means that you should assimilate your knowledge. If you have knowledge, you already have food. By this food you can survive, you can live. But if the food remains in your stomach, you become sick. So the food must be digested. It's very clear. If you have certain knowledge of the human world, human life, you have to take time to digest it. This is called "to accept." To accept requires you to take time to understand how to put your knowledge, your ideas, your hope into practice in your everyday life. This is not so easy; it takes lots of time to do this. But we should take the time. If knowledge is completely digested, there is no trace of knowledge, because knowledge turns into life energy, just life. All you can see is just life energy in motion every day. This is realization.

In the Dhammapada, number 228, Buddha says, "There never was, there never will be, nor is there now a man who is always blamed or a man who is always praised."[2] It is true. I cannot say I am a great teacher, because I know already how much trouble my existence gives to some people. I cannot say "good teacher," but, on the other hand, I cannot say "bad teacher" either. So you have to see one picture where two things exist, constantly interchanging. There is a poem by Gensho Ogura that I have translated:

> See at a distance an undesirable person;
> See close at hand a desirable person;
> Come closer to the undesirable person;
> Move away from the desirable person.
> Coming close and moving apart,
> how interesting life is!

Usually we only want to be near desirable people. When we see an undesirable person, we always want to keep away from him. It is natural, but, on the other hand, sometimes we have to come closer to that person. Then we really appreciate him. We cannot always keep our distance from the undesirable person and we cannot always be near the desirable person. So, is the place where we have to stand up a certain place in which we can always be close to the desirable person? Is this the place to stand up in order to see the total picture in equality? No. Should we keep away from the undesirable person? This is not our place either. So the place where we have to stand up is the total picture where we can see many things always interchanging. Nevertheless, this place is very stable, steadfast, immovable. If you don't understand, there is a way to experience this. You must be magnanimous, generous, kind, compassionate, and you must be joy. This joy does not mean pleasure; this joy comes from the bottom of your heart naturally. If you are generous, even for a moment, joy comes up from the bottom of your heart. Joy means appreciation, gratitude. Even though you don't see that appreciation or gratitude, if you become generous or magnanimous in whatever situation you may be, joy, appreciation and gratitude come up from the ground, just like spring water, because you are a great being, because you are buddha. That is to know, to accept and to realize. That is the meaning of to realize the truth that all beings are buddha.

The second point signifying the entrance to the Buddha Way is the profound and steadfast aspiration for living our lives with all beings in peace and harmony. This is the Buddha's world where we can see the total picture of life interchanging, one being with another, constantly interweaving. The world is always changing, so we always feel uneasy. Practically speaking, our minds, our lives are always wriggling and wobbling, always complaining because there are too many hindrances. But, basically, all we have to do is to continuously carry on this profound, steadfast aspiration, this vow, to try to live in peace and harmony with all beings. And we must live this vow in terms of the Buddha's teaching, the Buddha's life, not in terms of individual ideas. That is what "in the light of the Buddha" means.

The third point signifying the entrance to the Buddha Way is to help all beings. We can help in many ways. Using toilet paper carefully is helping others. Don't expect helping to be a big deal. In our everyday life, we can help someone or something all the time. This is Zen teaching. This is the goal of entering the Buddha Way.

To see the opportunity to enter the Buddha Way is to see the way to turn over a new leaf. It is the first step to enter into a different world even though you don't know it. To enter the Buddha Way we should see and create this opportunity, but, if you don't understand this opportunity, don't punish yourself, don't withdraw, and don't be a coward. "Don't be coward" means you should take the initiative to create this great opportunity in a positive way. Most people, if they don't understand, will withdraw; you should go ahead.

More or less, everyone is seeking for something supreme, consciously or unconsciously. You may not understand, but that's why you come to *zendos* and practice zazen. How much do you understand zazen? You don't understand exactly, but something compels you to do this kind of practice. This is really a positive way of life. You are creating this great opportunity because you want to seek for something supreme even though you don't understand what this means. Everyone has this capability.

Repentance

In the ritual of formless repentance the following verse is chanted:

> All the karma ever created by me
> Since of old through greed, anger and self-delusion
> Which has no beginning, born of my body, speech and thought,
> I now make full open confession of it.

In Buddhism, repentance does not mean to apologize to someone for an error or a mistake. The ritual of repentance is not to ask forgiveness from someone for what one has done. Repentance is not a preliminary stage to enter the Buddha's world or to become a good person. If repentance is understood in this way, we fall, very naturally, into the trap of dualism; a big gap is created between us and whatever object we try to make repentance to and that will always cause some confusion. Real peace cannot be found in dualism.

Repentance in Buddhism is to lead us to be present right in the middle of peace and harmony. It is the perfect openness of our hearts that allows us to hear the voice of the universe beyond the irritation of our consciousness. Repentance, itself, makes our life perfectly peaceful.

When contemplating the significance of repentance in Zen Buddhism there are three conditions to consider: that we should realize the world of the compassionate heart; that the self must readily accept the compassion of Buddha's world; that we must set in motion the interactive communion between us and the universe.

The first condition, that we should realize the world of the compassionate heart, is to accept and forgive all beings without any exceptions. The buddhas and ancestors are human beings who realize this truth: that the same and one ground of existence, where all sentient beings coexist in peace and harmony from moment to moment, is profoundly compassionate, accepting all sentient beings without exception. If you realize this truth, you are called buddha. This truth is called Dharma or Dharma body. Whatever we feel from our lives, animate and inanimate beings are peacefully embraced by this compassion. This is why we can live every day beyond making mistakes or not making mistakes, beyond failure or success, beyond pros and cons. We have to live to appreciate and to express this compassion. It is not something we need to try to understand. Even though we may be able to explain the total picture of the universe using many words, practically speaking we don't really understand it. All we have to do is to put ourselves in the heart of this compassion, right in the middle of the vastness of the universe.

For instance, the *dōan* hits the small bells and the big bells during the Buddhist service and chants the titles of the sūtras. It seems to be a simple task, but even though we understand the procedures for hitting the bells and think we remember, when we actually start to do it, we become easily confused, forget the order and may not be able to do it. If we see something at a distance every day, we feel we are intimate with it. But if we really participate in that simple thing, we find that we don't know what to do, because that simple thing is not so simple; it's a huge world we are seeing. If we see our object, our life at a distance, our understanding becomes very narrow. But if we participate in one thing, like the dōan's task, we can see one thing from many angles and it brings up many questions for us; we can see the broad picture of the dōan's task rather than just one corner of it. Even though we say, "I understand," we don't understand completely. So first of all if we understand something in one sense, we have to participate in it instead of looking at it objectively. This is called experience, direct experience. But human beings always create attachment to actual experience and become arrogant. So, very naturally, the goal of Zen Buddhism is to be free from that strong attachment to our own experience. The harder we live our life, the more we attach to it, because we are really proud of ourselves. So the real goal, real peace, real freedom is to be free from that attachment.

The troubles in the human world are very complicated, but you should not ignore them. However, neither can you stay with them. You have to take care of them. But we also must take care not to attach to something good or pretty or sweet. It's not so easy, particularly if we do something good; we want to be proud of ourselves, we want to attach to our lives. But it is essential that we attach to neither the mistakes nor the good actions of our lives.

Repentance is to realize exactly the oneness of merging all sentient beings and buddha, delusion and enlightenment. All sentient beings are allowed to live and are, from the beginning, forgiven for living their lives in this world. Everything, whatever it is, has some reason why it exists: evil, good, even something neither evil nor good. You cannot destroy devils just because you don't like them. Even though you don't like monsters, still there is some reason why they exist. Everything is entitled to live in this world in peace and harmony beyond our judgment, our evaluation. This is the first condition we have to realize—everything is buddha.

The second condition we have to realize is that the self must readily accept the compassion of Buddha's world. "Buddha's world" means the Truth, or the same and one ground, or that which is beyond good and bad. Whether we like it or dislike it, we have to accept this. What is meant by readily accepting Buddha's compassion? It means we must actualize Buddha's compassion in our everyday lives. We have to live our lives in the complete realization that we are already forgiven, that we are already allowed to live, and that we, ourselves, must make our lives come alive. It is most important that we take this attitude toward our lives if we want to realize and accept the compassion of Buddha's world. We are already embraced, so we have to live our life in the realization that we are forgiven. But who is it that lives? We live by our effort, but this is a narrow understanding, so we have to live our lives with the understanding that we are allowed to live. This means we should appreciate our life. Then, if we appreciate our life, we can make our life come alive. To do this, we must be not only passive, but also active. Someone may say, "The universe takes care of me, so I don't have to do anything." Of course, it is true, but this does not mean we can take a nap in the universe. The universe is always working with us, so if we become lazy, the universe appears as laziness. Then very naturally we are confused. So, constantly we have to take the initiative. When we do gassho, we have to practice gassho with the forgiving universe, with appreciation for our lives, making gassho come alive. This practice is not a matter of discussion.

Buddha's world is completely pure and serene, quiet and also dynamic; it is dynamism in motion beyond our thoughts and ideas. So very naturally, in order to accept it, we have to put aside our understanding, our thoughts, and put our body and mind right in the middle of that dynamism in motion. This is samādhi or actualizing Buddha's compassion. When we do zazen it is a very simple opportunity to be present there, to put aside our thoughts and preconceptions. That's why it is called the practice of egolessness, and for this, zazen is the most important practice. If we practice in this way, discussion comes after; ideas and teaching come after. If we take care of our lives in this way, teaching and ideas are the contents of our lives. So, very naturally we can think, we can teach, if we live like this.

The founder of Buddhism is Shākyamuni Buddha. In Chinese, *shākya* is translated as *no-nin*. *No* means subjectivity; *nin* is human. *Shākya* is the self as subjectivity, which we cannot lose. *Muni* is *jaku moku* in Chinese. *Jaku* means tranquil; *moku* means silence; so *muni* is sometimes translated as holiness. Holiness is exactly tranquil silence, but it is also something upholding all sentient beings. *Shākyamuni* means that the self as subjectivity must practice tranquil silence. So Zen Buddhism emphasizes that the truth is to be practiced constantly, in silence, because truth itself is really tranquil silence. The moment when we touch the truth, there is no way to explain the self as a subject who touches the truth. So, very naturally, the subjective self who touches the truth becomes silent. But it is a deep silence; the truth is really something alive in you. And people are very impressed by this silence that you give forth from your whole body, your whole personality. In this way you can help people. Shākyamuni is the person who attains the self as subject, who practices tranquil silence exactly. This is called buddha; buddha is exactly the total manifestation of tranquil silence. Buddha is Truth. If you experience this, buddha gives forth its own light from your whole body. Then people are moved by your experience.

The third condition is ritual. Ritual in Buddhism is attaining *kannō dōkō*, which means "the interacting communion of appeals and response." Ritual is constantly painting a portrait of our life, setting in motion the interactive communion between us and the universe, not between us and something small, between us and the universe. Without ritual we cannot do anything. The poem "To Paint the Portrait of the Bird,"[1] by Jacques Prévert, is a good example of the interacting communion of appeal and response that is ritual or the essential nature of repentance:

> First paint a cage
> with an open door.
> Then paint
> something pretty
> something simple
> something beautiful
> something useful
> for the bird.
> Then place the canvas against a tree
> in a garden
> in a wood
> or in a forest.
> Hide behind the tree
> without speaking
> without moving . . .
> Sometimes the bird comes quickly
> but he may take long years
> before deciding.
> Don't get discouraged.
> Wait.
> Wait years if necessary.

How fast or how slowly the bird comes
has nothing to do with the success
of the picture.
When the bird comes
if he comes
observe the most profound silence
till the bird enters the cage
and when he has entered
gently close the door with a brush.
Then
erase all the bars one by one
taking care not to touch any of the bird's feathers.
Then paint the portrait of the tree
choosing the most beautiful of its branches
for the bird.
Paint also the green foliage and the wind's freshness
the dust of the sun
and the noise of the creatures in the grass in the summer heat.
And then wait for the bird to decide to sing.
If the bird doesn't sing
it's a bad sign,
a sign that the painting is bad.
But if he sings it's a good sign,
a sign that you can sign.
So, then, so very gently, you pull out
one of the bird's feathers
and you write your name in a corner of the picture.

The cage, in the first line, means our whole body—the six senses, six sense organs, six sense objects and the five skandhas.[2] This is what the whole world consists of; this is our cage. Everyone has an individual cage. We are nothing but the cage. The poet says, "First paint a cage with an open door." "Open door" means we should accept the vastness of existence. Usually we don't open the door. We make the cage and then shut ourselves off. But, if we do this, how can we attract the bird? "Bird" means the Truth, the same and one ground. How can we attract the truth if we close the door? So the poet tells us to paint a cage with the door open.

Next he says, "Then paint /something pretty/something simple/ something beautiful/something useful/for the bird." We have to paint something pretty, simple and beautiful, not for ourselves, not for the cage, but for the bird. "Something beautiful, something simple" means something beyond our intellectual sense. It means we have to see ourselves and also the vastness of space in which all sentient beings exist. This is our practice, constantly. Even if we don't understand it, paint it, paint something pretty. Even if we don't believe it is something beautiful, that's all right, we are following the Buddha's teaching and we should see the total picture. We should put ourselves in this position. This is to paint something beautiful.

"Then place the canvas against a tree/in a garden/in a wood/or in a forest./Hide behind the tree/without speaking/without moving . . ./ Sometimes the bird comes quickly." When we paint something beautiful, we shouldn't attach to it. Leave the painting in the wood, in the forest and then hide ourselves. This is to practice the truth. When we do gassho, we have to practice samādhi. Samādhi is really silence. We must be behind the gassho, but we cannot move. If we move, even a little, immediately our intellect comes up and argues. That's why this poet says, "Hide behind the tree/without speaking/without moving . . ."

Then the poet says, "Sometimes the bird comes quickly," but strictly speaking, the bird is always there. The bird is there, but because we don't always experience enlightenment through zazen we say "sometimes" it comes. However, Buddha's compassion is open to everyone; there is always a bird whether we realize it or not. We don't know when it will come. But according to this poet it doesn't matter when it comes or how long it takes. How fast or how slowly the bird comes doesn't matter, because that has nothing to do with the success of our life. Real success is just to put ourselves in zazen when we do zazen, to put ourselves in gassho when we do gassho, because compassion is open to everyone. "When the bird comes . . ./observe the most profound silence/till the bird enters the cage/and when he has entered/ gently close the door with a brush." Not with our hand, please, close the door with a brush. "Then"—and this practice is very important— "erase all the bars one by one/taking care not to touch any of the bird's feathers." This is egolessness, the practice of egolessness. How beautiful it is. If we want to paint the portrait of a bird we have to practice egolessness.

"Then paint the portrait of the tree/choosing the most beautiful of its branches/for the bird./Paint also the green foliage and the wind's freshness/the dust of the sun." When we do this, all things become alive. We can make our lives come alive; simultaneously we can make the lives of the trees, the air, the autumn come alive. But without this practice, we cannot paint the autumn, the air, "the dust of the sun" or "the noise of the creatures in the grass in the summer heat." We cannot.

"And then wait for the bird to decide to sing./If the bird doesn't sing/it's a bad sign,/a sign that the painting is bad." This means that perhaps enlightenment is attained, or a Ph.D. degree or the degree of medical doctor, but our life doesn't work. When it doesn't work, we need to pay more careful attention to what that degree means or we have to pay attention to our own experience, until the bird starts to sing. When the bird starts to sing that is our experience, our life, so we can sign the painting. But don't sign with arrogance. The poet says to sign your name in the corner of the picture. We shouldn't show off, because the whole of life, the whole world is alive. We are just a corner, that's enough. We are the whole world; the whole world is working. "One of the bird's feathers" means take buddha. Take one of the ideas of the universe that we believe, for instance, "the universe is the same and one ground," and use that feather. With that feather we can write our name, not in the middle of the canvas, but in the corner of the picture. This is the poem, a very beautiful one. Throughout this poem we can see ritual in action.

The Triple Treasure

The Triple Treasure in Buddhism, "I take refuge in the Buddha, I take refuge in the Dharma, I take refuge in the Sangha," is the foundation of the precepts. The precepts in Buddhism are not a moral code that someone or something outside ourselves demands that we follow. The precepts are the Buddha-nature, the spirit of the universe. To receive the precepts is to transmit something significant beyond the understanding of our senses, such as the spirit of the universe or what we call Buddha-nature. What we have awakened to, deeply, through our body and mind, is transmitted from generation to generation, beyond our control. Having experienced this awakening, we can appreciate how sublime human life is. Whether we know it or not, or whether we like it or not, the spirit of the universe is transmitted. So we all can learn what the real spirit of a human being is.

Wherever we are born in this world, we have many opportunities to learn about the depth of existence. We should awaken to this spirit of the universe because it is constantly present through all the ages. In a broad sense, there is constant transmission of the exquisite image of human life throughout all generations. This is why, finally, we appreciate human life and we try to help human beings. And then, very naturally, we can create human culture and we can build the human world in peace and harmony under all circumstances through all the ages. This is the human effort we make repeatedly.

The Triple Treasure is the very foundation of the precepts, the first step to enter into the universe or the Buddha Way. No matter how much our life and body may change, we should respect and we should take refuge in the Triple Treasure throughout countless lives over an immense span of time. My family were Shin Buddhists and chanted the name of Amitabha Buddha every day, and Christians are mindful of God in many ways. If you become a Buddhist, then you must be mindful of the Buddha, Dharma and Sangha.

Buddha is the universe and Dharma is the teaching from the universe, and Sangha is the group of people who make the universe and its teaching alive in their lives. In our everyday life we must be mindful of Buddha, Dharma and Sangha whether we understand this or not. We have to be mindful from day to night, through countless lives, over an immense span of time. Then our life will be very stable.

To "take refuge" does not mean to escape from the human world or from one another. In Japanese, to "take refuge" is *namu* or *namu kie;* in Sanskrit it is *namo. Namo* means full devotion or throwing away the body and mind. Full devotion is just like the relationship between your mind and your body. The body seems to be different from the mind, but actually the relationship between them is very close. For instance, if your thoughts make you nervous, your stomach becomes upset. They are separate, but they are not separate; they work together without leaving any trace of the stomach or of the thought. This is the meaning of full devotion. In English we also say to "take refuge in" or sometimes to "go to Buddha for guidance."

We take refuge in the Buddha because Buddha is our great teacher. "Great" in this sense is completely beyond the human evaluation of good or bad. The spirit, the essence of the universe, the merit of the universe, and the functioning of the universe are great beyond our speculation. When we realize this, we become the universe and we are called buddha. So Siddhārtha Gautama realized the essence of the universe, the merit or virtue of the universe, the attributes and functioning of the universe. Then Siddhārtha Gautama became Buddha. We take refuge in the Buddha because he is our great teacher.

We take refuge in the law, in the Dharma, because it is good medicine. Dharma is teaching; this teaching is completely beyond human evaluation, beyond moral sense or ethical sense. Dharma is the Truth, something coming from the Truth. It really benefits everyone, all beings, just as rain nurtures grass, trees, pebbles, human beings, air, everything. Dharma is good medicine.

We take refuge in Buddha's community, or Sangha, because it is composed of excellent friends. Sangha is a community, but it's not the usual sense of community, because this community has many people who try to follow the Buddha's way, so they are excellent friends for you. They are not good friends in the usual sense of friendship. "Good friend" has three meanings. One is good friend in the usual sense. If a friend benefits us in some way, we say he is a good friend. The second meaning is the person who commands respect from others beyond a sense of give and take. Even though this person cannot give material things or anything of practical benefit to others, one can deeply respect this person. The third sense of good friend is completely beyond either a sense of respect or of give and take. Even though this person lives far away he or she always influences our life in a broad sense. Even if we think of this person for just a moment, the presence of this person really helps our life. It's not merely our imagination. This third good friend is always helping us in many ways. So, you see, the community we call Sangha is quite different from the usual sense of community. In the usual sense, people just gather and live together. But in the Sangha, each person has to be an excellent friend to all the others. Because we must be following Buddha's teaching, we must be following the essence, the virtue, the functioning of the universe, and therefore we become an excellent friend to others. Usually it is difficult to act in this way. This is why, in communities in the United States, there are lots of problems. Most people think Sangha is just a usual community. This is understandable because the people who practice in the community are no different from other people; all of us are just human beings. This is true, we are human beings, but, at the same time, we are not human beings, we are buddha. Don't forget this point. If we forget our Buddha-nature, we become just an ordinary human being. The reason we forget is simple—we don't understand that we are buddha. But the meaning of "we are buddha" goes beyond whether we understand or not, we are exactly buddha. Being buddha means the total qualification for living in this world under all circumstances. There are no excuses. We have to respect each other and all sentient beings. But when we forget our Buddha-nature, we do not have a chance to communicate the spirit of the universe. This is really a senseless way to be a human being. If we are mindful that we are buddha, it is really the driving force that gives life to our everyday activity.

Only by taking refuge in the Triple Treasure can we become disciples of the Buddha. In other words, we can become a child of the Buddha. Being a child of the Buddha means that we have to accept completely the universe where all sentient beings exist. There is no excuse for ignoring anything in this world. If we accept ourselves, we have to accept all sentient beings, not as something separate from our life, but as the contents of our life. So in other words your life, each of your lives, is not different from me. But if I consider all of your lives to be something separate from me, that viewpoint comes from the intellectual world. Then, very naturally, I can discriminate between you and me. There is no sense of human warmness created by the human heart or spirit and, very naturally, we cannot communicate with each other. To be a disciple or a son or daughter of the Buddha means we are people who accept the lives of all sentient beings as the contents of our life. The universe is vast. The universe completely accepts us, accepts our lives as the contents of the universe. The universe never separates its life from our lives. The tree's life, the bird's life, our life, winter's life, spring's life, all are accepted as the content or quality of the universe. This is why the universe is buddha. We are children of the Buddha. If we realize this, then we can put this spirit into practice. When we accept others' lives as the contents of our life, then others' lives become very close to us. Examples of how others lived their lives are not just stories of others' lives separate from ours. Their stories are exactly the contents of our life. So, very naturally, others' lives become a mirror for me and my life becomes a mirror for others. My life is reflected in others' lives, and theirs in mine. There is always a very close relationship. This is why, whatever kind of problem you bring up, or whatever lifestyle you follow, I cannot ignore it. I have to be a good listener under all circumstances, constantly practicing the six pāramitās, that is, giving, practicing the precepts, being patient, giving my best effort, meditating, practicing total calmness and practicing wisdom. Practicing those six pāramitās, I have to be a good friend continually, I have to be a good listener to all of you. Then, we can really communicate. You become a good friend for me, I become a good friend for you. This is called being a disciple of the Buddha or a child of the Buddha. We have to digest this teaching because the universe completely accepts all sentient beings as the contents of its life. By taking refuge in the Triple Treasure, the Buddha, Dharma, and Sangha, we have a chance to become children or disciples of the Buddha and we become qualified to receive all the other precepts. And then, total devotion to the Triple Treasure turns into the motive power or energy of everyday life.

How can we touch this spirit of taking refuge that then turns into energy for our daily life? The spiritual communion between the Buddha and the practicer, the Buddha and you is the interacting communion of appeal and response. The usual meaning of "appeal" is to ask for help. But in this case "to ask" is too strong a term. I appeal in many ways, spiritually, materially, but I don't ask for something in particular. I appeal to you constantly for help, but this appeal is not to you in particular, it is to the whole universe. There is nothing to ask for help from in this world, but there is something we can appeal to beyond the human world, even though we don't know exactly what it is. To do that we pray, for our lives, for others' lives, to the vastness of space and existence. How do you do this in a concrete way? You look up into space and pray. Why look up? We don't know. The sky or space is called *ākāsha* in Sanskrit. Ākāsha is characterized by no obstruction, no interruption, allowing all beings to function in peace and harmony. When we look up to the sky and pray, we don't know what space is, but spiritually, in a deep sense, we understand what space is. So, naturally, we look up to the sky and pray. The altar in the church and the altar in the Buddhist temple are a little higher than we are, so always we look up when we pray. And when you pray you kneel down to the floor, you become lower; in other words, you become humble. Intellectually, we don't understand it, but spiritually everyone knows. This is the meaning of appeal.

Then, the response comes from the whole universe; from space, from ākāsha, it comes. If we feel this spirit of the universe completely and appeal for help, or appeal that we may come alive in our everyday life, very naturally, we can be one with the universe. This is response. In other words, if we reach out our hands to the universe, the universe sticks out its own hand to us. Then, the path of your life and the path of the universe cross each other, become one, interconnected. In Japanese, this is *kannō dōkō*. *Kan* means appeal, *nō* is response, *dō* is path, *kō* is to cross. Appeal and response cross very quickly. This is wholeheartedness, exactly.

If we see deeply the total picture of the human world, how transient the world is, how fragile human life is, then we can hear the cries of the world. The cries of human beings are simultaneously the one who listens. So we can appeal for help and simultaneously the universe reaches out its hand. That is, simultaneously we can see the path through which we and the universe are crossing. This is the manifestation of our wholeheartedness. When we chant, when we repeat the name of Buddha, when we do gassho, wholeheartedly, this is exactly the total presence of our life, which is exactly the same as the total presence of the universe before we poke our heads into it, trying to analyze it. Then, simultaneously, we feel peaceful. This is sitting zazen. We don't know this, but even though we don't know it, if we sit with wholeheartedness, some part of our body feels it directly. We can feel peaceful because our presence and the presence of the universe are exactly in the same place. This is what we call wholeheartedness or "with all your mind."

It is not possible to take refuge in the Buddha, Dharma and Sangha intellectually. We cannot attain spiritual security or peace in this way. It is not necessary to throw away our intellect, but please, let the intellectual sense just join in, and practice with wholeheartedness. Then, spiritual security is present. This is not something we can know, but it is something we can touch. We can touch it directly by putting ourselves right there. I have to put myself right here and then talk. In Katagiri's life, the intellectual world is always coming up, but if I want to give you Buddha's teaching beyond our cultural backgrounds, all I have to do is be present right now, right here, with wholeheartedness and then talk. Then there is some communion. I can be very calm, I can be composed, and then very naturally you can be composed, you can be calm, and then communion goes between. This is called "taking refuge in the Buddha, Dharma and Sangha." This is why the three refuges are very basic practice for us in order to enter the Buddha's world.

Everyone, consciously or unconsciously, is seeking for something trustworthy, something dependable, beyond worldly affairs, from which one can feel relief. This is why we suffer. In Buddhism this is the "inception of suffering." Even though we feel happy, there is suffering, because we want to hold on to happiness. Constantly, whatever our lifestyle may be, whether we are happy or unhappy, there is always suffering, there is always some feeling of dissatisfaction. We want to grasp something perfectly trustworthy, or completely dependable. This is the goal. This goal is not something we can get in the realm of the conscious world, nor in the realm of the unconscious world. It comes from something more than these worlds. We don't know what it is, but we are seeking for it every day and no matter what we achieve in the realm of worldly affairs, we aren't satisfied. We still seek for something more than we have. This is pretty deep; no one knows what it is, but we are all seeking.

This goal, which everyone has, is the lofty, sublime, ideal image of human beings from which peace and harmony originate. Sublime means high spiritual, moral, and intellectual worth. We have to appreciate our life because our life is sublime; this means our physical and mental life has spiritual, emotional, ethical and intellectual worth. This is why everyone should respect others.

The three refuges refer to that which is our goal in life. We have to understand, we have to accept the three treasures in terms of spiritual, ethical, intellectual and emotional worth. This is called "faith." If we do this, very naturally faith comes up from the bottom of our life. This is why I say that the three refuges are the lofty, sublime, ideal image of human beings, how we should live in this world in peace, in harmony. As long as we are born in this world as human beings, there will be this goal in life, there will be this goal in human society. Everyone's effort should be directed towards this goal because we exist in this particular society of sentient beings.

Let's look at the three treasures in terms of spiritual or functional worth, ethical or virtuous worth, emotional worth, and intellectual or philosophical worth. If we ignore intellectual worth our effort directed toward the three treasures becomes very emotional. And if we depend on intellectual worth alone, we ignore the emotional aspect of human life. But we cannot do this; it is not the right way of faith. So we have to accept faith or the three treasures in terms of the whole situation of our lives—emotional, intellectual, spiritual and ethical.

First let us look at the three treasures in terms of philosophical or intellectual worth. Buddha means exactly Truth itself, the whole universe itself. The essence of the universe, the essence of being itself, we

call the Truth, we call the universal life, common to all sentient beings—trees, birds, human beings, pebbles, rivers, mountains. This is
Dharma. Dharma refers to cleanness and purity, which allow all beings to be free from worldly dust. For example, look at winter. According to our individual emotional pattern of life, some accept winter,
some don't, some hate it, some love it. So various styles of life appear.
But according to the Dharma, in terms of philosophical worth, I think
winter is a constant manifestation of beauty itself. When you see winter,
you are impressed by it, because winter is Dharma, which shows us
the cleanness and purity that allow all beings to be free from worldly
affairs, free from our thoughts and evaluations or judgments. The
Dharma allows everything to be free from any dust. This is why at the
very moment of meeting winter, we are really moved. The next moment we don't know why we are moved, but we are moved. This
means we are connected, we have had real communion with the universe. So, from this point of view we say winter, bare trees, snow, sky,
all are Dharma. All sentient beings are really peaceful and harmonious, perfectly clear and pure. This is the state of all sentient beings
in terms of philosophical worth, completely beyond our judgment or
evaluation. Sangha means, in this case, peace and harmony that allow
all beings to be free from confusion, perverted views and misunderstanding. Originally, all sentient beings are very peaceful, exactly
peaceful and harmonious. This is called sangha. In terms of philosophical or intellectual worth, Buddha is truth itself, Dharma is the form of
all sentient beings regarded as purity and cleanness, and Sangha means
all sentient beings are originally peaceful and harmonious. This is
why, if we open our hearts, we communicate, naturally. We can have
spiritual communion between us and the universe. This is the philosophical worth of the three treasures.

Second, let us look at the three treasures in terms of virtue or ethical
worth. From this point of view, Buddha means actualized realization
of the supreme way. Buddha means that the universe, existence, is
nothing but the total manifestation of the truth. Temporarily, we use
the term "existence," but existence is something more than a philosophical concept. Very naturally, we have to see something more than
the philosophical sense of existence, so we say "nonexistent." Intellectually, we have to negate the usual concept of existence in order to see
something more than the philosophical concept of existence. So we
should forget this term, and then open ourselves and see, practically,

what is is, if we want to see existence as a whole. The truth is already actualized before we poke our heads into existence. This is why I say "actualized realization." Realization means to accept and to digest. Realization means we should accept subject and object, and then we have to digest both of them totally until they disappear, leaving no trace of subject and object, concept or idea. They completely turn into life energy. The world and all sentient beings are exactly the actualized realization of the truth. This is why we can live in the world.

In terms of the virtue of the three treasures, Dharma means that which the Buddha has realized. What he has realized is, "I have attained enlightenment simultaneously with all sentient beings." This is the Dharma. In other words, all beings are nothing but realized beings, enlightened beings, because Buddha realized this. So we have to see or hear with our whole body and mind and deal with all sentient beings in terms of enlightened beings. Then, very naturally, we can share compassion or kindness with everyone, with all beings in which the Buddha is amply present, or, in other words, in which the Truth is amply present. So everyone is the Truth. The form of everyone is the manifestation of Buddha, or truth, because this is the content that Buddha realized twenty-five hundred years ago. Even though we don't understand it, it is really true. Buddhas from generation to generation have transmitted this essence, this essential teaching, to the next generation.

In terms of virtue, Sangha is to learn, to study, to practice this Buddha, this Dharma. Very naturally, we can feel appreciation because the world, existence, is that in which Buddha or the Truth is constantly manifested. All beings are nothing but that which Buddha has realized. So all sentient beings are enlightened beings; there is no waste. We have to deal with all sentient beings with compassion, with kindness, with appreciation. Whether we understand or not, it doesn't matter. We have to continually study and learn and practice this Buddha, this Dharma in everyday life. This is the Sangha. These are the three treasures in terms of virtue or ethical worth.

Third, let us consider the three treasures in terms of functioning or spiritual worth. In this case, the Buddha constantly edifies all beings wherever they may be. In Buddhist psychology there are ten categories of existence in the world: hell, hungry ghosts, fighting spirits, animal spirits, human beings, celestial beings, *pratyeka* buddhas, *shrāvaka* buddhas, bodhisattvas and buddhas. And each of the ten categories of existence contains all the rest. This means that hell is not only hell; within hell are hungry ghosts, fighting spirits, animal spirits, human beings, celestial beings, pratyeka buddhas, shrāvaka buddhas, bodhisattvas and also Buddha's world. So within hell there is buddha. Even in the hell world, still there are all the rest of the worlds, always. Wherever you may go, you have great opportunities to be saved. Whatever you do, wherever you may be, you are doing it in the Buddha's world. Buddha's world means the universe. The universe is nothing but the total manifestation of the truth by which all sentient beings are supported, upheld, naturally, if we open our hearts. If we don't open our hearts, it's a little bit difficult. Difficult means it takes a long time. But, basically, the universe and truth are very compassionate and kind toward all sentient beings. Constantly the compassionate universe is helping, just like the rain. Rain is accepted by many kinds of beings; some of the plants that are rained on grow, but some of them do not. If we don't open our hearts it's pretty hard to grow, it really takes time. But still, the rain is just the rain. Rain continues to fall to support all sentient beings. So in terms of functioning or spiritual worth, buddha refers to a person who consistently edifies all beings, wherever they may be.

Dharma means to edify animate and inanimate beings by virtue of appearing as, for example, Buddha statues and as Buddha paintings. Truth manifests itself constantly by virtue of appearing as statues, paintings and as Buddhist scriptures written in words, because it's very difficult for human beings to have communion with the Truth itself. Human beings naturally have deep feelings and sensations and we try to make things through which we can experience a deep, compassionate communion with the universe. This is art, Buddhist art, religious art. This is a Buddha statue. The statue is not an idol. This beautiful art is the manifestation of perfect beauty coming from the human heart. This is the Dharma. From the point of view of functioning, not only paintings and statues, but also the form of the trees, the color of the mountains, the sounds of the valley streams, all are teaching us the truth. The Chinese poet Su Tung p'o (Sō Tōba) says, "The sounds of the valley streams are his long, broad tongue. The colors of the mountains are his pure body. At night I heard the eighty-four thousand verses uttered. How can I show others what they say?"

Sangha, in terms of the functioning of the Triple Treasure, means saving all beings from their suffering and freeing them from worldly affairs. This refers to the profound aspiration for letting all beings be free from suffering, all beings including subject and object, because generally, sangha means peace and harmony. There must be something actualized by you. This is refined human action and it must last for a long time, not only in your lifetime, but life after life. In order to carry on this refined human behavior for a long time, we need profound aspiration, or what we call the vow to help all sentient beings be free from suffering. Then, simultaneously, this profound aspiration based on the vow to let all beings be free from suffering naturally turns into human action to establish a world where all beings can live in peace and harmony. There are many ways we can help. This is Sangha.

We have to understand the Triple Treasure in terms of philosophical or intellectual worth, virtue or ethical worth, and functioning or spiritual worth. Then we can see a dim image of the lofty ideal of human life toward which our effort should be directed. Very naturally, we can establish our life as a whole personality that is profound, and that helps all sentient beings emotionally, philosophically, ethically, in many ways. This is called Buddhist faith.

The Three Collective Pure Precepts

The Three Collective Pure Precepts, refraining from all that is evil, practicing all that is good, purifying one's mind, are the teachings of all the buddhas. The first two lines, refraining from all evil and practicing all good, are precepts. The third line, purifying one's mind, is having pure faith in the Triple Treasure. Taking refuge in the Buddha, Dharma and Sangha is purifying one's mind.

Buddhist precepts are not moral or ethical imperatives or orders given by someone that people must follow. They are the ground of Buddha's world, through which we can manifest ourselves as buddhas. We are already enlightened and the precepts are already enlightened words. Each word is Buddha's mind completely beyond our speculation. If we take the precepts as Buddha's mind, Buddha's teaching, we can each behave as a buddha. But if we take them in the moral sense we become moral people. It is very difficult to understand this with our usual mind, so very naturally we think we are obeying Buddha's teaching in the moral sense. That's all right. Just keep going, accepting the precepts as the Buddha's teaching.

In the beginning, even though you understand the precepts as a moral teaching, all you have to do is take the precepts continually, and learn them in your everyday life. This applies to the precepts and to whatever else you may do. Practice everything you do like this. Before you are conscious of it, that teaching penetrates your life.

If we want to practice calligraphy, we should study the teaching of that art from a textbook written by a great master rather than from one by an ordinary person. Unfortunately, when the characters we have drawn do not look like the calligraphy written by the teacher, we become frustrated and decide we don't like the textbook. We want to have a book in which the calligraphy is similar to our calligraphy. But if we use a book like that, we will never progress. Even though we don't know how long it will take to master this calligraphy, we should take the book by the great teacher and learn. If we practice it continually, we will experience that where no evil is produced the true strength of practice is actualized. Very naturally, sooner or later we will master the calligraphy before we are conscious of it. At that time no particular effort is needed. The brush moves naturally, and the calligraphy matches the teacher's calligraphy exactly.

The moment you step inside of Buddhism you step inside an already enlightened world. So the first step is very important for us, and that's why it's a very important step to become a priest or a monk. The bodhi-mind must be aroused a hundred, thousand, million times, day by day.

In order to achieve the perfection of this faith and the precepts we have to sever three ties: the first is selfishness, the second is doubt or wrong view, and the third is wrong religious belief or, in other words, superstition or dogmatism.

In order to sever the tie of doubt or wrong view, we cannot attach to excessive, one-sided ideas. We have to see the human world, human life, in the light of the teaching of impermanence and the law of causation. This is a very contradictory situation. If everything is impermanent there is nothing to grasp and hold on to. But, on the other hand, there is the law of causation. If you do something, very naturally there will be a result. These two teachings are contradictory, and so, we are confused by the human world, by human life. But impermanence is a very basic teaching of existence. Impermanence is that which causes change to occur. It doesn't have any form or color or smell. Impermanence itself is a kind of energy, moving, functioning, working dynamically, appearing, disappearing, always supporting our life. Only through change can we see it and understand it. Through change we can see the depth of human life based on impermanence.

We have to plan for our life within impermanence. This means we can make a plan for our life, but we cannot attach to the result of our plan. We just make a plan and then follow it. Day by day we have to practice it. And then, very naturally, we can get a taste of impermanence, what a plan is, what our hope is, what human life is. We cannot ignore this right view of the human world. We have to be free from doubt about the teaching of impermanence and about the teaching of the law of causation.

Next, we have to be free from selfishness. Selfishness means always attaching to the self first. It's very difficult to be free from self. Do you know the children's story of the tortoise and the hare? The tortoise is one of the slowest creatures in this world. Common sense tells us that he would never win a race with a hare. But actually he did it. In order to win, can you imagine how much effort this tortoise made? He made an enormous effort. In order to make this enormous effort he had to be completely free from the label of the slowest creature or the fastest creature. In the race he just made every possible effort to keep moving. It is important to give quality to the effort, instead of expecting the result of the effort. All you have to do is just make your best effort, being free from a label or judgment that you are capable or not or that you are good or not. Forget it and just make an enormous effort.

If while making this effort you are also competing with somebody else or with an idea of how to become a buddha, it's very difficult to give quality to your effort. We always think that we are deluded, ordinary people who will never become a buddha. Such an idea is also competition. If we practice like that it's very hard; our zazen becomes "hell" zazen. If someone else attains enlightenment that is their story, not yours. If someone stumbles, help them; don't think about being first. Don't compete and don't expect results. This is the best way to be free from selfishness. This is called the practice of egolessness. This is our practice.

The third tie to sever is wrong religious belief. In Buddhism we take refuge in the Triple Treasure. Refuge in Buddhism is not someplace we go in order to escape from the human world. Refuge is a place where everyone has to go, like the terminal station. If you take the train of human life you have to go to the terminal station. And then from the terminal station you can go anywhere else. So it is an end but it's also a beginning. In Buddhism, that terminal station is referred to as the Triple Treasure: Buddha, Dharma and Sangha. Buddha is one who understands human life based on impermanence and the law of causation. His effort is going on continuously and if we participate in it, we are called buddha. But in everyday life it is very difficult to do this because we already have preconceptions, we have our own customs and inherited traits. That's why we have to come back to this way constantly, doing the same thing Buddha did. Every day we have to come back, a hundred, a thousand, a million times, to the Buddha's teaching. We have to come back again and again to the teaching, without a sense of competition or expectation. We have to follow this teaching that is given to us by a person who understands the human world, who lives his own life on the basis of impermanence and the law of causation. We have to grow by ourselves, but we need help. This is to take refuge in the Buddha, the Dharma and the Sangha.

Even though we have Buddha and the Dharma, we need human beings who exist now, who are practicing together. That is Sangha. People come together and practice Buddha's way, Buddha's teaching, and grow and become buddha in the same way that Shākyamuni Buddha did. Then we can transmit that teaching to future generations. We can make human history, we can make human culture. Without human beings who exist now we cannot transmit Buddha's teaching to future generations. We need all of us and we need a place where we practice the Buddha Way together. Buddha, Dharma and Sangha are the terminal station we have to reach. And then we can see our lives extending everywhere. We can see our life from the universal perspective.

The Ten Prohibitory Precepts

The word for "precept" in Sanskrit, *sīla*, means to form a habit. Habit, in the usual sense, may last for only a lifetime and there is attachment to self or an object or individual desire involved. Forming a habit of living in a way that is based on Buddha's teaching is the practice of spiritual life and is called vow. Vow is continually going on in the realm of eternity beyond time and space, life after life. There is no sense of self-attachment, no desire, no individual interest. We have to put this vow into practice in our everyday life. For this we practice the

Ten Prohibitory Precepts. They actualize the embodiment of living in vow. Every day, constantly, we have to form the habit of living in the way that is based on Buddha's teaching.

The deep meaning of precept is that it is Buddha-nature or Truth. To receive the precepts is to awaken to the Buddha-nature. Even though we don't understand what Buddha-nature or Truth is, to receive the precepts is awareness. For example, if we don't understand the value of a diamond, but somebody gives us one and we receive the diamond in our hand, there is already awareness of the value of the diamond. We may not be conscious of it, but more or less it affects our life in many ways. That's why it's important to receive the precepts. We always try to understand something in terms of our intellect, according to our individual knowledge, our individual education. And then we either receive it or we decide we don't want to receive it. But in spiritual life, regardless of whether we understand it or not, to receive the precepts means to receive Buddha-nature, Truth. In order to help our true nature grow we have to receive the diamond again and again, even though we don't understand what has been given to us. Receive it every day. This practice helps the seed of true nature grow. It is a simple practice. Our consciousness is always grumbling and complaining. Then life appears to be very complicated. But actually, spiritual life is a very simple life. Regardless of whether we understand or not, we receive the diamond as it is in order to help the seed of Buddha-nature grow.

The first of the ten precepts is to refrain from taking life. Our usual understanding of not taking life, from the dualistic point of view, is that in the present, life is here, and in the future, life will be extinguished. So we think it means, "Don't extinguish life." Strictly speaking we will never understand the reality of life and death from this point of view. We have to get a taste of it through practice. It's a little difficult, but we have to touch the core of the meaning of life itself and death itself.

Life is not something as compared with something else. Life must be understood as it is, life as "life-ing." Katagiri is Katagiri-ing; sitting is sitting; talking is talking; zazen is zazen-ing; awakening is just awakening. If I say Katagiri is awake, Katagiri does zazen, it is already a dualistic concept, it is already an idea of zazen before or after real zazen. From the view point of this conceptual world, we always ignore the most important world that we are passing through. Right in the midst of the reality of "awakening is awakening," "life is life-ing," "death is dying," there is no room to conceptualize, because it is nothing but practice in dynamism. Life is the full manifestation of total dynamic working; death is the full manifestation of total dynamic working. That's all. We are living from moment to moment and this life is moving very quickly. Now I am talking, next moment I may be dying. It goes very quickly. In the conscious world we always understand before or after. We have no way of consciously understanding this sphere of "moment." But if we stand up in this "instant" world we will be able to see the beautiful panorama of the vastness of existence, because "instant" means the eternal world, the source of our life.

What do you mean "to die"? Please, just die. That's it. Whether we scream or we say, "I am happy to die," it doesn't hit the mark. Within the screaming, within our feeling, within our experience, there is nothing for us to do. Our responsibility is right in the midst of reality in which death is dying. That's all. It's very simple. But our consciousness does not want to accept this, does not want to know what it is. Consciousness gets used to being in the conceptual world of before and after the sphere in which life is life-ing, death is dying.

The moment between before and after is called Truth or Buddha's world. We don't know what it is but we are there. Our life is completely embraced by this. We are present from moment to moment right there. That is what we call buddha, Buddha's world or Buddha-nature. That Truth is not something objective; it is the original nature of the self. Original nature of the self is not something different from the Truth. They are one.

The source of energy that helps the growth of our original nature is not in the conscious conceptual world. We are just going, so there is no room to say it is anywhere. It is continuous dynamic working and it is there we must stand up. Life is the full manifestation of total dynamic working. There is no room to conceptualize. It is just working. If we want to taste this, it is practice. We have to be right there, be present right there. We have to be in harmony with our original nature. If we are there, very naturally seeds of our energy grow, the source of our energy, our life, grows. But it is not an idea of "right there"; it is more than that; it is nothing but dynamic energy, energy in motion. It is going on eternally, regardless of whether the world is born or not.

When we do gassho, we do gassho, that's all. Gassho maintains gassho. Gassho is gassho-ing. This is the true picture of the world around gassho. If we want to taste real Buddha-nature through the form of gassho all we have to do is maintain this form in a pure sense. Then it is called undefiled practice.

In Buddha's world, to refrain from taking life means that we cannot take life. We cannot take life because in order to "take life" there would have to be before life and after life and in Buddha's world there is no room to let our intellect poke around with these dualistic ideas. There is just energy in motion, life itself in dynamic motion. We simply are not able to take life. How can we know this? All we can do is just go through it. Practice is to just be right in the moment. This is Buddha-nature, Buddha's world. It's the source of energy and it grows very naturally.

Our understanding is from the dualistic world, from participating in a completely different world from Buddha's world. When our understanding of Buddha's teaching itself comes from this different angle, we never know what Buddha's teaching really is. That's why we have to teach and transmit the real teaching of Buddha. Even though it seems to be difficult, we have to practice this because it is already the reality of our life.

Attaining enlightenment is not the main purpose of practicing Buddhism. This is false understanding, and to practice with the goal of attaining enlightenment in mind is false practice. It is already to be participating in the conceptual world of before and after, missing the most important point. From this point of view, we will never understand what human life is, we can only understand the surface. We may enjoy it because it is the usual, familiar way, but we aren't satisfied by that way of life. We will have many questions, but we won't know how to practice or how to touch the most important point of human life. Always we will be looking for a better life, without trusting, without feeling that it is the right way of life. We don't know any other way because we are always living in the conceptual world.

Buddhist precepts are difficult to understand. But it's not necessary to try to understand. Just receive them and form a habit of living them as a vow. It is important to have the guidance of Buddha's teaching, of the ancestors and of living teachers, all walking hand in hand with us, because we don't know how to practice, how to maintain the habit of a way of living based on Buddha's Way.

The main purpose of Buddhism is to form the habit of practice as a vow forever. This is just taking a journey in the universe, day by day, step by step. It is like walking in a mist. We don't know what the mist is, we don't know where we are walking or why; all we have to do is just walk. This is Buddha's practice.

Buddhist Faith and Practice

Right Zazen

HISTORICALLY, Eisai Zenji was the founder of Rinzai Zen Buddhism in Japan. He was one of Dōgen Zenji's instructors and Dōgen Zenji had great respect for him, mentioning him in his writings. In those days there were already many Buddhist schools in Japan, such as Kegon and Hosso; however, Zen Buddhism was not transmitted to Japan until Eisai Zenji brought it from China. Initially, Zen Buddhism was not accepted in the atmosphere of Japanese Buddhism at that time, but Eisai Zenji was eager to establish it. There were many religious enemies from other schools against his advocacy of Zen Buddhism, so the Zen Buddhism he taught had to be flexible, accepting the Tantric way of Buddhism, the Abhidharma teachings and the techniques and teachings of many other Buddhist schools. But finally he was successful in establishing Zen Buddhism in Japan.

Before Eisai Zenji transmitted Zen Buddhism to Japan, the practice of zazen was taught by other schools, but it was not exactly actualized in Japanese Buddhist life. So he tried to actualize the practice of zazen in everyday life. However, zazen was still considered a means to an end. After Eisai Zenji's death, Dōgen Zenji went to China and studied Zen Buddhism, and when he returned he wrote about zazen as being the "right entrance" to the Buddha-dharma.[1] He strongly emphasized that zazen is studying zazen-buddha. Zazen is not a way to reach the peak; zazen is exactly that we are buddha, we are already on the peak. This is a big difference from the usual understanding of zazen. Even now, many, many people still use meditation as a means to an end or as a way to reach the peak. But Dōgen Zenji emphasized that the Way is not a means to an end; the Way is exactly the same as the end itself. If using the Way, or zazen, as a means to reach a peak is the basis of our life, there is always a feeling of irritation and uneasiness; we never feel secure. This is our usual common daily life, whatever we experience, whatever we seek for. But the purpose of religion is to offer perfect security to human beings. If you believe zazen is a means, then why practice it as a religion? It is not necessary to do zazen—you could follow many other ways. Religiously speaking, the way is not the means to an end, the Way is exactly the peak itself. If we live our life in this way, there is stability and perfect security, and we can seek for the truth constantly.

Recently I have read articles in psychology magazines that clearly emphasize that Buddhism is gradually coming into the United States, not as a religion, but as a psychology. If Buddhism is accepted as a psychology, it will never be rooted in American life. Temporarily we can feel some satisfaction, some interest in it, but Buddhism will never penetrate American life. Sooner or later, when the times change, it will disappear. For a certain period of time, psychology and philosophy are fantastic, but I don't know that they give perfect religious security. In a sense, Buddhism as a psychology is still part of human culture, influencing, but not exactly penetrating American life. In order to penetrate American life, Buddhism must be accepted as a religion, and zazen must be practiced as an end in itself. Then it is really strong. Even though we don't realize it, it really penetrates human life.

Most religions have the important practice of prayer; without prayer religion doesn't make sense. Buddhism doesn't seem to have prayer and this appears to be a big difference between it and other religions. In the nineteenth century, Western people didn't accept Buddhism as a religion because it didn't seem to have prayer; it was not what is called revealed religion. Revealed religion emphasizes revelation from God or a higher source of being. Toward the end of the nineteenth century, several Western Buddhist scholars began to study Buddhism and gradually Western people have come to understand it and how it is different from other religions. Though Buddhism doesn't seem to have prayer, it does have *dhyāna*. *Dhyāna* means zazen (meditation), and dhyāna is exactly the same as prayer. Shākyamuni Buddha says Dharma is a light you can depend on, the self is a light you can depend on, but this self is really the self based on the Dharma. Dharma is the ultimate nature of existence, or holiness or the Truth itself. So, Buddhism is not a revealed religion, but an awakened religion—it is awakening to the self or to the Truth. This is the characteristic of Buddhism.

In Buddhism, however, this dhyāna or zazen, which is exactly identical with the practice of prayer, must not be a sort of means to an end;

even prayer in Christianity is not to pray to a divinity that exists apart from us. If we pray in that way, there is no religious security, because the more we pray to God existing apart from us, the more God keeps silent. Real prayer is completely beyond whether God speaks to us or not, or whether we feel satisfactory or not; all we have to do is just pray. That prayer is just process itself, the process of the prayer itself; that is all we have to do. This process or practice itself really manifests the source of our life or the ultimate nature of our existence. Within such a practice of prayer, there is no object to try to pray to or no subject who is doing the praying; this is real prayer.

Zazen, as the right entrance to the Truth, is universal. Whoever you are, a Christian or someone with no particular sense of religion, anyone can do zazen. At the minimum, all you have to know is information about how to sit. You cannot daydream in zazen; you have to sit in zazen physically and mentally. If your body is sitting, but your mind is drifting away, it is not *shikan taza* (in Japanese this means "just sitting" wholeheartedly). If your body is right in the middle of sitting, your mind is also sitting with it. But if you are always daydreaming, or if you are always trying to research what mental stage you have reached, it is not real zazen. Zazen is exactly the same as the manifestation of the basic source of energy (or right entrance); this is the basic practice of human life that is connected to the problem of life and death. Through this you can understand what human life really is. That is why zazen penetrates and is available to all circles of human life: skiing, basketball, dancing, whatever you do. For instance, how can you create something, how can you compose music? Music does not come from your intellectual sense; you don't know where it comes from. But many composers, pianists, painters, dancers and philosophers create their life from the basic source of energy. Even though we don't understand a person who creates a wonderful dance that comes from the basic source of energy and not just from intellectual sense, still great dancers always create like this, great pianists and great composers create music like this. So all we have to do is transmit this way from one to another. We have to transmit how sublime human life is. Dōgen Zenji says that Shākyamuni Buddha and many ancestors "gained the Way through zazen."[2] We must follow them. This is great historical universal proof; it is really true. This is the history of human life.

Even though you don't understand, do zazen. If you do understand, do zazen. If you are bored, sit zazen; if you find it fascinating, sit zazen. That is all we have to do. This is basic universal practice, because we create life anew, day after day.

Right Faith

Dōgen Zenji says that only a person who has right faith can enter the Truth or Buddha-dharma. He uses the term "whole faith-like body,"[1] which means your whole body and mind are exactly faith. You cannot discriminate between you and faith, you and zazen. We don't know who is sitting or what is going on or what should be known by whom. It is just like a fish swimming in the water. The water is exactly one with the fish; so fish is water, water is fish. Without the water the fish cannot swim. It is very difficult to explain exactly the state of oneness. It is dynamic motion between the water and the fish. The same applies to faith or the "whole faith-like body."

Faith is not spiritual greediness; it is free from oneself and also from others; it is not something given by somebody; it is not something coming from you. Where does faith come from? What is faith? Faith is completely nothing to comment on. In Japanese, faith is *jakujō* or complete tranquillity. *Jaku* means there is no one with whom you want to talk; *jō* means serenity or imperturbability. Imperturbability is something that permeates every inch of our daily life, from the top of our head to the tips of our toes. Serenity is really something alive, because it is a state in which human life is always ready to fit itself to any circumstances, and to act. But this fitting to any circumstances and acting is not doing something recklessly. If our head is not imperturbable, we cannot be ready to do something. If even just the tips of our toes are confused, we are not ready to do something. So our whole body must be imperturbable, quiet. There must be a very clear consciousness there.

According to Dōgen Zenji's understanding of faith, there is nothing that persuades us or pushes us or forces us to create faith. Faith means tranquillity, and complete tranquillity is the source of our nature and our existence. There is no need to talk about tranquillity or not tranquillity in our life or in our zazen. Everybody is already perfectly tranquil. That is why people who do not practice Buddhism seem not to seek for tranquillity, but in actuality, they seek for it and struggle for it in many ways. They work hard during the day and then they just want to come back to their home and sit down and relax regardless of whether that house is fancy or not, messy or clean. We should always be mindful of our original nature that is perfectly tranquil, because daily life becomes so busy that we may forget or ignore it. We should trust in this tranquillity and practice it within the original nature of tranquillity. Then we will be able to improve greatly in the practice of tranquillity. If we behave in a certain manner, so as to let this imperturbability break forth, it will really come up. If we do not behave in such a way, we will never have a chance to know, to realize the imperturbability we already have. Zazen is to adjust our body and mind to exactly fit this imperturbability, so it naturally comes up. Zazen is exactly identical with the original nature of existence, which is called tranquillity, imperturbability.

There is a Zen story that talks about this. The seventeenth ancestor, when walking with his disciple, asked about the wind bells suspended from the four corners of the temple roof. He said "What is ringing, the wind or the bells?" The disciple said, "The wind is not ringing, the bells are not ringing, the mind is ringing." This is really true. What is ringing, the wind or the bells or both? Whatever we say, it doesn't hit the mark. So finally we find a solution, that the mind is ringing. This is very true, but still there is a question. What is the mind? To this question the disciple replied, "tranquillity, imperturbability." The seventeenth ancestor was really pleased with this answer. The mind is completely vast, nothing to say. This is the original nature of existence inhering in the bells, wind, human beings, our mind, whatever it is. Dōgen Zenji had a very interesting comment about this story. He said, "It is the wind ringing, it is the chimes ringing, it is the blowing ringing, it is the ringing ringing."[2] "Ringing ringing" means that ringing entrusts itself to ringing, settles itself in ringing, and manifests itself in creative activity. At that moment, ringing is all-pervading without having any obstruction.

Tranquillity does not mean inactivity. In other words, tranquillity is not something we should hold on to by keeping away from human society; it must be something alive in our life. If we are completely isolated from human society, wherever we may go, our life does not work. Going to live in the heart of the mountain seems to be a way to have tranquillity. There it seems that we can handle our object, our circumstances as we like, but actually we cannot do so. If the tranquillity we have is not expressed in our daily living, that tranquillity is isolated, a limited form of tranquillity. Accordingly, it results in a lack of sharing it with people. We just want to keep it to ourself because it is nice. If we stay in our home it seems to be nice because no one interrupts us. But is is really just like a frog swimming in a small well. It is not the real state of human life. This tranquillity must be backed by the unconditioned; the unconditioned means purity, joy, peace, the unadulterated and also nonregression in our daily life. Nonregression or nonwithdrawal means perfect stability or religious security. So tranquillity must be backed by the unconditioned, wherever we may be. At that time our life is really embossed in the universe and not in the small scale of "I." If our life is embossed in the small scale of "I," we cannot have tranquillity, and very naturally we are irritated and restless. We want to get out and do many new things. It is fun, but basically there is always a sense of irritation and restlessness. It is not faith. It is not religious relief or ascertainment. Religious relief or ascertainment means nonregression; wherever we may go, there is nothing that causes us to withdraw. Faith is always there. At that time, very naturally, we can understand what human life is.

Faith in Buddhism is to trust in perfect tranquillity, which means to trust in something greater than just our conceptualization. We gradually develop this by listening to Buddha's teaching and practicing Buddha's teaching. So first, there is trust. But trust is not just trust without doing something. What is it that we have to do? It is to listen, contemplate and practice Buddha's teaching. This is the actual manifestation of trustworthiness. For instance, if we trust in somebody, we want to express ourself in a concrete way by doing gassho, bowing, opening our hearts or talking. We can tell our suffering to the person we really trust in. So trust is not just trusting somebody in our head, but simultaneously it is doing something practically. This is really tranquillity, and this tranquillity comes up just like spring water from the earth because we already have it underground, regardless of whether we are conscious of it or not.

So if we trust this tranquillity and practice it, it is alive in our life and very naturally our life becomes joyful and peaceful and we can share our life with people because we know how to live with people. And then there is very strong religious relief or ascertainment wherever we may go. Sometimes, however, if we look around the human world and see lots of miserable things happening, it is very easy to ask why we have to practice to establish a peaceful world. It seems to be useless. But when we ask this, immediately it is nothing but losing tranquillity. We shouldn't lose this tranquillity right in the middle of a miserable human world. We must still be tranquil and share our life with people. We shouldn't be withdrawn from the world, but should constantly listen to, contemplate and practice Buddha's teaching. Finally we can touch the core of human life. We just nod and say, "Yes, that is right." Then understanding comes from our heart and cannot but help us to love all beings. This is faith. This is expressing deepest appreciation for human life and also it is transmitting this deepest appreciation of human life to the next generation.

In the second chapter of the Lotus Sūtra, one of the major disciples of the Buddha, Shāriputra, asks the Buddha to explain the teaching of the One Vehicle, that everything is buddha. Buddha tells him that it is difficult to explain and that the monks and the lay Buddhists would not understand, so he is hesitant to teach it. But Shāriputra asks him three times and finally he accepts. So he starts to teach about the reality that all human beings are exactly buddha. Then five thousand monks and nuns and Buddhist laymen and laywomen start to leave because they find it too difficult to accept. These monks, nuns, laymen and laywomen are just like all of you. Don't you believe it is ridiculous to listen to the Buddha's teaching, which you don't understand, when there are many things you can understand? There are many people who teach wonderful things everyone can understand. But if we always listen to something we understand, we will never understand the human world, because the human world is still something we don't understand. Because of this we have to listen to things we don't understand, and sooner or later, what we don't understand will be understood. But Buddha allowed them to leave. Even though we grab people and say, "Stay here, listen to the Buddha's teaching, it is wonderful," whether they are able to stay and listen depends on the person and also on the circumstances.

There is a very interesting story about this. There was a monk who was spending lots of money drinking beer and whiskey in bars at night instead of practicing zazen. His teacher was very concerned about him. Several times he asked him not to do it, but he continued. One day he asked the monk to come to his room and when the monk entered, the teacher screamed, "Get out!" The monk jumped a little because he didn't expect his scream, and then thought, "This is a good chance to escape from this ridiculous temple life." So he immediately accepted and said, "Yes, sir." He was about to open a door to leave, when the teacher said, "It is not your door through which to get out." So he tried another door and again the teacher said, "It is not your door to escape." He tried three doors and each time his teacher said the same thing. Finally the monk became angry and said, "What should I do? You said to get out, but how can I get out?" The teacher said, "If you cannot get out, stay here."

Sometimes people are very stubborn. Even though the Buddha teaches again and again, still people don't accept. At that time there is nothing to do. So, on Vulture Peak, Buddha allowed the people to leave. But this doesn't mean that the Buddha completely gave up on them. Buddha felt pity for them and still he could express compassion toward them at any time, and if they decided to come back he could accept them. That is why Dōgen Zenji says, "Even on Vulture Peak there were some the Buddha allowed to leave. If right faith arises in your mind, you should practice religious discipline and study under a master."³ So if you have right faith, start to listen, to contemplate and to practice the Buddha's teaching. We should not keep away from human society, but we should practice together under the guidance of a teacher.

Dōgen Zenji goes on to say, "If it does not arise, you should cease for a while, and regret the fact of not receiving the benefits of the Dharma from the past."⁴ This doesn't mean we should turn our backs on people in need, but we should call upon them to reflect seriously upon themselves and their lives. We are already right in the middle of the Buddha's compassion. If we cannot see this, it is just like being in the midst of the ocean looking for water.

Have you ever thought how wondrous or strange it is that you are practicing zazen right now, right here? It is really something unexplainable, but it is a fact. This is your life. This is the time of the zazen you do now. What is meant by "the time of zazen"? Zazen is a being that is right in the midst of the stream of time. Then, when time occupies a certain portion of space, it is called occasion. This occasion is represented as washing your face, having a meal, walking, doing gassho, or chanting. What is the quality of this occasion? This occasion did not happen by chance. It has a long history. Why do we do zazen? We don't know. We have never been forced to sit zazen, but we do. The quality of the occasion of sitting zazen is not a shallow river or creek. It is really a deep ocean called causes and conditions. Why did I become a monk? I don't know why. Maybe I did something good in the past. This is a cause, but simultaneously there are lots of conditions helping this cause. My parents were very religious people, and it really helped me. There were lots of conditions helping me to come to Minneapolis to practice zazen: San Francisco, Japan, my parents and ancestors. So look at the quality of this occasion. The whole world comes into this occasion, the zazen we do together.

Time arises just like this, by time, occasion, causes and conditions. It just arises. "Just arises" means unadulterated motions or unconditioned activity. There is nothing to say about it. So why don't you trust in zazen, trust in tranquillity or, in other words, in the truth that you are buddha. If you don't trust in this, how can I take care of you, how can you take care of others? There is no way.

What is meant by trust? Listen to the Buddha's teaching. With wholeheartedness, try to live in peace and harmony with all beings. When you do zazen, do zazen. Do not sleep in zazen. Many people are studying theology, philosophy and psychology very hard in order to be free. But when you do zazen, do zazen wholeheartedly, because this is the occasion you are confronted with. It is the universe. We have to throw ourself away into the universe. Then, very naturally, magnanimity, compassion and illumination come forth from our zazen. If we don't do this, how can we live in peace and harmony with people? It is impossible. Zazen is a simple practice. If we cannot do this simple practice we will never have a chance to live in peace and harmony.

Each of us should think carefully in order to understand what Buddha's real practice is. Always we are seeking for something outside ourselves such as the practice of chanting names, sūtra recitation or reading the Buddhist scriptures and treatises. This is a very common practice. Dōgen Zenji points out that we have always done this in our daily life. So he wanted to tell us what Buddha's real practice is. His emphasis is that first we should have right faith. If we don't have right faith, no matter how long someone explains how important practice is, we won't understand.

In the zendō of Komazawa University in Tokyo there was a famous Zen master. His voice was very large and came from the *hara*, and he would scold the students as he walked behind them, so everyone was wide awake. One day he had a hemorrhoid attack that caused him a lot of pain and he couldn't sit on his cushion, so he stood up and started to walk behind the students. They really woke up. Then he said, "When you do zazen, you should leave zazen to zazen. Then, at that time, you can attain zazen." I didn't understand it then, but now I understand. Dōgen Zenji says almost the same thing: "When you leave the way to the way, you attain the way. At the time of attaining the way, the way is always left to the way."⁵ This is one of the explanations of giving. In other words when you give something, just give something. This is not an instinctive human act. To give something you must have a clear understanding of before and after giving, the person and the circumstances, and then all you have to do is just give. At the time of attaining the giving, giving is always left to giving; then giving comes into existence. This is really giving.

For instance, let us imagine you are climbing up a mountain cliff. That situation is just like being on the verge of life and death. There is no way to escape; you cannot complain. If you are there, all you have to do is just be there. If you act instinctively, you could die. If you are nervous, you could die. Should you depend on the intellect, you could also die. So you have to depend on the mountain, your mind and all circumstances. You have to watch carefully and understand. Your consciousness must be clear and know what is going on there. Then, after using your best understanding, your body and mind should depend on just one step. This is action. This is the process of one step without being nervous about what will happen in the next moment, or thinking about when you will reach the peak, or how far down the bottom is, or who is climbing, or how much farther you can keep going like this, or that you could die. There is nothing to think about, nothing to depend on. All we have to do is just be there using all the things we already have: consciousness, mind, mountain and weather. Then we have to act. Just take one step, a pretty simple step.

What is this one step? Is it to understand about living by studying philosophy or psychology? I don't think so. Finally they must be thrown away. All we have to do is just live. Take one step, and that one step must be stable. This means, after using your consciousness with your best effort, then act, wholeheartedly. This one step is really not just one step; it is the universe, including the mountains, your mind, and your consciousness. All things are completely melted into one step. What is one step? One step is the mountain. One step is the weather. One step is you. One step is the true way to live. It is really to attain the Way.

So the Zen master from Komazawa University said, "When you want to do zazen, you should leave zazen to zazen." That is all. When we want to climb the mountain, what is the true way to climb? Leave climbing the mountain to climbing the mountain. Just take one step. Then you can continue to climb, step by step. This is called right faith or imperturbability.

Buddhism is not a revealed religion, it is a self-awakening religion, because it is based on the ultimate nature of existence. Faith in Buddhism does not depend on something extra, something outside of ourselves. Faith is based on self-awakening and consists of very simple actions. Even though we don't understand this ultimate nature, all we have to do is just continue to approach it. This is Buddhist faith. This is the pure sense of practice. Nothing contaminates it. It is very realistic, but simultaneously it is vast, connected with the universe. This is the actual practice for us, leaving the Way to the Way, leaving zazen to zazen, leaving one step to one step. This is the true way to attain the Way. This is all we have to do.

Usually we seek for something outside: "I want to do this." Then we look for sweet candy, and if we see it, then we are really inspired to do something; if we don't see it, we are not interested. But if we always seek for something outside ourselves, if in zazen we consciously or unconsciously seek for something outside, this is not real zazen.

Dōgen Zenji says, "To read the words, unaware of the way of practice, is just like reading a medical prescription and overlooking to mix the compounds for it; it will be altogether worthless."[6] We just look at the prescription and forget to mix the parts of the medicine together, and completely forget to drink the medicine. We enjoy reading the prescription, saying, "Oh, this is wonderful medicine!" It is ridiculous, but we do this always. We think zazen is wonderful because Buddha says if we do zazen we become strong. From where does the strength come? Does it come from outside of you? We look at the scriptures and depend on them, and then we are really happy. But who must be strong, the scriptures? No, you must be strong.

When I was in college I studied hard, and one day I really attained a sort of enlightenment while reading a book. I felt very pleased and went to see a friend of mine, Yokoi Roshi, and told him about my enlightenment. Immediately he said, "How stupid you are!" My friend accepted that happiness of enlightenment, but he had to say how stupid I was. That was wonderful. It was really true, because that enlightenment was not my enlightenment. It was from a book. The book tells us about enlightenment, saying, "Someone says," "Dōgen Zenji says," "Buddha says," but this is not enlightenment. The experience of enlightenment is important for us, but it is not enough. Again and again that enlightenment must become more profound, until it penetrates our skin, muscle and bone.

Right Teacher

Dōgen Zenji suggested to us that first we have right faith and that then we have a teacher under whom we can practice. Right faith is not waiting until we understand something and then doing it; faith is to do something even though our consciousness tells us we don't have faith, and even though we don't know what right faith is. Right faith is to do something because it is exactly the total manifestation of the ultimate nature of existence. In order to let the original nature of existence manifest, we should behave in a certain manner. This is very important for us. So to have faith is to do something, to do something is to live. But to live by ourselves and still know human life in a broad way is pretty hard, because each of us already has our own territory, preconceptions, egoistic sense, heredity, and characteristics. So it is pretty hard to know human life from a universal perspective. We have to get out of this small well. We always feel comfortable there, but even if it is only once, we have to get out and for that we need guidance.

Dōgen Zenji says, "Only you must know without fail that the wondrous Dharma of the seven Buddhas can be received and maintained with its genuine essence manifested if the practicer whose mind is in accord with enlightenment closely follows and receives the right transmission from a clear-minded master who has attained the Way. There is no way for this to be known by a priest who studies only words. Therefore, you should have done with these uncertainties and illusions, and negotiate the Way in zazen under the guidance of a true teacher, and gain complete realization of the *jijuyū samādhi* of the buddhas."[1] This means that the most important point is that sooner or later we have to take responsibility for transmitting the genuine essence of existence, how sublime human life is, to the next generation. This is our responsibility. This is called Dharma transmission and it is most important in Zen Buddhism. If we have a teacher, and practice the religious life, it is necessary to have Dharma transmission from one to another. Just to pour water from one cup to another cup is exactly Dharma transmission. Only when you become the practicer whose mind is closely in accord with enlightenment can you follow, can you be in accord with the teacher's teaching. It is not something difficult. You may think that you are not able to follow because you are deluded, but I don't think so. Buddhist practice starts from "you are buddha." It is not something specific that you have to reach. You are already buddha.

Buddha means you don't understand buddha; buddha means complete digestion, nothing left. If you eat something that is perfectly digested, there is nothing left. Even if there is the slightest bit of dregs at the bottom of the bottle—it is not buddha. So the main purpose of Buddhism is to make sure that through and through we don't leave any dregs. This is perfect digestion. When we have a meal, the food must be digested. After digestion, the dregs come out from the body; then after the dregs have come out completely, what is left? Just aliveness: your blood, flesh, brains, consciousness, heart, everything working dynamically. But if there is even a slight bit of dregs in your stomach, it is a cause of sickness. That is pretty hard to realize. If you have studied Zen Buddhism, you are pretty easily attacked by the sickness of enlightenment. If you say you are happy, you are already a sick person. Zen always pins that down, but we don't realize it. Complete digestion is called buddha. Your life is really aliveness. Right in the middle of the process of life, dynamic motion or activity, there is nothing left. This is called buddha.

What is it that we call buddha? It's not a matter of discussing some aspect of metaphysics, philosophy or psychology. It is nothing but daily living. That is why Zen Buddhism, particularly Sōtō Zen, emphasizes just daily living. If you become a student of a Sōtō Zen teacher, you will always be given suggestions as to how to behave as a buddha; that is all. I was never praised by my friend and second teacher; he always scolded me. Because we are already buddha all I had to do was just do something as a buddha, but I didn't realize that. That is why he would point out things and say, "Oh, you made a mistake!" But his way of suggesting was not gentle. We don't understand this. This way really seems ridiculous, because if we are always scolded by someone, our ego-sense, our life, our self-consciousness gradually fades away. This is pretty hard for us to accept. But this is not done as a way to shrink our life. It is just pointing out that we should behave as a buddha. For many, many years we have become accustomed to developing self-consciousness; that is why we don't know how to behave as a buddha. But Zen teachers know pretty well how to develop self-consciousness in the proper way. That is why they always scold. But that scolding is really the Dharma seal, a certificate of enlightenment, only we don't realize this.

There is a beautiful story about Kishizawa Roshi, a famous Japanese Zen master. He was a high school teacher before he became a monk at the age of thirty and practiced under the guidance of Nishiari Roshi. Nishiari Roshi's face was unique; he was very serious and had lots of pimples, so his face looked like a potato skin. Kishizawa Roshi was always scolded by him, no matter what he did. Good or bad, right or wrong, he was always scolded. Then Kishizawa Roshi thought that he wanted to quit; he really wanted to because he did not understand why he had to suffer so much like this. Very often he wanted to quit, but he couldn't quit. So in a sense everyday life was sort of like a person doing undignified skips to catch up with somebody who bustled along—like a little boy trying to catch up by skipping along. Desperately he always had to do that. Daily life was always there so he had to bustle along to catch up.

One day his teacher gave a lecture about Dharma transmission and explained some of the Dharma transmission diagrams. One of the diagrams was called *dai ji* or "great matter," and it diagrammed the philosophical background of Zen Buddhism. The complete diagram was beautiful, going from Shākyamuni Buddha to Dōgen Zenji to us. Also there was another diagram that had the phrase "Here the iron man is." Iron man means a person who has perfect faith, a nonretrogressing spirit. An iron man is just like a huge mountain. This first phrase also means there is no second phrase; this first phrase is complete purity, just one step off the cliff. We cannot expect a second step off the cliff. All we have to do is just take one step; there is no second step or previous step. So if we become an iron man, then we say, "Here I am." This is a great man who is never moved. This is exactly no second person, nothing else, just "Here it is."

When Kishizawa Roshi heard this the tears streamed down his face incessantly, and afterward he wanted to ask his teacher for a calligraphy of "iron man." However, he was afraid to because whatever he did his teacher always scolded him, never accepted him. But he really wanted it, so one day he decided to ask an old man, who was favored by his teacher, if he would ask for the calligraphy for him. Whenever the old man went to see his teacher, the teacher was thoroughly pleased; even when he was in a bad temper, he would just smile and talk with this old gentleman. At first the old man was a little bit hesitant, but finally he agreed. So one day the old man went to see the teacher carrying a bottle of *saké* as a gift. The teacher really liked saké and wheat noodles. So the old man went to see him and said, "Here I am, let's have noodles and saké." The teacher was very pleased and said, "Come in, come in." They started to drink saké and eat noodles, and then, when the teacher was really feeling good, the old man decided to ask about the calligraphy. He said, "Roshi, I would like you to write a calligraphy for me." The teacher said, "Oh, yes, I am pleased to write a calligraphy for you. What do you want me to write?" The old man said he wanted "iron man." Immediately the teacher's face changed to a scolding look and he said, "It is not for you; someone asked you for it didn't he?" The old gentleman said, "Yes." The teacher said, "It was my student, Ian Kishizawa, wasn't it?" The old gentleman admitted it was he. After mentioning the name of his student the teacher paused a little, then his voice became a little lower, tears streamed down his cheeks, and he said, "My disciple, Ian, was ripe. He wanted me to write 'iron man'; that's wonderful." When the teacher had talked about the iron man, it had pierced Kishizawa's heart and tears had streamed down his face. The teacher knew about this and had waited for him to come and express his understanding. The calligraphy that he sent the old man for was really a great seal of enlightenment, and finally Kishizawa received Dharma transmission from his teacher.

Practice is not something particular, because practice is nothing but the total manifestation of human life itself, which is completely digested. All you have to do is discover how to accept that you are already in the middle of the ocean. This is nothing but constantly expressing a debt of gratitude. But we don't know how to behave as a buddha, so the teacher points this out in daily life. This is Buddhist practice. So very naturally Sōtō Zen accepts our life as completely digested. First of all, there are no dregs; but we don't realize this. So the teacher's responsibility is to help our life bloom without leaving any dregs; that is all. That is the teacher's responsibility. For this, the teacher has to know what complete digestion is, what buddha is, what real practice, which is called zazen, is. Zazen is not a means to attain enlightenment by seeking something outside ourselves. Zazen is nothing but expressing the debt of gratitude in our life.

Someone said to me that every teacher of every religion emphasizes that his own way is best. I understand this. In a sense I experienced the same thing in the past. I was really fed up with that. I wondered why every teacher had to say his way was best. But in a sense we can understand this, because any religion you follow is the way to reach the peak, and then this peak is Truth. This Truth is absolute. Through the spiritual teacher's way you can reach the peak. There is nothing wrong with this, because he reached the peak this way. This is his religious security. Through this way you can reach the peak, so we should accept it, we should respect the teacher's way; otherwise we cannot follow the teacher. If the teacher says, "I don't know," how can you follow him? If you follow such a person, how can you find spiritual security in your life? There is no way. It is ridiculous. Spiritual leaders in particular are very stubborn in a sense, because they always say, "This is best." That is why you can follow them.

First you should understand the stubbornness of a spiritual leader and respect it and accept it. Second, it is not important whether the spiritual leader has reached the peak or not; it is not important. It is secondary. The most important point is how much the truth that has been experienced has been digested, how much it is manifested in his or her life. Even though he doesn't say so, the truth is completely digested in his life. This is most important.

Buddha's teaching is how we can digest our experience of the truth. To reach the peak is not the goal, because Truth is emptiness. We cannot stay there, and we cannot personally hold on to the Truth. The problem is if the spiritual leader hangs on to the truth he has experienced and says, "This is best," then that becomes his truth. Truth is universal, cosmic. No one can hold on to it, whatever it is. If you find it, let it go. This is emptiness. This is why we cannot stay on the peak. No, never—we cannot do it. Buddha also experienced other teachers with this same problem, because religious teachers and philosophers always emphasize, "My way is best," and then fight with each other. Buddha said, "Why is it people have to fight over this experience of the truth?" Truth is one. So to experience the truth is not important. The important point is how we digest the experience of the truth in our life. Emptiness is that the truth must be perfectly digested in our daily life. Truth is something always sustaining our life, giving religious security to us. This is the truth. If so, where is the truth? It is you. Zen Buddhism emphasizes, from the beginning to the end, not leaving any dregs of the truth in our lives. This is pretty hard.

There is a Zen story that is a very good example of this. A monk went to see a Zen teacher and said, "I am here without carrying anything at all." The teacher said, "Put it down." The monk said, "If I am not carrying anything at all, how can I put it down?" Do you understand this? "I am here without carrying anything at all" is already something that he carries. That is why the teacher said, "Put it down." But the monk didn't understand, so he got angry. Finally the teacher said, "Please take it back to your home." This is wonderful but it is very delicate. It is really sickness, but we don't realize that sickness; it is a very delicate sickness. We all have this sickness, always; this is called having dregs. How can we completely leave these dregs? First we need to do zazen. This is the best way because zazen doesn't leave any dregs; we, zazen, good, bad, just sit down there. This is the best way. We don't believe it because our stubbornness, our ego, always wants to get something in our hands. If we have dregs, we feel good, because they make noise. We are always shaking the little bit of dregs at the bottom of the bottle to find out how much benefit we get from zazen, and then we want to practice more. Finally, if we have a bottle perfectly filled with dregs, there is no sound. At that time we know what dregs are, and we can understand why zazen is best. Still we don't believe, and this is why we need the guidance of a teacher who has experienced this zazen.

I say zazen is best, but immediately you feel like leaving when I say that. I experienced this in Los Angeles where I lived with a young American boy. He could speak Japanese pretty well, so we discussed things every day. I didn't like discussing Dōgen Zenji and other aspects of Buddhism because I was very exhausted psychologically; this was the first time I had lived abroad, and circumstances and lifestyles were completely different. Everything made me exhausted, even though I didn't do much, so I didn't have extra energy for discussions. But he continued to ask me questions every day, so I started to talk. I said, "I am a Sōtō Zen priest, but I am not talking about Sōtō Zen, I am talking about Buddhism, because Buddhism is learning human life. So strictly speaking, I am talking about human life, the original nature of human life, the taking off of lots of cultural clothes. Whatever it is, take it off. And then what is left? Just a human being. I'm talking about this." Then I quoted Dōgen Zenji. Finally he asked me, "Why did you use Dōgen's words?" We are already Dōgen Zenji and to bring up denomination is ridiculous. Do you understand? If we discuss in that way, we will be splashing water at each other constantly; it is ridiculous.

Can we thoroughly learn the naked nature of a human being? If we try to do it we are always looking at ourselves in our own territory. It is sort of like playing hide-and-seek or putting new knowledge into a hole. We feel good, but on the other hand we find another hole. We put that new knowledge into a hole and then we see another hole. Always we do this. We take out old knowledge and put in new knowledge constantly. This is human life. It is fun. But it makes us exhausted and finally we cannot play hide-and-seek with ourselves. Then we must throw ourselves away into the universe; that is practice under the guidance of a teacher.

First, do zazen. That is pretty hard. Zazen is best because zazen is ridiculous. It is perfectly ridiculous. I don't recommend that you do something wonderful, because everyone else gives you something wonderful to do. I want to give you something ridiculous. Then if you do this, it is really best. But spiritual leaders usually hang on to their own individual experience and always emphasize, "This is the truth; this is best." I understand this, but it is not important for us. The most important point is how can you let go of the dregs of the truth. When the truth is completely digested in your life, there are no dregs. Just show your life. Just be there. That is an iron man, here I am. Even though you don't bring any religious terms or spirit, you just show your life. At that time you are never tossed away or moved and you do not wobble. Always, "Here I am," that is enough. But can you stand up in "Here I am," in the completely naked nature of a human being? It is very difficult. Very naturally we want to have something outside of ourselves, Bibles, scriptures, what the Buddha says, what the iron man's truth is. But strictly speaking, there is completely nothing. When there is completely nothing, how can we live?

We live right in the middle of modern civilization, but we don't know how long modern civilization will last. According to the Christian sense, sooner or later the end of the world will come. At that time, what do we do? Nothing. All we have to do is stand up in "here I am." Zen Buddhists always emphasize this—we cannot leave any dregs. Just stand up there. And then our life ends with the world. That is all. Can you do this? Can you end with the world? This is exactly the genuine essence of human existence. This is our life and death. There is nothing there, even slightly, to leave any kind of dregs. We have to live in that way. We don't understand, because we are in too comfortable a situation to see it. This is why we have to put ourselves into certain circumstances, such as climbing a mountain cliff, where we are completely on the verge of life and death. At that time we really understand how important one step is, how important our rope is, how important others' help is; we understand. But if we put ourselves in a comfortable situation, we don't understand. So we have to practice in this uncomfortable situation. At that time the spiritual power of practice really penetrates our skin, muscle and bone. No matter how long we practice there is no proof that at the exact end of the world we can just be there; no proof. But all we have to do is just continue to practice like this. Because this is life, this is death.

The teacher has to know human life and has to know zazen. This is exactly the same as the problem of life and death; it is not a means. If we do zazen, that zazen is exactly life and death. There is no gap between them. But we don't understand, and that is why the teacher has to know and has to transmit this kind of practice to people. But we don't always give something like sweet candy in order to reach the goal, enlightenment. It is wonderful in a sense, but it is nothing but the dregs which will be left at the end of our life. You will understand after my death. Now, when you don't understand, all you have to do is just continue to practice this pure sense of zazen. I am sorry for you, but you have to do it.

Sooner or later, I want to have a monastery. The monastery will be a place where wonderful teachers can come for all students to see. Just see them. Even though you don't understand, you can see them. This will be wonderful for you. According to Dōgen Zenji's understanding of the idea of a teacher, how many teachers would he accept in the United States? Maybe Dōgen would accept no one as a teacher. Maybe I would be the first person to be fired, but I can't escape. So don't trust me. But please trust in Buddha's teaching that I talk about. I do my best to talk about Buddha's teaching directly even though you do not understand; even though you feel bored, I continue to do this. Trust this. Trust Buddha's teaching. You may say you can accept the teaching but not me. But if you want to drink the tea, please accept the kettle too. The kettle and the tea are the same, but they are also different, so that is why I say don't trust me. But I want to teach Buddha's teaching. Trust this and practice with each other, hand in hand.

To Live Is Just to Live

I told a student, "Let's practice forever!" She said, "Forever?" I said, "Forever, three thousand *kalpas*." Three thousand kalpas. In the Diamond Sūtra, a bodhisattva says Buddha was born in this world because he practiced for many, many years—countless numbers of years, maybe three thousand kalpas in the past, and because he honored thousands and thousands of buddhas in his past lives. Do you know how long one kalpa is? Let's image a huge field that is forty square miles in size and is completely filled with poppy seeds. A celestial being, a beautiful lady, descends to this field once every three thousand years and picks up one poppy seed. When all the poppy seeds in this forty-square-mile area are gone, it is called one kalpa. Can you imagine this? We have to practice three thousand kalpas. Can you do that? Well, if you can't, I think you had better quit right now.

You know if you walk in the desert and can't see the end, it's not necessary to become irritated. Usually, if we don't see the end we don't know what to do, or if the end is far away we become upset. When we think of how to master zazen or attain enlightenment or try to understand zazen as taught by the Buddha, we become exhausted. We can't practice. Sometimes, particularly when we feel lazy, we should think of those questions. But when those questions make our head ache, we should forget thinking. Just practice, that is wonderful. Forget about the end and take one step like an elephant or a turtle. This is our practice. In Buddha's world, it is really wonderful and beautiful. There is no end. So let's practice for three thousand kalpas.

The Shingon school says it is not necessary to practice for three thousand kalpas. "It teaches that 'the genuine enlightenment of the Five Buddhas is attained in a single sitting, without going through many kalpas of practice."[1] But Dōgen Zenji strongly emphasizes zazen or shikan taza: "You should know that for a Buddhist it is not a matter of debating the superiority or inferiority of one teaching or another, or of choosing the depth or the superficiality of the teaching that matters; all we have to know is whether the practice is authentic or not."[2] This is most important. If we discuss about whether the teaching is good or bad, there is no end. Finally, we fight each other. The important point is whether the practice we are doing now is deep or shallow, true or not true. We are always debating some aspect of the teaching, whether it is good or bad, or right or wrong.

If we compare our experiences with the experiences of other religions, we can see something very similar. But the experience itself is a sort of doctrine, a sort of result we can have and discuss about. It is something set up or fixed by an individual. Through certain practices, we can reach the Truth, but when this truth comes into us and we consciously experience it, at that time truth is not real Truth, that truth is our individual truth. This is religious experience; it is something already fixed by individuals. Then when we pick a point and discuss it, it is fun, because we can discuss it endlessly. I don't mean we shouldn't discuss religious experiences, but it is of secondary importance, because it is not real human life; it is not dealing with how to live. The important point is can you have faith in God. If the answer is yes, then go pray. That is all. Do you believe in zazen? If the answer is yes, go to the zendō and sit. That is all. Real human life and how to live is a very practical matter. It is sort of like a television set. Most of us don't try to understand the electrical system or how a television set works before we turn on the switch. The television set is already there. It is part of our life. If we want the TV to communicate, we turn on the switch. This is a very simple practice. Turning on the switch is an urgent, practical aspect of human life, completely beyond how much we understand the universal energy behind the tiny switch, or how complicated the electricity is in a TV set. If we turn on the switch, it all comes together and we can see it. This is human life. But usually we don't do this. First, we want to understand our life by making a list of our experiences, their benefits and deficits, and then by discussing them with other people and trying to find out about certain results. Then after all that, we believe in our life. But that takes time.

Usually, we practice religion according to a system of three stages: teaching or doctrine, practice, and enlightenment. This is a very common system. First, we read the teachings, and then practice, and then, finally, through practicing we attain the result, the experience itself, or enlightenment. But Dōgen Zenji's way is completely opposite. First, there is enlightenment, then practice and then the teaching.

Enlightenment is Buddha's zazen. Buddha said that he attained enlightenment simultaneously with all sentient beings. In other words, he experienced that all sentient beings were already enlightened along with him. Already enlightened! That is the quality of the zazen he did. The quality of zazen or quality of experience the Buddha had was simultaneously the same as zazen itself; zazen is not a means to an end. For instance, I have the title of head priest of the Minnesota Zen Meditation Center. If so, are this body and mind separate from the position of head priest? No, they are exactly the same. The position of head priest is simultaneously the quality of this body and mind, of Katagiri's existence. Without this body and mind, I cannot have this position.

Zazen is not a means to an end, but exactly the Truth mentioned by the Buddha, that he attains enlightenment along with all sentient beings. In other words, all sentient beings are simultaneously in his zazen, and at that time zazen blooms. It is really a total manifestation of the human world, of all worlds. This zazen is jijuyū samādhi. This is the actual practice we do. But this is not a matter of discussion. This is something we have to do right now. Even though I constantly tell you that you are already an enlightened person, you don't believe me, but this is really true. You are already enlightened. All we have to do is just practice.

Dōgen Zenji emphasizes that zazen is not a means to an end, but that zazen is jijuyū samādhi. *Ji* means self, *ju* means receive, *yū* means use and *samādhi* means oneness. This means you receive your life and simultaneously the whole universe. That is why samādhi is translated into Japanese as "right acceptance." Right acceptance is to receive yourself and simultaneously the whole universe. We have to receive the whole universe and use it. You are you, but you are not you, you are the whole universe. That is why we are beautiful.

If we wholeheartedly paint a certain scene from nature on canvas, it becomes not just a portion of nature that we pick out, it represents the whole picture of nature. At that time, that picture becomes a masterpiece. That is why painters practice hard. How can we master this practice? Just practice day by day. Drawing one line is not one line, this one line is simultaneously the whole picture. That is called jijuyū samādhi. It is not a matter of philosophical or metaphysical discussion. It is what is called enlightenment.

Enlightenment comes up first and it means to just be present. If you want to be what you want to be, be present. Just stand up straight, with stability, and then simultaneously your effort turns into practice. Then from this practice, the teaching will come up later.

The teaching of how sublime human life is comes from us; it is in us. At that time we can accept the Buddhist doctrine of how sublime human life is very naturally, because it is coming from us. Usually we forget practice and try to mold our life into the doctrine, and then we practice. But, day by day, human life is constantly changing. The Mahāyāna doctrine was compiled right about the beginning of the first century C.E. Can we mold our life into the first century? We have to respect that doctrine because it comes from enlightenment and practice, but if we don't understand the real significance of the doctrine, it becomes something objectified; it doesn't come from our lives. When we read the doctrine in papers and books, we say it is wonderful and then discuss it. If everyone says it is good, we start to practice, but if everyone says it is not good, we throw it away. Usually the doctrine comes first, then we practice and then attain enlightenment. But we cannot take care of human life like this. Practically speaking, it is completely the opposite. First, enlightenment, then practice and then human culture, human thought, human history come up. And that history, thought and doctrine are that which we have now. Don't accept them as something objectified, apart from us. We should understand the doctrines in the proper way; they come from human life. If I say, "When you do zazen you become buddha", that is beautiful, but it is still words, still doctrine, still the moon in the water. Put it aside and just do zazen.

First you should trust in you, because you are you, but simultaneously you are already an enlightened person. We are beings embossed in the universe whether we trust this or not. It is completely beyond trusting or not trusting; it is super trustworthiness. So do zazen, not as a means but as jijuyū samādhi. In the zazen you do, simultaneously the universe must be there. This zazen is really beautiful; it supports you and includes your past life and future life. They really come together. This is the zazen Dōgen Zenji mentions. This fits into human life exactly. Dōgen Zenji has to say that this way is best, because we don't do this. But he doesn't hold on to his own ideas. We should understand this deeply. Sometimes he has to say this because everyone is ignorant. We all believe in our own way of developing self-consciousness. That is why he says that this way is best—this is a big shock. But we don't feel it as a big shock, we hate it. We think Dōgen Zenji says the same thing as other spiritual leaders. But Dōgen Zenji's criticism is not criticism, it is encouragement and deep understanding. It is paying attention once more to what zazen is. He gives us the suggestion to open up our eyes. We have to practice. That is why Dōgen Zenji's answer is that we should know whether our practice is authentic or not. This is really practical.

There is a very interesting story about two monks who were talking with each other about their lives on a boat. One monk was a Tantric Buddhist and the other was a Zen monk. After landing, a dog began barking at the two monks because they wore shabby, dirty *koromos*. The Tantric school of Buddhism always encourages chanting *mantras*, so the Tantric priest began chanting a mantra to keep away all the devils and to obtain happiness. He was holding a stick on top of which was a symbol of strong spiritual life, and he was shaking it, making noise as he chanted the mantra again and again. The more the priest chanted, the more the dog barked; it was a funny situation. Even the dog could understand this. Then the Zen monk said, "The dog hasn't stopped barking, what is wrong with you?" The Tantric monk really became angry and said, "Can you stop the barking?" The Zen monk said, "Well, let me try." Then he took some bread out of his koromo sleeve and gave it to the dog, who stopped barking and ate the bread. That is nice. I don't know if it is a true story or not, but it doesn't matter. Such things always happen in our lives.

For instance, in my case, I always had to go back to my temple at midnight. It was in the mountains and no one was living near there. I would hear sounds and it would scare me, but I would tell myself that it was all right, not to worry, nothing would happen. But, still I felt as though somebody were following me. Sometimes I looked back and there was nothing there, but I could not walk quietly. Finally, I chanted the Heart Sūtra and I felt good; but immediately when I saw a rabbit or other animal, I jumped. So the Heart Sūtra didn't work. In a sense it was good. I don't mean you should ignore the Heart Sūtra; temporarily, it was nice. But don't expect anything when you chant the Heart Sūtra. Just chant the Heart Sūtra, that is enough. That practice is very important, just like jijuyū samādhi zazen. This is really invisible spiritual power. It penetrates us, and finally, very naturally, wherever we walk, we don't feel fear.

I really admired my master. He lived in my temple for many, many years and that temple was really scary. Japanese temples are not like American churches. Churches are very bright inside, but a Japanese temple is very dark and scary, particularly at night. Behind the temples there are graveyards. The country village people try to take care of the bodies organically. They dig a hole, set up wood in a particular way, put the dead bodies on top, cover them with rice straw that has been soaked overnight in water, and set it all afire. It burns all day, and sometimes in the evening the wind would bring the smell of the dead bodies burning into our temple. The first time this happened, I said to my master, "Is someone cooking fish?" My master said, "No, it is not fish, somebody is cooking the dead bodies." I said, "Dead bodies! Where?" My master said, "In the backyard." My master was really amazing. He was never surprised at anything; he was very calm. One time I asked him, "Don't you feel frightened living in this scary, mysterious temple by yourself? Do you think there are ghosts in this world?" He said, "Don't worry, don't worry." He didn't care, but I was very scared. This is our practice, very practical, very simple.

If somebody asks you about doctrines, sometimes you can discuss them, but sometimes you can say you are busy. It may be particularly difficult to discuss Buddhism with your parents because they feel it is weird. So a really good teaching is to practice jijuyū samādhi. This means to just be present at your home with your parents with whole-heartedness. When you get up in the morning, just say good morning and take care of your parents. Finally your parents may be very curious about what you are doing, because you have changed. You are you, but you are not you. Maybe your parents will ask you, "What is Buddhism?" You may say, "I don't know." Then they will ask why you practice something you don't know about. But if you knew everything it would not be necessary to practice. You don't know, that is why you have to practice. Very naturally your parents will be curious about you because you have really changed. You are not the usual person your parents have understood. If you continue to practice shikan taza, wherever you may be, very naturally your parents may visit you to see what you are doing. This is called you and the whole universe coming together. It is just like the Zen monk giving the food to the dog to make him stop barking. It is a simple practce; it is really human life, just human life. That is the quality of the zazen that Shākyamuni Buddha did. Then the Buddha tried to bring it into the world because people didn't understand what zazen was. But even in the present world people misunderstand. So century after century we have to explain what real zazen is.

Based on Shākyamuni Buddha's experience and the experience of the buddhas in the past, the main point of Dōgen Zenji's teaching is that zazen is to just become present in the process of zazen itself; this is shikan taza. It is not something you acquire after you have done zazen. It is not a concept of the process, it is to focus on the process itself. It is very difficult to understand this because even though we are always in the process, we don't focus on it. There are even many schools in Buddhism that still handle Buddhism as a concept. But real Buddhism is to focus completely on the process itself. The process is you.

Zazen is completely different from other meditations. It is not a matter of philosophical or metaphysical discussion. All we have to do is do what we are doing, right now, right here. Whatever kind of experience we have through zazen is secondary. Whatever happens, all we have to do is to be constantly present right in the middle of the process of zazen. This is the beginning and also the end. You can do it; it is open to all people, whoever they are. This is shikan taza.

We are already exactly peaceful and harmonious. But still, when we do zazen, we want to try to be peaceful. Trying to be peaceful is no longer to be peaceful. Just sit down. We do not have to try or not try or say that we do not care. If I say something is this way, immediately you rush and try to grasp it. And then if I say it is not this way, you immediately try to grasp that. Then I say it is not that either, and then you are confused. Finally, you say you are neutral, but that is not good either. What we have to do is realize we are buddha; this is a big *kōan* for us. This practice is called shikan taza and is our kōan for our whole life. There are hundreds of kōans, but those kōans are just leaves and branches, that is all; the root is shikan taza. We have to understand this. This is perfect peace, perfect harmony.

We are always thinking about something, always trying to acquire something. Some people criticize Sōtō Zen, because it teaches not to expect enlightenment, to just sit down. They say if one cannot expect enlightenment, then what are we doing? Even Sōtō priests do not always understand what shikan taza is. Then if they are criticized, their faith starts to wobble. This is very common. This is to be a human being, and includes not only my friends, and others, but it includes me. If someone criticizes us, then our faith starts to wobble. If we look around, there are many things for people to be interested in. Very naturally, we think some other way would be better. So we pick it up and use it. But if we are wobbling, our feet are already not completely grounded. It is just like walking during a big earthquake. Even though we believe we are walking stably, we are not. If we are going to walk, we have to walk stably, no matter what happens. This is completely beyond being a matter of discussion. To walk in stability means to just walk. "Just walk" is to be present in the process itself. The process of walking is exactly that our body and mind are nothing but the process. There is no gap between us and the process. This is shikan taza; this is to be peace. We are peaceful, we are harmonious from the very beginning. That is why we should not expect to acquire peace. Take off all conceptual clothes, and then what is left? Finally, there is nothing to think about. All we have to do is just plunge in.

For twenty-five hundred years the Buddha has been teaching us that we are buddha, that we lack nothing of the highest enlightenment. Still we do not completely understand, and even though we understand, it has not settled down in our hearts. That is why we have to practice constantly. We have to practice because we have a mind.

Mind is tranquillity; it means peace and harmony. What is wrong with mind? Nothing is wrong with mind. What *is* wrong is that for many years we have given our mind the chance, the environment, the circumstances for it to be a monkey mind. Monkey mind means the mind is always going out, in many directions, picking up many things that are fun and exciting. If we always leave the mind to take its own course, finally before we are conscious of it we are going in a different direction than we expected and we become completely confused. That is why we have to take care of mind. We have to take care of chances, circumstances, time and occasions.

For zazen, we arrange the circumstances in the zendō so that it is not too bright or too dark, not too cold or too hot, not dry or wet. We also arrange the external physical conditions, such as our posture and the amount of food we eat. If we eat too much we fall asleep pretty easily, so we have to fill just sixty or seventy per cent of our stomach. Also, we keep our eyes open, because if we close our eyes we might fall asleep, or we are more likely to enjoy ourselves with lots of imaginings and daydreams. Next we arrange our internal physical condition, that is our heart, our intestines, our stomach and our blood. But these things are beyond our control, so how can we take care of them? The only way is to take care of the breath. If we take care of the breath, very naturally, internal physical conditions will work pretty well. This is important. If we arrange the circumstances around our body, our mind, and all internal and external conditions, then, very naturally, the mind is also engaged in our activities. Then we are not bothered by the workings of our mind; the mind does not touch the core of our existence; it is just with us, that is all. When all circumstances are completely peaceful, just the center of ourself blooms. This is our zazen; this is shikan taza.

Shikan is translated as wholeheartedness, which seems to be sort of a psychological state or pattern. But shikan is not a psychological pattern. Shikan is exactly becoming one with the process itself. Literally, *za* of *taza* is zazen and *ta* means to hit; so, from moment to moment, we have to hit the bull's-eye of zazen itself. This is not a technique. In the practice of *kendō*, one has to hit right in the middle of the opponent's head to get a point. This is not a technique; it is the practice that has been accumulated day after day. Our practice must be very deep, unfathomable, and then we can hit the bull's-eye. Shikan is exactly taza—full devotion to zazen itself, that is to the process itself and not to a concept. This is the practice of zazen mentioned by buddhas and ancestors.

Dōgen Zenji says in "The King of Samādhis Samādhi," "Even though some may have known experientially that sitting is the Buddha-dharma, no one knows sitting as sitting."[3] Even in Dōgen Zenji's time, no one knew this except his master, Ju ching. Sitting as sitting is just the process of zazen itself; this is exactly life and death. If we look at our life, it is very clear. How often in our lives have we had feelings of happiness, unhappiness, pros and cons, success and failure? Countless numbers of times. But we are still alive. Regardless of whether or not we awaken to how important the essence of human life is, basically we are peaceful and harmonious. In other words, our life is just a continuation of living, that is all, "being living" constantly. That is why everyone can survive, no matter what happens. Is it our effort that makes it possible for us to survive for twenty years or forty years? No. Is it our judgment? No. Strictly speaking, it is just a continuation of becoming one with the process of living, that is all. This is the essence of living. The truth of living is just to live. This is a very simple practice.

How can we communicate "just living" with people? In Sōtō Zen Buddhism, communication is life to life, living to living. That is what we have to learn from the teacher. We do not know what it is, because it is just living. We have to learn this dynamic living. My teacher never changed his attitude or feelings. Of course he had feelings, but he was very calm. Sometimes he expressed loneliness, sometimes anger, but in a different way. Basically, his life was just going on. If we practice under such a person, we can learn what the truth of living is. The truth of living is not a technique or concept; there are no words. It is a communication of how to know the truth that to live is just to live.

In many schools of Buddhism, this is not considered enough. That is why kōans are used. Through the kōan, we try to communicate by checking our practice. The teachers give us kōans and then check our practice to see how much progress we are making. Then they tell us when we have attained enlightenment and we say, "Thanks." The moment when we say thanks it is already something else. It is not real communication. Many teachers know this, but they can't stop this practice. It is not the fault of the teachers, it is the fault of human beings. People around teachers always push the teachers to give them something. That is why there is a long history of this kind of practice. It is very difficult to stop, because in a sense it is a nice way of teaching that nurtures self-development, self-consciousness, very naturally. If there is completely nothing to teach or communicate in words, it is very difficult to live. I used to think it was a weird way to teach, because I really wanted to get something from the teacher. Otherwise, why did I become a monk? My purpose in becoming a monk was to become a good monk. I wanted to be free from suffering. I did not care about my teacher's suffering, I only cared about what I wanted. That was my energy when I was young. But my teacher did not give me anything. He just lived. That was very strange and the temple was strange and the food we ate was not very nourishing, just rice and stinky pickles. Sometimes there was no food, and then my teacher would say, "Why don't we wait, maybe somebody will bring it." I thought, "This is a way of human life?" I could not believe it. But he did it. He was very calm and he could wait.

In the novel *Siddhartha*, by Hermann Hesse, a merchant asked Siddhartha what he had to share with people. He said that he could think, he could wait and he could fast. To fast means even though there is nothing, no reward, you can just be present, just practice. He was able to fast, think and also wait. That is pretty hard practice; it is a great capability. But the merchant did not understand and asked him if that was all he had to share with people. Siddhārtha said it was all. This is very important for us to understand.

I learned what the real essence of the Buddha's teaching is from my master, even though I did not understand his way at the time. All we have to do is to continue to show this. But usually teachers do not show this. They accommodate human desires and give candy. Of course it was very hard for my teacher to live with me, because I was young, and he was old. I was nineteen years old and you can imagine how strong the energy in a nineteen-year-old boy is. It was very hard for me too. My energy was very strong and desiring everything. But this way of living is very good for us; this is the essence of Buddha's teaching, shikan taza. Usually the teacher does not have patience under such circumstances, because human beings have too many desires and are always groping for something. No matter what field we are in, science, philosophy, psychology and even religion, we are always groping for something. But shikan taza is "sit down and just be present," right now, right here. Become one with being present. This is a continual process. Process is really dynamic energy; it is not a concept of energy or concept of process. Process is process. If there is even a slight gap between the process and us, it is not process. We must be process. For this we must always be present. If we are exactly right in the middle of the process of time we do not realize it. It is exactly us, it is very peaceful, very harmonious. Even though we do not realize or get a taste of how much we are in the process, or how much we can benefit from the process, that's all right. All we have to do is continue being process itself. This is why Dōgen Zenji says the most important thing is to know whether the practice is true or not, true life or not. Whether we experience something or not or whether we care or not, we cannot say anything. Whatever happens all we have to do is just be right in the middle of process continuously. Broadly speaking, even though we are not conscious of it, our life is already going in that way. Remember this. It is why Buddha says that you are buddha. We are already there, even though we do not realize it.

Why do we have to realize this? Without realization, even though we are right in the middle of process itself, we slide off. How can we realize calm mind? We cannot tame the mind to become calm because the mind is already calm. The mind itself is peaceful and harmonious. All we can do is create calm circumstances, that is enough. This is shikan taza. And then, very naturally, sitting in zazen, our mind is calm. When our mind slides off, we begin thinking; immediately we try to be calm, but already this is not to be calm.

Why do we create circumstances that nurture the mind to be monkey mind? Actually, there is no reason; this is called ignorance. But if I say ignorance makes our mind confused, then immediately we try to find ignorance. I do not think ignorance exists as something like an avocado seed that we can get hold of. No matter how long we try to find ignorance like this, we cannot find it. Ignorance is something we have to get a taste of through the truth that to live is just to live. Teachings are important, but where do they come from? They come from the truth that to live is just to live, from the process itself. It is a very simple practice for us. Teachings are not teachings apart from us; teachings are us. Teaching must be something coming from us. That is the real teaching. To study the teaching is fine, but it is a mistake to believe that the teaching we have studied is true religion. Religion becomes true when the teachings we have studied penetrate our skin, muscle, bone and marrow and finally disappear. Then they become energy to support us. Teachings have no form because they are energy, our life. We do not understand this and so we create concepts. But, although we stumble on the way, the great Way is already present. We are existing there, and it supports our life. But we misunderstand the great Way. We always pick up the concepts and then discuss and believe that is religion. But that is nothing but the dregs. The important point is how we can accept or handle the truth so it becomes alive in our daily life. This is not a matter of discussion. Through discussion we can communicate, but it is not real communication. Real communication is the direct demonstration of how to live. This is the point of religion. It is very hard, but we have to learn this. We do not like it, because consciousness immediately thinks it is strange. No one believes this. If you know, it is fine; it is not necessary to teach. But we do not know, that is why we have to teach.

Dōgen Zenji says, "Because of these intellections, flowers in the air of various kinds appear."[4] "Flowers in the air" are the Buddhist teachings of emptiness, interdependent co-origination and mutual interpenetration. They are really beautiful flowers blooming in the sky. Then we believe that is religion. We poke our head into it and discuss it. But we should ask ourselves if we are okay. If we can say fine, that is great.

Zen Master Gonmyo always woke up in the morning and said, "Good morning, sir!" to himself. Then he said, "Are you okay? Yes, I am fine this morning." Then he would say to himself, "Do not be cheated." What do we mean by *fine? Fine* is not a concept. *Fine* is really the process of living itself, right now, right here. This life must be peaceful and harmonious, completely beyond peace or not-peace, or harmony or not-harmony. It is perfect peace. This is what is called *fine.* Zen Master Gonmyo says, "Fine," and "Don't be cheated," because we are always chasing after something, groping for something.

My motivation for going to college to study Buddhism was to be free from suffering, because when I was in the temple I thought my teacher was not teaching me anything. So I went to school to try to learn Buddhism and end my suffering, but the complete opposite happened. The teacher gave me many books on Buddhism to read, which I did.

Finally, he gave me a book on the Buddhist philosophy of emptiness. It is a collection of many simple sentences, but if you read it, it is really strange and hard to understand. Finally I thought, "Why did I become a monk?" It made me suffer more. Such is human life. We should remember the following point too. If we hear Dōgen Zenji's teaching that the truth to live is just to live, and then completely ignore the study of Buddhism, that is also too much. We should keep our life balanced. Keeping our life in balance is shikan taza. Shikan taza does not make us suffer or give us a headache; it makes us more simple. There is no mess, nothing to stick in our intestines, no diarrhea; it is very wonderful. We feel good because nothing is there. Whatever we eat is digested very smoothly. In other words our life becomes completely, absolutely digested through zazen. This is a perfect, peaceful life, which is called "we are buddha." This life is just the process of energy itself. Very naturally this energy process supports our life. This is the best way to communicate with people, with the universe. Intellectualization is fine, but, we should remember, it is nothing but the dregs. It is not bad. It is important for us, but we should realize that intellectualization has its own limitations.

We are buddha; as Dōgen Zenji points out, "we lack nothing of the highest enlightenment."[5] We should drop off all things, and single-mindedly do zazen. This is nothing but process itself or zazen we are doing from moment to moment. In the practice of Buddhism, particularly Zen Buddhism, we emphasize attaining enlightenment. Enlightenment is perfect peace and harmony. If you think enlightenment is something you can get, then it appears right in front of you and you rush to get it; but the more we rush to get it, the more enlightenment eludes us. We try with greater effort, and finally we become a frantic screaming warrior. Then we become exhausted. This is very common. But enlightenment is completely beyond enlightenment or not-enlightenment. It is just perfect peace and harmony.

I do not want to say the zazen we do is best, because if I say so, it becomes a means to an end. The important point is how we handle the zazen we do right now, right here. This is really the question. This question should always be with us. Who is alive from moment to moment? If we don't realize this, we can create a big gap. Whatever we think, let it go. Then what is left? All we have to do is keep our mouths shut and just do it. Then we can see many things in a broad universal perspective. The whole world comes into our zazen. This is the truth that to live is just to live. Very naturally, teaching comes from this life, and we can transmit how sublime human life is to the next generation. Day by day, year after year, we have to practice this and understand it.

Clarity and Purity

Faith in Buddhism is that which makes the mind clear and pure. It is the continuous process of gazing at the truth under all circumstances. If we really are gazing at the truth continuously, our life becomes very generous, very accepting of the world. Faith also includes understanding, practice and realization. Realization is the final goal of Buddhist practice; it means to leave no trace of the practice of zazen. Real realization is perfect oneness; there is no "I," no zazen. It is nothing but activity, the movement of you and zazen. That realization corresponds to making the mind clear and pure. If we become one with zazen, without leaving any trace of "I" or zazen, how can we think something such as, "I am a bad person or a good person," or how can we say good zazen or bad zazen? We cannot say anything. All ideas drain away right in the middle of realization, oneness. This is "making the mind clear and pure." This is ultimate, thoroughgoing practice.

Clarity is to gaze at eternity without a sense of mystery. By our knowledge of biology, physics, theology, "Buddhology," *I Ching*, astrology and all the sciences, we can understand the ultimate nature of existence very clearly. For instance, we can research what the ultimate nature of water is. We can know how many molecules water has and what kind of molecules relate with each other. We analyze these molecules and give them certain names, such as A, B, C, D, and then we try to understand how they communicate with each other. So according to scientific understanding A falls in love with C and D, but never falls in love with B. We really systematize and we think we understand very clearly. But reality is completely reversed. It seems to be clear, but still, sometimes A molecule falls in love with B molecule, which is very illogical. Then the reality of the water's life is completely reversed because we don't know why A communicates with B. According to our understanding, A shouldn't fall in love with B. Finally, we have to know something more than the human world that we understand by our knowledge. Buddhism accepts this illogical situation of the water as something clear. So even though for scientists it is mysterious, for Buddhism it is not mysterious; it is very clear. Clarity means to accept that which is clear and that which is not clear in the human world. So everything is clear. It is not mysterious when you practice it because it is the motion of molecules, the function of molecules. This is reality.

Our life is going on logically and illogically. We don't know why Katagiri becomes Katagiri connected with you. Katagiri is constantly functioning day by day and then something happens. People ask me why I chose Minneapolis as a place to teach. I don't know why, but it happened. It is mysterious, but it is very clear; there is some reason why that choice was made. We don't know why because the original nature of our life is functioning very quickly, at super speed. This is the original nature of our life. Very naturally, what we have to do is just practice day by day, just function. That is all we have to do, and then something comes up; it's not by chance, it is very clear, but our intellectual sense cannot reach it. All we have to do is let the flower of our life force bloom constantly. This is the function of the molecules of water. This is what is called mysticism in Buddhism. We don't know what it is, but this mysticism accepts all things as being clear.

For instance, in Japan, there is a Buddha statue of Maitreya Bodhisattva with very beautiful eyes. Before Buddhism came to Japan, Japanese society was based on Shintoism, and life was very simple and not logical. The Japanese are still not logical, but when Buddhism came to Japan, it brought with it more information about human life. That was the time when this bodhisattva was made. It was the turning point, when the Japanese people opened their eyes to know the human world, human life, with clarity. There is much feeling in this bodhisattva statue. Its face is always gazing at something that is clear; it is very sharp, and also, there is a sense of aloneness.

Aloneness comes out of mysticism, out of not knowing how original nature functions. The original nature of existence is just motion. We cannot get anything to hold on to from that. It makes us pensive and we feel a little bit dissatisfied. We cannot stand up there.

This aloneness is based on the primordial awareness of human existence. Loneliness is a little bit different; it is awareness of the human world through our experience. But aloneness makes us just a drop of water in the immensity of the ocean—just pfft, that's all. Simultaneously, aloneness is not aloneness, because that drop of water extends everywhere in the immensity of the ocean. So if we understand real aloneness, we can be free from it. Realization of aloneness is leaving no trace of aloneness. Sometimes this is expressed in a smile, the smile of a bodhisattva who is constantly gazing at the Truth and simultaneously feels a sense of aloneness. Then, through and through, aloneness reaches its own source and defuses. Our individual daily life is a drop of water constantly falling into the immensity of the ocean. If we completely understand pensiveness or pain, we can smile. This is a bodhisattva's smile. It's not smiling on purpose. It is not smiling to curry favor. It is just a smile, like a baby's smile. A baby's smile is wonderful because it has no purpose. That is a beautiful smile. But our smile is a little bit complicated because it is created by human speculation. A real smile very naturally comes up from the bottom of our mind. This is clarity.

Purity is practice itself. It is no gap between you and zazen, between you and me, you and the trees, you and a poem, you and the piano, you and friends. This is perfect purity. This is our original nature; very naturally we become one. But unfortunately, human knowledge, human empirical awareness is still very narrow, very limited. This is why we have to gaze constantly at the clarity of human life. Gazing at this clarity really deepens our life day by day. Then we can deepen our personality, and really understand each other. If we first try to understand zazen intellectually and then practice it, it is too late. The span of our life is not long enough; we will die before we understand. Whether we understand what zazen is or not, we can accept it as clarity, and just practice. This is called purity. And then finally, faith makes the mind clear and pure. This is realization, or leaving no trace of oneness; it is just functioning. This is perfection, and perfection is fullness.

When we want to understand the mountains, we should research them intellectually, as well as the clouds, ropes, boots, and we should examine our mental and physical condition. Also, we should learn the illogical aspect of the mountain. If we accept the illogical aspect of the mountain through our intellectual understanding, when we climb the mountain, we can confine trouble to the minimum. But if we depend on our intellectual understanding only, it is pretty easy to make mistakes, because the mountain has an illogical aspect, which the mountain shows us if we climb it. The illogical and logical aspects of the mountain's life communicate with each other and with us and then something happens. We fill the bottle of our life as a mountaineer, and then we know the mountain's life, the tree's life, the cloud's life, the sky's life, and the emotional and spiritual aspects of ourselves. This is called perfection.

Finally, practically, climb the mountain. That is all. Just climb the mountain, and then there is no gap between the mountain and us. The mountain climbs the mountain. The mountain is our life, so we can learn about our life from the mountain. There is no subject, climbers, and no object, mountain. There is just climbing. Delusions drain away, drop off naturally. This is called perfection. This practice makes our mind clear and pure.

Buddhist faith includes understanding, practice and realization. It is not a belief; it is not something that seems to be true, mentioned by somebody else. Dōgen Zenji warns us not to believe Buddha's or the ancestors' messages as the truth completely. Even the Buddha and the ancestors can make a mistake. This doesn't mean you should be arrogant and create Buddha's teaching as you like. We should accept the Buddha's and ancestors' teaching, but still keep our eyes open. This is very important, because it's pretty easy to fall into the trap of mysticism; there are lots of things we cannot know. But if we totally accept something we don't know, it becomes clear for us. This is our practice: faith is to make the mind clear and pure.

Understanding Life and Death

Buddhist faith is to live one's life in clarity and purity. Purity is oneness between subject and object; there is no gap between them. Clarity is to gaze at eternity that is no mystery. It is to see human life including death. This is most important for us.

When I became a monk, there was only one thing I really disliked and that was performing funeral services. I tried to escape from doing them, but it was too late, because I was already a monk. In a sense I was very lucky, because there was no excuse; always I had to face death directly. We don't usually think about our own death. Death always happens to somebody else. So it was really hard for me to see death exactly. When I went to the monastery, I thought I could escape from doing funeral services and facing death, but reality was completely the reverse. There was a wooden gong hanging in the monastery that said, in big Chinese letters, "The important matter of life and death, everything is impermanent." Every day I had to see this gong, and I thought, "My goodness, here is death again."

In "Shushōgi," by Dōgen Zenji, which talks about the meaning of practice-enlightenment, the first sentence says, "The thorough clarification of the meaning of birth and death—this is the most important problem of all for Buddhists."[1] Boom! That's it. A big shock. We don't see our life including death. We just see birth and living and we ignore death. For instance, if Zen centers were to offer lots of things that are good for human happiness and health, such as yoga exercises, vegetarian food, macrobiotics, *I Ching*, astrology and various kinds of meditation, then maybe Zen centers would develop pretty well. Many people would probably come to them because people want these things in order to be happy and healthy. But where are we heading?

When Dōgen Zenji was studying in China he was asked by a teacher why he was reading the Buddhist scriptures. Dōgen Zenji said, "I want to learn what the ancestors did in the past." The teacher said, "What for?" Dōgen Zenji answered, "Because I would like to be free from human suffering." The teacher said, "What for?" Dōgen replied, "I would like to help all sentient beings because people are suffering so much." Again the teacher said, "What for?" So Dōgen Zenji said, "Sooner or later I would like to go back to Japan and help the village people." The teacher said, "What for?" At last Dōgen Zenji didn't say anything at all. Finally, there is nothing to say. Nothing to say means this constant questioning led him into a corner; he could not say anything. This is touching the core of human life, so-called death. But we don't say death; it is just keeping silent, that's all.

For what reason do you become happy? For what reason do you become healthy? I don't mean you should ignore your health or happiness. Everyone wants to be happy, but it is not the final goal. We cannot always hang on to it or depend on it, because when we die, we are inevitably completely unhappy and completely unhealthy. How can we hold on to a healthy body? When we die we are completely at the bottom of unhealthiness. There is no way to escape. Sooner or later, we know without exception, we are going to die. This is why life is beautiful. Remember this. If we lived forever we would never have a chance to let our life force bloom. We are fading away from moment to moment. Consciously or unconsciously, we know this, but we don't want to see it. We use a lot of toys to forget this fact and just struggle to live. But it is not a fair way to understand human life, because we *are* going to die. We have to see the total picture of human life.

Sometimes, at a restaurant or the bank, you can see beautiful flowers, and often they are not real flowers, they are plastic. People like plastic flowers very much because they don't die. Plastic flowers are cheap and economical and if we buy only one bunch, that is enough for our whole life. But even though we try to make plastic flowers exactly the same as living flowers, we never see the real beauty that we see in a living flower. A living flower is fading away and that is why it is beautiful. A plastic bowl is just like a plastic flower. It's pretty and cheap, and even though you drop it, it doesn't break. But many people don't like plastic bowls even though they are economical and beautiful. They like very expensive, real china bowls. In Japan, people interested in the tea ceremony buy beautiful china tea bowls. If you drop one, it breaks pretty easily and then a thousand dollars is gone. But nevertheless, they are really interested in buying these bowls because they are so fragile. They are fading away and dying. That is why they are beautiful. The same applies to our life. We are going to the grave. We are fading away. That is why we can really live. This is gazing at eternity with no sense of mystery.

We should understand how to live within the limitations of human life based on the very dangerous situation of our life fading away. We don't know when we will die. So we have to do our best to live wholeheartedly. This is called purity. It is very beautiful.

The other day on the news I saw a famous Russian ballerina teaching young American ballerinas in New York. This teacher's ballet was completely different from that of the students. Her series of movements in the ballet were just like frames of film moving. They were fading away—appearing and disappearing, appearing and disappearing. But each form of this ballerina was perfect, her body and hands, everything about her was perfect. She had a very long neck, twice as long as mine. I was very surprised. Her body had been completely reformed by the ballet. Her body was not her body, her body was ballet itself. Each movement was beautiful and completely independent, but simultaneously each movement was connected. It was just rhythmically going on, like frames of a movie or smoothly running water. That is why it was beautiful. There was no gap between her and the ballet. Within the limitations of her life fading away, she took care of each form with wholeheartedness. That is why her body completely became ballet. When we see her ballet there are two things we can see. One is that her ballet is always fading away, appearing and disappearing. This is the impermanent world, which changes constantly. But in addition to this, we can see the perfect beauty of the ballet. There is no gap between her and the dance. They are just one. We don't know how such wonderful beauty can be created right in the middle of impermanence. Right in the middle of appearing and disappearing, there is a beauty that is eternal. Faith is exactly to live like this.

Dōgen Zenji says this in a different way. He says, "To study the Way is to try to become one with it—to forget even a trace of enlightenment. Those who would practice the Way should first of all believe in it. Those who believe in the Way should believe that they have been in the Way from the very beginning, subject to neither delusion, illusive thoughts, and confused ideas, nor increase, decrease, and mistaken understanding. Engendering belief like this, clarify the Way and practice it accordingly—this is the essence of studying the Way."[2] He explains clarity and purity in a little different way. Clarity and purity is that there is no confusion, no delusion, no misunderstanding. It is perfect. But we always say it is impossible for subject and object to become one. We don't believe in that way because we already have our preconceptions, so-called "I." I have a certain type of life, or I have a certain type of body, so I can't do it. If we think in that way, we cannot do anything at all. The body and the mind of that ballerina were completely flexible. There were no delusions, no misunderstandings. If we train ourselves, we can create a wonderful body and mind. Even though we say our body is stiff and we cannot make our neck any longer, if we want to be a ballerina, we can do it. Everyone can do it. But becoming a ballerina doesn't happen without doing anything. First we have to move toward becoming a ballerina. So we train our body. This is purity. This is true not only for ballet, but photography, painting, sports, whatever it may be. This is very important for us. This is Buddhist faith.

Faith is to long for establishing perfection of the human personality to the highest pitch. This is a bodhisattva's life. Perfection is water oozing from the ground and naturally filling a bottle with water. This is our practice. If we say, "I am not perfect, I am immature, and I would like to have a mature personality," that is already dualistic understanding. In Buddhism it's not real practice. Real practice is that we are already a great being. So why don't we accept ourselves as a great being first. Even though our nose is a little bit crooked it is a great being. But we see our nose as crooked and say, "Oh, maybe I can correct it a little bit." My brother's little finger was short and crooked at the end. As a child he hated his little finger and tied a chopstick to it with a piece of string to make it straight. Once a week, he would take it off and look at the finger to see if it was straight. Then he would say,

"Ah, I did it!" but then an hour later it was crooked again. So he tied the chopstick on even tighter and the same thing happened, week after week. Finally, he gave up.

Of course this finger was not normal, but it should be accepted as a buddha, as a great being, because it is already a great being in a wonderful world. Accepting the finger as a great being means to handle it as a great being instead of hating it. If you hate it, immediately you hurt this finger in many ways. This finger doesn't say anything even though we hate it, but if we take care of human beings, our friends or our mind in that way, we create a big problem. Look at your mind. If you see hatred come up and try to fight with it, it grows even larger. You don't know what to do. But our practice is to do zazen as a great being. Let us accept our body, our present life, as a perfect being. This is very simple practice, day by day. When sitting comes, just sit. When you see your nose, just take care of your nose as a great being, with compassion, with kindness. If you see hatred, be generous toward hatred or anger or whatever it is, and accept it as a great being. Next, with a calm mind, you can see hatred as hatred. So you can handle hatred with compassion. If you say, "I don't like hatred," there is already a gap between hatred and you. This is the dualistic world. This is understanding hatred through the intellect.

Our practice must be grounded, zazen must be grounded, our breathing and our concentration must be grounded, day by day. This is our zazen right now, right here. This is all we have to do. Just move the handle of the water pump, and then, very naturally, water comes up. But in everyday life we easily become irritated, so if we move the handle of the water pump for five minutes and then don't see any effect, we become mad at the water pump. Finally we destroy the water pump. This is very common. More or less, we do things in that way. This is not an appropriate way of life. Our practice is water coming up from the bottom and filling our bottle. In order to do this, we have to gaze at eternity that has no end, no sense of mystery, and then we have to become one with our object completely. This practice is just doing zazen as a great being, as a buddha. This is faith, this is perfect happiness.

Many people like being a vegetarian very much. People ask me, "Are you a vegetarian?" and I say, "Almost." If you want to be a vegetarian, that is wonderful. If you want to listen to beautiful music, that is wonderful. If you believe it is good for your happiness or your health, that is wonderful. But once more again, we have to think about what happiness is. If we accept vegetarianism as a certain rule or doctrine, it becomes dogmatic. If we do zazen to obtain something, then we should ask ourselves where we are heading. Can we carry this kind of zazen or happiness to heaven? Eventually, we have to say good-bye to everything. Suzuki Roshi's final words were, "It's all over." "All over" means he really touched the core of human life—where are we heading? For sixty-eight years he worked hard and taught Buddhism in the United States, and then where was he heading? In such circumstance, could we say that because we do zazen we can die in peace and harmony, or that by doing zazen our mind will become calm and strong? If we believe zazen is like this, what's the difference between us and a bank robber? By doing zazen, we can become a bank robber with a calm mind, and steal money from the bank with a calm mind. It is ridiculous if we believe in zazen in that way.

Finally, we should ask ourselves where we are heading. Without doing this we cannot see eternity. When we have to do zazen, just sit zazen. Just sitting zazen is not just sitting zazen; it is gazing at eternity with no sense of mystery. Right in the middle of the limitations of human life we do our best to do zazen wholeheartedly. This zazen is apparently nothing but a fading away, appearing and disappearing; it appears as a flashing light—good zazen, bad zazen. But beyond this, right in the middle of this kind of zazen, there is beauty. That is the eternity of zazen. If we think, even slightly, that we would like to be happy by doing zazen, at that time it is not perfect happiness. It is not real zazen. It is very simple, although not many people understand this. But this is exactly life and death. There are no exceptions. Everyone has to live and everyone has to die. There is completely no choice. For many, many years we have trained ourselves to use something as a means to find happiness, always to use something as a means. But when we die where are we heading? To ask this question constantly is Buddhist faith. Our zazen must be grounded in no misunderstanding, no delusion, just like a ballerina. She had no delusions like "I am a good teacher" or "I am a perfect teacher" or "I have a stiff body." She just trained, just practiced in the world of impermanence. Our great responsibility as human beings is to manifest eternity, perfect beauty, right in the middle of this impermanence. If we want to help human beings, this is our responsibility. Then, very naturally, we understand human life and death.

The Ten Steps of Faith

In Buddhist scriptures, the word faith has many meanings. In Sanskrit the words for the three basic meanings are *shraddhā*, *prasādha*, and *adhimukti*. The first, *shraddhā*, means trust, certitude or confidence. When we listen to the Buddha's teaching and meet the Buddha face to face, then, very naturally, we experience a sense of certitude and trustworthiness. The second term is *prasādha*, which means to experience joy and satisfaction through shraddhā. When we experience this confidence and certitude in our life, very naturally joy and satisfaction arise. It comes from a very steady, confirmed religious life from which we can never withdraw. This is prasādha. The last term, *adhimukti*, literally means faith, confidence and understanding. However, to understand in Buddhism is not to understand with our knowledge, but to accept or receive something with a strong feeling of conviction. For instance, if we listen to the Buddha's teaching, sometimes we have an understanding and say, "Ah, that's right." This comes up from our heart. It comes in, penetrates our heart and settles down at the bottom of our mind. This is understanding. So adhimukti means belief and also understanding. The final goal is religious security in which we accept how sublime the Buddha's teaching and Buddha's life is. Then we can depend on his teaching, his life, with complete conviction. This conviction is not only to understand intellectually, but also through our experience. To experience is to do something under the guidance of the Buddha's teaching. We need guidance, and then, very naturally, our understanding, our knowledge, gradually penetrates our skin, muscle and bone. This is adhimukti. Usually I use the English term faith in place of these three Sanskrit words, but maybe through this explanation of these words you can see a little clearer image of what Buddhist faith is.

Buddhist faith is always focusing on the primordial state of existence. For instance, Dōgen Zenji comments on this kind of faith when he says, "Faith is that which is free from oneself and another. It is not that which is brought up by one's intentional compulsion nor by one's creation, nor by another's persuasion, nor by regulations. Faith manifests itself at the stage of buddha."[1] Faith is not something created by ourselves or others. It is really the basic, fundamental primordial state of human existence. Simply speaking, we call this Dharma. If you try to acquire faith through the practice, it is something else; it is not real faith. Dōgen Zenji says that if you convey yourself to your object first in order to get something, it is called delusion. This is very natural. Whatever our objective is, we always try to understand it first. We are always living at the conscious level. This is a fact. Without human consciousness, we cannot exist.

For instance, this table that I see before me is not a real table; this is an image of my understanding of the table. Even though I try to keep this table as a table, someone may come in and see it and create another image through his understanding. He may say it is not a table, it is firewood. He can then easily break up this table and put it in the fireplace to keep his body warm. So we are all conveying ourselves to our object first and then trying to understand. This is delusion. It is a perverted view. Fortunately or unfortunately, everyone already has a perverted view of the world. "Fortunately" means that through this perverted view we can realize what the truth is. Without it, how can we know? How can we seek for the truth? So from this point of view we are lucky. But unfortunately, we don't realize it is a perverted view and so we stay with our image of the table. Then someone comes and takes it and breaks it and we really get mad at him and fight with him. This is not the proper attitude to take in order to see deeply into the fundamental nature of existence.

Faith is not something created by someone. It is not something that forces you to believe something expressed by others that seems to be true. People always try to force us to believe this truth or that faith. But real faith is not something like this. It is not religious regulations or something you should believe. Usually we believe the teachings, but not the real, ultimate nature of existence. The teachings are a form of the ultimate nature or Truth, but they are not the real truth. So someone experiences the real truth and then teaches that truth to people. Then people try to analyze, synthesize and eventually build up the teachings. Then we say, "Believe this, this is the truth." We say the truth is in the Bible or the sūtras. The teachings are a part of the Truth, but they are just ideas. If we believe in these ideas our life becomes dogmatic. So whatever teachings or "isms" we study, they all must be digested in our life.

Faith is something more than we have thought. What is it? It is the absolute or primordial state of existence. But is the absolute apart from human life? No, it is not. So Dōgen Zenji says, "Faith manifests itself at the stage of buddha."

Buddha is also called tathāgatha and this name has two meanings: the first is "just going and coming," and the second is "not coming and not going." Just coming is, when we do gassho, just do gassho without leaving any trace of "I." It's pretty hard, because our consciousness immediately picks up "I" and also an object. But we can reach this stage that is called buddha, tathāgatha, or just going and just coming, not going, not coming. It is not contradictory. It is the real picture of our life.

For instance, when we dance on the stage, we have to just move our body and mind, just going and just coming. But if we think of "I" as a dancer, or the audience or the composer, it is sort of an object. If we have an object in mind, right in the middle of just dancing or just doing, it really interrupts us. In karate, when we hit a board with our hands, if we have "I" as a subject in mind, we will hurt our hands. But if there is no "I" and no object, then the board is exactly our hands, our hands are exactly the board. That is why our knuckles can be very hard. Whatever we do, this kind of practice is very important for us.

When the primordial state of existence inherent in us manifests itself in our life, this is faith manifesting itself at the stage of buddha or tathāgatha. This primordial state of existence works constantly, but we don't realize it. When we realize it, this first stage of realization is called faith. Faith is not something we can conceptualize. It is not an object of worship we can see objectively, but it is in us and it comes up from the bottom of our life. This is nothing but activity. Faith is something completely pure and clean, with no stain, no contamination. Faith is the hands of clarity and purity. We are always in a wonderful treasure house, but if we don't have these hands, how can we accept faith? Faith must be manifesting itself constantly as activity.

There are ten stages or steps of faith. The first step is aspiration. Aspiration is the longing to develop one's whole personality in one's life. Everybody has this longing in many ways. People study, go to school and run businesses. Through running businesses they can learn what business is, and through relationships with people they can learn how to deepen their personality. But deepening one's personality through running a business and through relationships is very complicated. So, as best as we can, we try to find the simplest way to develop our total personality. This is the religious way. This is aspiration.

The second step is mindfulness. If we really long to develop our total personality, we cannot be egoistic. So very naturally our eyes are

open to ourselves and simultaneously to others, not only human beings, but trees, birds, our boots, our clothes, toilet paper and water.
We must be mindful of others' presence. Without this, we cannot develop aspiration for the truth. We have to understand others.

The third step of faith is endeavor. When we see the presence of
others, trees, birds, the ocean, the sunrise and sunset, very naturally
we endeavor to live in peace, in harmony with them. This is human
effort. This effort is not to develop individual egoistic life. If we try to
develop our personality egotistically, the reverse happens. We destroy
our personality and hurt others. Egoistic effort is always a trouble-
maker. It is not real faith.

The fourth step of faith is zazen. This is how to live with all sentient
beings in peace and harmony. Usually we convey ourselves to the object first, then try to understand it, and then become attached to this
understanding. We say, "This is the way I am," and when someone
suggests we go another way, we say we don't want to. We always hang
on to our way. Finally, our mind is burning, excited and confused, and
then we fight. This is not the appropriate attitude toward human life.
So, at any cost, we have to keep peace and harmony so that we are able
to see everything in equality under all circumstances. When conditions
are favorable, it's really easy to see everything in equality, but under
unfavorable conditions, it is very difficult to do. That is why we need
practice. This is zazen.

The fifth step of faith is wisdom. Wisdom is to know how to maintain one-pointedness. This is very important. Through zazen we can
dwell in one-pointedness, but in daily life it's very difficult to do this.
Actually, in zazen it is also very difficult, but then our life is arranged
in a simple way so it's a little easier. Wisdom is to figure out how to
keep one-pointedness in zazen, in gassho, in eating a meal, in working
in our office and even right in the middle of anger, hatred or love.
Wisdom is to figure out how to keep our eyes open. To keep one-
pointedness right in the middle of anger means to stay with it. To stay
with it means to accept the anger and do something about it in a positive way. Even a little bit, we should try to do this. This is wisdom. It
is to see people, anger, pleasure, unwholesome or wholesome things,
everything, as existing simultaneously in a big horse pasture.

The sixth step of faith is discipline. In daily life, lots of crises can
happen. If we don't have discipline in our life, we are completely swal-
lowed up by these crises. We don't know what to do. So how can we

maintain one-pointedness or wisdom? Our life must be disciplined in many ways.

The seventh step of faith is *eko*, which means to transfer one's merit to others. This is a very important practice, and also it is one of the beautiful ways of life in Buddhism. If we discipline our life and maintain one-pointedness, our life becomes very simple and we can understand others and live with them in peace and harmony. If at that time we say, "I did it," this is not so good. We have to return to the source of existence, which is called emptiness. That is to let go of whatever we have in our hands. Let go of "I did it." This means let go of stinkiness. If you become a doctor and say, "I am a great doctor," that is stinkiness. If you become a zen teacher and say, "I am a good boy," this is really stinky. We should return our merit to emptiness, and then that is simultaneously to give merit to others. People realize how beautiful this is. For instance, through discipline, ballet dancers manifest their dance, living in peace and harmony with the orchestra, music, composers and audience. Next, they return to emptiness. This means they just continually dance—dance, return to emptiness, dance, return to emptiness. This is the perfect beauty of dance. We cannot know what this beauty is, but we can see it. We are really impressed by this kind of dance. This is the beautiful practice of eko. In Buddhism, when we chant, we dedicate the chanting of the sūtra to someone; this is also eko.

The eighth step of faith is protection of Dharma. The protection of Dharma means to protect our body and mind in order to practice the Buddha Way. Our body and mind are great Dharma containers; without them we cannot seek for the Truth or lead all sentient beings to the Buddha Way. This includes our desires and instincts, our consciousness, our wholesome and unwholesome traits, everything. To return to emptiness doesn't mean to throw away our body and mind. We have to take care of our body and mind as a Dharma container, so that we can practice the Buddha Way in order to help all sentient beings.

The ninth step is nonwithdrawal. If we practice the Buddha's teaching and do zazen, then simultaneously we receive merit and we give it to others. People receive this merit, which means they accept us with respect. Very naturally, when we are respected by others we feel joy and satisfaction. Because we protect others, simultaneously we are protected by all, and then satisfaction and joy ooze from the bottom of our life.

The tenth step of faith is living in vow. This is the final goal. Living in vow means your life is completely secure. Not just in this life, in but life after life we can have an aspiration to live in this way. Every morning, in the Buddhist service, we chant the three refuges (or Triple Treasure). The first is, "I take refuge in the Buddha, vowing with all sentient beings, acquiring the great Way." This great Way is the universal path along which everyone can pass. It teaches us what supreme mind is. We believe our mind is really stinky, but our real mind is a great mind that can pass along the universal path. Even monkey mind is nothing but one of the beings in the big horse pasture. Monkey mind is just going and coming, without leaving any trace. At that time, monkey mind turns into supreme mind. This is to vow to Buddha, to respect Buddha with all sentient beings, constantly seeking the great Way and experiencing the wonderful human mind and body. Next, we take refuge in the Dharma or the Buddha's teaching. It teaches how great and sublime human life is. We deeply enter into the Buddha's teaching, which is wisdom as vast as the sea. It is just like an ocean where we can live in peace and harmony. Next we say, "I take refuge in the Sangha, vowing with all sentient beings, bringing harmony to all, completely without hindrance." The determination to live in peace and harmony is not something we try to follow only in this life, but life after life. This is the final step of faith, and is called bodhi-mind or awakening the Way-seeking mind.

Faith is not something we think about. It is practice that very naturally comes up from the bottom of our life. So all we have to do is live. How? Just follow the ten steps of faith one by one. If we live like this, very naturally faith comes up. But before we do so, still we have questions. We want to know we can live, how we can have faith. Human speculation always comes up. So I say, "Why don't you believe in Dharma? Why don't you follow me?" The Buddha says, "Please follow me, walk with me," because Buddha is a person who has realized Dharma, who knows how to live based on just going, just coming, without leaving any trace.

Commentary on "The Bodhisattva's Four Methods of Guidance"

In the chapter "The Bodhisattva's Four Methods of Guidance" from the Shōbōgenzō, Dōgen Zenji teaches that the four methods for guiding people to live in peace and harmony with other human beings are giving, kind speech, beneficial action and identity action.

Giving

In Buddhism there are three kinds of giving: giving materials, giving teachings (Dharma), and giving fearlessness.

The Buddhist monks in eastern Asia do not participate in productive labor, so they cannot give material things. Instead they concentrate on Buddhist practice and particularly on giving fearlessness and giving teachings.

Most people want to teach only after mastering something completely. Of course it is right, but sometimes we may be face to face with an opportunity that compels us to give Buddha's teachings regardless of whether or not we are ready. In such a case, no matter how we feel, we must just teach with our utmost effort. It does not mean, however, that in our daily life we just open our mouth to talk impetuously about Buddha's teachings; we have to keep our eyes open to see when and how there is an opportunity to give.

To give a talk is particularly beneficial for the teacher, because when preparing for the talk we have to study, but we cannot use all the information that we have learned in preparation, and many aspects of the teaching are still left in our body and mind. So there is much benefit for the teacher as well as the listener. That is giving the Dharma.

Along with giving the Dharma, giving fearlessness is very important, particularly if we are practicing a spiritual life. According to the Buddha, there are four kinds of fearlessness: first is fearlessness arising from the awareness of something omnipresent in the world; second is fearlessness arising from perfection of character; third is fearlessness arising from overcoming opposition, that is, being free from the dualistic world while in the midst of it; fourth is fearlessness arising from the ending of suffering.

Buddha teaches that life is characterized by suffering. Suffering is the real picture of human existence, regardless of whether we like it or not. To live is suffering for us. To be is already suffering. Because we do not participate straightforwardly in what we do, there is human suffering.

We dichotomize all the world holds, but we must be free from dualism while we are right in the middle of it. If we were not in the dualistic world it would not be necessary to be free from it. But we *are* there and we must awaken to what we do and to how the world is misused. We have to awaken thoroughly to what suffering is and from where it comes. To awaken to this we have to practice. Thoroughgoing awakening is to realize the Truth.

Century after century, buddhas and ancestors have done zazen—shikan taza—without reward and have become free from suffering by understanding human beings very deeply and by helping all sentient beings. Even though intellectually we may be skeptical about the idea that "zazen is realization," still we can do it because of the practice of the buddhas and ancestors in the past. This really gives us fearlessness.

Through understanding the structure of human existence philosophically and psychologically, and through directly experiencing human life, we can build up perfection of character. A person's character must be perfectly beautiful, allowing us to be generous, tolerant, compassionate, kind and strong. Perfection of character is something that makes us free from human suffering, even though we are in the midst of it. Our presence is very important for all sentient beings, whoever we are. If our life wobbles and is shaky, it is very difficult to be present from moment to moment. So we must be stable when we are around people. Even if we have been thrown into despair, we should constantly be mindful of the many people who have stood up straight in the midst of their despair and whose examples can give us strength. Their attitude, their way of life, gives fearlessness to others. Our present life is supported by the past and future. Even though we fall into hell in the present life, there are still great possibilities for the future. Even though we may believe that we don't have any future, that idea comes from our limited understanding. If we really don't have any future we cannot exist. That we exist now shows that we already have a future. The possibility of that future gives us fearlessness and enables us to exist from moment to moment. We cry, we struggle, we despair and we have many difficult experiences, but those experiences are good signs that we exist. They inspire us and encourage us to live in peace and harmony. This is why we can practice the giving of Dharma and fearlessness. We have to stand up straight continuously, in whatever realm of existence, suffering, pain we find ourselves, and then, very naturally, we can see something omnipresent.

That omnipresence is not absolute. In Buddhism the absolute is absolute, but, at the same time, absolute is not absolute, because the absolute is something changing constantly, interconnected, dynamically working. Absolute is usually understood as something that exists eternally, without change, but in Buddhism everything is interconnected, changing constantly, and interpenetrating; it exists forever in this way from generation to generation regardless of whether we live or die. When we stand up straight continuously, no matter what circumstances we are in, we can really feel, we can really understand something omnipresent. This is the practice of giving fearlessness.

We must give without expecting a reward. In many aspects of human life, greediness appears. Whatever we do, studying science, philosophy or religion, or even when we are trying to understand human life deeply, greediness comes up. If we see the truth, we want to hold on to it without being interrupted by anything. This is, in a sense, pretty good, because greediness gives us energy and vitality to live, but we have to awaken thoroughly to this situation. If we don't, greediness interrupts and hurts others, because the primary characteristic of greediness is exclusiveness. We want to be a big shot and we kick everyone else out.

With greed comes covetousness. Coveting is very sticky, very deep-rooted. Buddha calls this thirsting desire. That is a very sticky string at the bottom of human life; it is always there. When we covet something we are likely to curry favor. This means to seek favors by fawning or flattering, like expressing your emotions or affections in the manner of a dog wagging its tail. Consciously or unconsciously, if we are covetous, we try to gain favor in this way. That makes our life complicated. For instance, when we try to gain favor by doing gassho, we are always saying something to the gassho: "I like gassho," "I don't like gassho," "I hate gassho." Lots of feelings come up. When you do gassho, just do gassho. Even though we understand the meaning of gassho intellectually, practically our body must be there, and then simultaneously our mind is there too. Our mind must be clear about what it means to do gassho; that is, gassho is just gassho, not a way of currying favor.

Giving is just to give, but just to give does not mean to give blindly. Our mind must be clear; otherwise we cannot give. For example, when we jump into the ocean our body must stand up straight, and simultaneously we must be clear; psychologically, we have to prepare for jumping. We must first understand our feelings, affections, circumstances and people, and then our body can "just jump into." "Just jump into" doesn't mean to jump carelessly, ignoring the function of consciousness. The function of consciousness is very important and is a unique characteristic of human beings. We must concentrate on how to deal with giving, practically, in our daily life. Whatever kind of giving we are dealing with, material, mental, psychological or spiritual, the question is not within the things we are about to give, but within us, who are trying to give something to others. Just actualize giving without currying favor. This is the most important practice for us, just simple practice, day by day.

Even if we become great spiritual leaders, we have to practice nongreed in order to lead people to live a spiritual life. For this we have to convey the right teachings, but when we give the teachings, they must be given without greed, in order to improve the life of all beings. To practice giving without currying favor is just like giving away unnecessary things to somebody you don't know, or offering ungrudgingly to the Buddha tiny flowers blooming in the heart of distant mountains. This is a very simple offering, a very simple way to give. Wherever we may be, or whatever position we have, the practice of giving is very important for us in order to convey, in order to transmit to future generations how sublime, how valuable human life is, how valuable daily living is.

The body-mind you have is a treasure, retribution for the virtuous quality you planted in your former life. You cannot understand this, but it is really true. Our body-mind is very important for us, for others, and for all sentient beings. Without this body-mind how can we practice the Buddha Way, how can we study, how can we live? So it is very important for us, first of all, to keep our body-mind healthy, mentally and physically, for all sentient beings. We should appreciate our body-mind. Appreciation is not something to think about or to believe; it is to do something practical with our body-mind, helping all beings. This appreciation is seeing and handling all sentient beings from a universal perspective. Very naturally we can be grateful for our life, for our presence and for the presence of all sentient beings. That is the practice of giving. Whether the gift is of teaching or of material things, the value worth giving is inherent in each gift. People have their own virtuous quality worthy of receiving something from others, and the teaching itself has its own virtuous quality worth giving away.

There is a story about a famous Zen master in China in the eighth century, Tennō Dōgo. A shopkeeper who sold rice cakes made it a rule to offer the first ten rice cakes to Zen Master Tennō Dōgo every morning. Every day the master ate nine and gave one back to the shopkeeper. The shopkeeper felt funny about this because the ten rice cakes were his gift, his contribution. One day he asked, "Why do you give me back one rice cake?" Tennō Dōgo said, "You brought ten to me, that is why you have the virtuous quality to receive one." The shopkeeper, whose name was Ryūtan Sōshin, was so impressed by this that he became a monk and a disciple of Tennō Dōgo.

If we were not already buddha, we could not bow to the Buddha. When the Buddha receives our bow, we become one with him. At that very moment the practice of bow is actualized. The Buddha does not force the practice of bow upon us, but that which has been offered is brought back to us. That is all, nothing else.

In Buddhism we should think carefully about the law of causation. We cannot be stuck in the law of causation, thinking if we do something good the result will be good, because even though we have good motivations the result is not always good. Sometimes something unknown to us comes in and creates a certain result that we could not foresee. Between the motivation and the result many things change, because everything is impermanent. Everything is ours, but simultaneously, not ours. We cannot hold even to the teachings. Buddha's teaching is ours, it is open to everybody, but if we believe Buddha's teaching is best and hold onto it, Buddha's teaching is not good for us. Buddha's teaching is not something to be monopolized by individuals or forced upon others; it is that which is always given without greed or currying favor. You can give very naturally. There is no reason to interrupt the practice of giving.

Even though we give a wonderful gift, sometimes it is good, but sometimes it is not good, because such a gift might be used for amusement. For instance, sometimes in rich families parents give children lots of money. When that gift is not used for helping others, but only for amusement, sometimes it can cause trouble. That gift is not good for us. It is not important whether the gift is valuable, the important point is whether the merit is actual. If we give something to others, we may be opening their eyes to a chance to live, or they may have a chance to find a job, or a chance to live a more stable life, or a chance to find spiritual security. If we give something it is very important to be aware of whether or not we are actually helping someone.

The practice of zazen is connected with the mainstream of life and death where we have to practice continually without greediness and without currying favor. When we are sitting zazen, there is nothing at all between life and us or death and us. We are always right in the middle of life and death. Whether life and death have value or not, whether things have value or not, is not the point. The point is how we deal with life and death when we are right in the middle of life and death.

The universal path is fair, clean, quiet, serene and, at the same time, dynamic. All sentient beings without exception are already passing along and functioning on the universal path. So all we have to do is leave ourselves to that Way, and then, very naturally, we can settle ourselves in the self. Our existence is very fair, the presence of zazen is fair, there is nothing to say. Even though we don't like it, if we sit like this, whoever we are, very naturally we return to our own spiritual home. Zazen itself is home. When the zazen we do is real, very naturally we attain the Way and we improve, raise, deepen and enrich our lives.

We don't usually handle zazen in this way, however. When we try to mold zazen into our own preconceptions, feelings and understanding, zazen becomes a kind of plastic home and not our real home; it is not real zazen. If we always handle our life and others' lives—flowers, spring, rain and snow—according to our own feelings and emotions, at that time how can we understand the human world, which is perfectly beautiful? Our feelings and our emotions are important for us because we have them, and we have to deal with them day by day. But first of all, we must be fair to ourselves and to our feelings and emotions, and then we can handle each situation as it is. We know we cannot stay at a certain stage called sadness or happiness; we may believe that happiness is something that exists, something we can reach and hold on to permanently, so we say it is real. Of course it is real, but it is also not real, because it's temporary and constantly changing, so we cannot stay with it for long; every day, life is manifested in many situations, therefore we cannot see our life from only one angle such as sadness. For instance, if we attend sesshin immediately we feel uncomfortable and say, "Why is it we have to do such a ridiculous practice with constant pain?" We handle zazen and the sesshin with discomfort and stay with that, and finally the whole world becomes painful and ridiculous. All we have to do is handle zazen as it really is, nothing to complain or comment about. It is really something to support our life, to help and to develop our life. This is the practice of giving.

The body-mind is not something we can think of in terms of our own telescope. Our telescope is just our own limited viewpoint. We have to use a universal telescope, because our body-mind comes from the universe, past, present and future. It's really a treasure for us. We must be fair to the treasure, the body and mind; that is, whatever we think with our body-mind, like hatred or anger, is just our feelings. We complain, we grumble, we always hang on to an image of body and mind, but before we create an image of body and mind, the real body-mind is already there. We should accept it; from beginning to end we should be fair to this body-mind as it is. At that time, treasure becomes giving. Our body-mind gives away something to us to help support our life and the lives of others.

We have to think about ourselves, because we are already beings that exist from moment to moment. When we have to think about ourselves, we must think carefully, not egoistically; we have to think what is most important in life and death. In order to grasp what is most important in life and death we need zazen.

Because Zen always emphasizes "just do it, just be present," sometimes Zen students misunderstand this, thinking it means not having to take care of body and mind. But if we don't take care of our life, our life becomes desolate, because without thinking, we cannot do anything at all. We cannot always do what we consider to be valuable, important things or favorable things; however, if we deal with unfavorable conditions carelessly, we create problems. Many beings exist, favorable and unfavorable. Even though we don't like them, they are really a fair existence completely beyond our speculation about how to handle them. So when we have to think, just think. To think is really to dig out our wisdom. This is great, this is really giving yourself to yourself. It is real wisdom. In the universal perspective, we have to think of ourselves, we have to think of others, and then we can give others treasure.

If we give zazen to zazen, the merit of this zazen permeates and influences all beings visible or invisible. The image of the Buddha carved in wood is not merely a work of a sculptor, nor the fruits of his scriptural technique, but his universal heart, which is inherent in everyone. Sanctity and majesty are manifested in it beyond its being just a kind of work. The same applies to our practice. Gassho and zazen are venerated by all beings in the universe.

If we can practice giving in the true way mentioned above, the merit of giving reaches at once to all beings, and all beings are in a position to receive it. Thus the relationships of practicers and all beings create an endless, agile interconnection and interpenetration. When we do zazen, we have to cast the pebble into the ocean first. The ripples caused by this action are forms, the doing of zazen. "Do zazen" spreads endlessly everywhere just like ripples. From this aspect zazen as the practice of giving is a great universal activity disclosed in personal practice. If we practice like this, people notice very naturally.

There was a young couple staying at the Sonoma zendo who were Canadian citizens and were having passport problems. Though they didn't know what to do about this problem, I clearly noticed that their lives were very stable, going on. It's true, people notice such a practice even though we don't notice it by ourselves. Even though someone says, "I am a Zen master," that isn't the important point. The title of roshi or Zen master is given by all sentient beings, that's enough. A teacher can give us a certificate and a title, but sometimes it doesn't work in our daily life. When all sentient beings give the title, at that time there is a real teacher. The communication of such a person is completely beyond human speculation. When we see a person like that, immediately there is communication on a deep level. That is real communication, human communication, subtle and completely indescribable. That is the practice of giving.

If we go rushing into giving the truth to people blindly, carelessly, we create problems. We should think about when, how and what kind of teaching to give people; with great careful consideration give a phrase or verse of the Truth. We can give a phrase of truth not only through words, but also through body and mind. When we are at home with our parents, and they don't understand what we practice, what we have learned, and we cannot explain what Buddhism is, we can still practice giving, being present there, taking care of our lives day by day. That is also a great verse, a great phrase of the Truth. All we have to do is to plant a good seed, day by day, year after year, even though our parents do not notice at the time.

Zen Master Rinzai was asked by his master Ōbaku why he was planting young pine trees. Rinzai gave two reasons for his action: one was to make the scenery of the temple beautiful, and the other was to benefit future generations. This is an example of planting a wholesome seed for us and for the temple. Intellectually or consciously we can see this. Why do we want to do zazen? We may have a conscious reason why and depend on this reason for doing zazen, and hang on to it, but finally all we have to do is just put it aside and sit without expecting anything; all we have to do is handle zazen as it is, planting good seeds, day by day, year after year.

After planting, then we can see the result. Usually, we pay a lot of attention to the result, stop to grumble about it, and finally, we cannot move an inch at all toward the future. I don't mean we should ignore the result, or ignore what we have done. Of course, we must take responsibility for what we have done, no matter how we feel, but Buddhism doesn't care so much about the result. The result is something we have to carry on our backs, completely beyond criticism. This is very good for us. We can't ignore it, we can't hang on to it, we can't be stuck there; we just carry it on our back and reflect upon it, and then all we have to do is to walk ahead day by day. That is the Buddhist way.

Everything we have is valuable. Teaching coming from our lives is valuable, words of wisdom from our lives are valuable, one word, one phrase is valuable. Even a penny is important for us. I saw a person on the news a while ago who had collected pennies for many, many years. He had several bags of pennies, and with those pennies, he bought a Cadillac. So a penny can be very valuable. Even a blade of grass is important. Without grass the soil cannot exist. Constantly from beginning to end, when we are exactly fair to our life, our life turns into valuables and we feel life is worth living. For instance, if climbing mountains is just a sport or an amusement, it's not really climbing mountains. To climb the mountain must be the practice of giving. This means handling the mountain as it is. At that time, the mountain teaches us something we have never seen or known. The mountain turns into the vastness of existence. Zazen, mountains, everything turns into buddha. Buddha means supporting life, enriching life, deepening life. Teaching the life of the mountain, teaching the life of the trees, the birds, clouds and the whole universe, that is climbing the mountain, that is Buddhist practice. We don't know what makes us climb the mountain; something inspires and encourages us. It is aspiration coming from the depth of our life. Whatever happens, whatever disturbances occur while climbing the mountain, we can overcome them; we just continue to do it. At that time aspiration turns into joy.

There was a prime minister in the Tang dynasty who became sick; the king felt sorry for him and asked a doctor how to cure his sickness. The doctor said that the power of a person's roasted beard would be good for this sickness. So the king shaved his beard, which he considered of great value, roasted it, and gave it to the prime minister, who recovered completely from his sickness. The prime minister really appreciated the king's spirit. It doesn't matter what the king gave, it was his spirit that was important. That attitude, that spirit made him take his beard and roast it and give it to the prime minister. Because the prime minister was very impressed by this act, he vowed to serve the king for his whole life.

The story of King Ashoka, which we can read in Buddhist scriptures, tells about a former life of this king who helped develop Buddhism in India. In King Ashoka's former life he was a child who offered sand to the Buddha. As a child he didn't have any money to give to the Buddha so he took a handful of sand and offered it to him. By the merit of this giving he had a chance to be born in this world again as a human, and he became King Ashoka.

Zen Master Ōbaku bowed to the Buddha without expecting a reward from Buddha, Dharma, Sangha. He just bowed. That is planting a wholesome seed constantly, day by day, for us, for all sentient beings, for generation after generation. This means we should do our best to do something with the capability that we have now. That is, with our best, we share our life with people. Ōbaku really shared his life with all sentient beings by just bowing. That's why Ōbaku's practice of just bowing has been handed down from generation to generation, up to now.

There is a great reality that causes the gift of material things to stabilize people's minds. After the Second World War in Japan we didn't have enough food and clothes. The United States helped in many ways, but still there was a lack of food, housing and clothing. When I returned home from the air force, I built a small hut and started working in a company. I was very hungry every day. I understood what a hungry ghost was from experience. One day some strangers gave us some food. It was not much, just a little bit. Even though it was very difficult to share that amount of food with everyone in our family, we were still very happy. It's really true. That gift of material things caused my family members' minds and lives to stabilize spiritually. It is not a matter of discussing the quantity of the gift; the important thing was that there was really spirit in the giving. All my family felt stable even though we didn't have enough food. We appreciated that small gift. It was really proof of the greatness of giving.

Making something in the kitchen, sewing,, working in a company, whatever we do is really the practice of giving. Dōgen Zenji's understanding of giving is very deep and profound, completely different from our understanding. If we say *giving* we immediately think of giving away our time or material things and then we say that we practice giving. It is giving, but it's just the surface. All beings that exist in this world manifest themselves as the practice of giving just by being whoever they are. That is a very deep understanding of the practice of giving. Real zazen is exactly zazen as it is. Birds flying in the sky, flowers blooming when spring comes, everything exists as it is with no contamination. However, when we think about flowers in the spring, immediately we speculate about them. They are late or early, spring is too cold or too short. This is just human speculation. Even though it may make us happy, it is not fair to all sentient beings. So, whatever we do, we have to be fair. If we use zazen as a means to attain enlightenment, at that time we can't be fair in our dealings with Zen Buddhism, because we are already handling zazen as something other than zazen. We are already seeing zazen in terms of our preconception, our understanding, our view, our telescope. At that time, how can zazen manifest itself? All we have to do is let the life force of zazen bloom when the time for zazen comes. That is fair to zazen and to us too.

When we do zazen we have to completely give away our body-mind to zazen. This doesn't mean to destroy our body-mind or to be confused about it. With our best effort we have to deal with how to give away our body and mind. If the practice of giving penetrates our life, we can understand this. We cannot curry favor from zazen; when we deal with zazen we must be completely fair. At that time we accept our body and mind and can give them to zazen.

Our present life comes from the practice of giving, the act of giving, what we have done so far, day by day. When we do gassho, when we bow, this is nothing but the act of giving. Get up, go to work, go to school, this is a very simple practice of giving for us. Because we took care of our life in that way in the past, our present life right now, right here, is great.

When you give something, there is no need to discuss the thing you are about to give; you are not doing it to curry favor. The important thing is your psychological and spiritual attitude, how you give it. Wherever you may go, whatever you do, you can practice giving. You can make an effort to give and can also be mindful of every opportunity to give, day by day.

Of course, we should also practice giving to ourselves. To give to ourselves means to think of ourselves. To think of ourselves is not bad. Most people believe that thinking of ourselves is very egoistic. Of course, there is always a certain egoistic sense there, but it doesn't mean we should ignore thinking of ourselves. We have to think carefully of ourselves in order to be aware of what wisdom we have. To think of ourselves in this way is not to create an egoistic sense, or our own individual life. It includes all sentient beings for generations. That is really a great practice of giving for us. If we practice like this, very naturally people around us learn who we are.

We must use ourselves, our bodies, our words, our minds, carefully; that is also a part of giving. Through this practice people allow us to understand what we do. When we were teenagers with rebellious feelings toward our parents and we said, "Good morning," that "Good morning" was completely different from the "Good morning" we say now. Very different. The words are the same, but how we use them is different. We have to use this good morning without currying favor. This is a great practice of giving. Then our parents gradually begin to understand us. We have to be present, to just say good morning when it is time to say good morning, taking care of our parents with compassion and with patience. Very naturally, people will understand us. This is a great practice of giving to people around us.

This practice, actualized from moment to moment, is temporarily called buddha, but that buddha is not an idea. Our life is really alive when it leaves no trace of an idea of buddha. This practice is not something we have to observe, obey or try to keep, because it's always there. For instance, if we climb a mountain, we cannot constantly obey, or maintain, or try to keep the discipline of a mountaineer. It's not necessary to maintain an idea called mountaineer. The mountain is there already, we cannot ignore it; that's really why we climb the mountain. The same applies to Buddhist practice. It is not something we try to obey, it's not a discipline. It's already there. Just actualize it.

The purpose of human life is not a matter of discussion. Whatever we say, it doesn't hit the mark. First we must be alive. All we have to do is just live day by day. How we live is the important thing. Practice is nothing but giving, day by day. At that time that practice of giving really penetrates and extends to the past, to the future. The purpose of human life is just to plant good seeds day by day. That's enough. If we do this, we create human culture; we can leave a wonderful culture, not only for us and for the people around us but for people from generation to generation. Simultaneously we can transmit Buddha's teaching to future generations. We should rejoice, we should be happy, we should accept ourselves and our zazen with joy. We are really bodhisattvas.

We know pretty well that the mind of all sentient beings is very stubborn and difficult to change. We know, as a member of human society, how egoistic and stubborn we and the people around us are. Even though we practice zazen for many years, still, the harder we practice the more we realize how stubborn we are. To change the stubbornness of all sentient beings is great practice for us. The mind is really difficult to change, but you should keep on trying to change the minds of all sentient beings. It is not necessary to try to change human society quickly by having strikes, carrying placards, fighting with each other, or participating in radical activities. We cannot change things quickly, so how do we change the minds of all sentient beings? It must begin with giving, just being there and greeting each other with compassion. It's pretty hard for us because we can't see how much we change people's minds. It's a very quiet practice; we must be stable, first. There is no way to change people's minds except to practice like this. You have to act in the enormous scope of Buddha's world. When you say good morning, just say good morning without being swayed by feelings and emotions, such as hatred or malice. If we just plant good seeds for ourselves, simultaneously we can plant good seeds for others.

When we give something to others we say our mind is big mind or universal mind. But what is big mind? There is no particular form called big mind. Big mind is nothing but just to give something, such as good morning, to others. That's all we have to do. When that one thing is alive for us and for others, helping us and others, at that time, we temporarily call this big mind. However, in the next moment, maybe big mind is gone and small mind appears. We say, "Oh, I should say good morning with a little bit of a smile because my mother seems to be angry." At that time small mind is present. Temporarily, we say "big mind," "big self," or "small self," but they are provisional beings, appearing and disappearing. They are just flashing lights, nothing but visitors to us. We cannot keep visitors for long, nor can visitors stay with us for long. Even though we say, "Would you please stay a little longer?" sometimes they have to leave. This is big mind, small mind, delusion, enlightenment. They are just visitors, coming and going, but because we have to know how to take care of them, these visitors are very important for us. We have to take care of ourselves and visitors as best we can. As soon as possible, we have to do something, we have to be hospitable to them.

Let's look at our zazen for a moment. Many visitors visit us, and so we become completely confused. We are sitting, not doing anything, and many visitors come and say many things. How should we treat these visitors? In zazen we should take care of them as simply as we can. "Hello, good morning. I am busy now, I don't have time." That's enough. However, if we seem to have lots of spare time, then the visitors want to stay and talk. At that time zazen is no longer a full-time job, it's really a part-time job. With a part-time job we have lots of spare time and can do many things. But it's not zazen. When we sit in zazen without creating spare time, we are really alive. There is no space for visitors. Big enlightenment or small enlightenment are nothing but visitors, flashing lights. Just see it. It's a good signal for us. Should we go now, or should we stay for a while, should we go straight or should we turn?

If we practice giving through using the words "good morning" with our whole body-mind, this giving really transforms the mind. Mind means we completely penetrate one dharma, we are proficient in it, we complete it with wholeheartedness. It doesn't mean empathy, because with empathy there is still some gap between us and "good morning." However, penetrating one dharma means that there is no space between us and "good morning." That "good morning" really pierces people's hearts, even though they don't understand. They don't realize it at the time, but eventually they will understand. It communicates beyond words. Already the vastness of existence is alive between us and others. Here, very naturally, we can feel human warmth. This is the great Buddhist practice of planting good seeds day by day.

The practice of giving is not to exploit something or someone for a certain purpose. We not just material beings; we are human beings who have consciousness or mind. So, from this standpoint, we have to help each other with our mind, with our body and with our words. In other words, we need human warmth, which simultaneously means Buddha's warmth, not egoistic or individual warmth. Buddha's warmth is huge. At that time we can really communicate. We can help somebody and simultaneously somebody can help us. We may complain, saying, "How can I find such a way? Wherever I may go I cannot find anybody who practices in that way, so how can I live in that way?" It doesn't matter. All we have to do is be a bodhisattva and try to live in that way. That is our vow. We should take our vow in that way. If we do this, we can light candles one by one. It's not necessary to imagine a huge, beautiful, ideal image of human life, where all sentient beings live in peace and harmony. Of course it is important, and Buddha constantly mentions that we should move toward that ideal. But actually, we should do small things, just small things in order to move toward a life of peace and harmony. This is really the practice of giving. It is a simple practice. Buddhism is not asking us to do something big, to be a big shot. If we can be big shots that's fine, but everybody cannot be one. We should know ourselves, who we are, and then if we want to be big shots in the future, fine. However, right now, let's do small things as we move toward the idea of being a big shot. That is Buddha's teaching. Buddha's teaching is always patting our heads and saying, "Fine. Your idea is beautiful. Why don't you have some more big ideas; but take it easy. Do something small." When you say good morning, just say good morning. At that time, we can understand the meaning of helping all sentient beings, and of changing human society. We can really understand what we have to do.

Kind Speech

The second of the four methods of guidance is kind speech. Kind speech is not merely to speak with an ingratiating voice, like a cat purring. If we speak of something with an ingratiating voice, very naturally, consciously or unconsciously, we are trying to get a favor by fawning or flattering. This is not kind speech. Kind speech is not the usual sense of kindness. It can appear in various ways, but whatever kindness appears in our speech, we should remember that it must constantly be based on compassion or deep love. Under all circumstances that compassion is always giving somebody support or help or a chance to grow.

Compassion is a little difficult to understand. Kindness is part of compassion, friendliness is also part of compassion, but as a whole, compassion is rooted more deeply in the human mind. Everyone has this compassion. Buddhism always focuses on the ultimate nature of existence, which is manifested as compassion.

The ultimate nature of existence is open to all sentient beings, whoever or whatever they are; without this we cannot exist. Whatever happens, all is going on in this vast expanse of the ultimate nature of existence. If you cast a pebble into the quiet ocean, the ripples extend in all directions and finally melt into the ocean. This is really human life. So from this vantage point, whatever kind of ripples you can see—suffering, up and down waves—whatever kinds of things come up, remember they are happening in the vastness of the ocean, and sooner or later they melt back into the immense ocean. This is characteristic of the ultimate nature of existence, in which all sentient beings are present from moment to moment.

The original, ultimate nature of existence functions just like a filter; we don't know what it is, but it is sort of like our lungs. Our blood comes into our heart and is pumped to our lungs, so our lungs are sort of a filter to clean the blood and send the pure, oxygenated blood to our body, to make our whole body and mind work well. When a person goes through the filter of the ultimate nature of existence and then comes out, he or she is of course the same person, but a little bit different—sort of a transparent person—what we call an enlightened being or buddha. Then this transparent person is exactly like a mirror, reflecting and accepting all beings in equality—trees, birds, tulips, spring, winter, all of life. For instance, this person sees a dog and simultaneously the person and the dog go through the filter and then come out, and then the dog and the person are the same—transparent. Then, the dog is not a dog, the dog is buddha, or an enlightened being, bodhisattva. That is why when this person hears the precept, "Do not kill," he does not moralize, thinking "Don't do it;" he cannot do it, because he and the dog go through the filter and come up, and are the same thing. What it is? A person? A dog? Some particular soul? No, they are buddha, universal life. Just universal life comes up. This universal life is exactly our life and the dog's life, so it's really the same, simultaneously. We cannot hurt the dog even though we may not know about the precept "Do not kill." We cannot do it. So the person goes through the filter and comes out and this person is not the same. Still this person must be alive as a human being, that is, this enlightened being must, at the same time, be in the human world. Everything is always simultaneously going in circles like this.

It is characteristic of human beings to have a mind seeking for the truth. Whether we know it or don't know it, it doesn't matter. We have this mind already. It goes through the filter: that is practice; it goes through the filter and then comes out: that is enlightenment. This enlightened person cannot stay in enlightenment and comes back to the form of the human being again; that is called nirvāna. So arousing mind, practice, enlightenment and nirvana are going on like this constantly, just like the circulation of our blood. This is our practice.

If we do zazen, simultaneously we become a filter. A filter is exactly zazen. When we do zazen with our body and mind, immediately we go through and come out and are an enlightened person. So all we have to do is just sit down. There is nothing to trick us. All we have to do is just be a filter.

If you become a priest, you must be a filter. You must function as a filter, not only in zazen, but in everyday life. That's pretty hard for priests because everyday life appears in many ways, its patterns never stay the same. That is why enlightened beings practice continuously, forever.

Sometimes we get tired of practicing, because we always have in mind to practice for a certain length of time, maybe seven days or a year. We focus on our practice for seven days, wanting to attain enlightenment. That is fine, if we can do it, but it is very hard, because our effort is just focusing for seven days. After seven days, then what? But if we focus on countless lives in an immensely long span of time, all we have to do is focus on right now, right here, without looking around. This is to practice in the eternal world. At that time we become calm step by step, just like a turtle, step by step.

This turtle must pass through the filter and come out again, and then come back to daily life. This is very good for us, but usually we don't do it. Instead of passing through the filter, we use a sort of prismatic device, analyzing and synthesizing how many colors there are in it. Consciously, we don't want to pass through this filter; we really want to pass through the prism. It's much more fun to see the wonderful, different colors—philosophy, psychology, suffering—it's wonderful! And then we just go on and never come back, because it's a lot of fun just going on, constantly keeping away from human life. This is modern civilization.

Sometimes we miss what we're aiming at and fail to pass through the prism. Consciously we want to go toward the prism, but nature is also constantly going on, so very naturally we pass through the filter and come up—pop! At that time loneliness, despair and depression come up, but it's not real loneliness or emptiness. This is what we have to know; we have to awaken to this filter. This filter is really a fantastic device for us. We can accept our life not only in a passive way, we also have to send our life to the universe in a positive way. This is why we are living. For this we have to go through the filter.

If you are not a priest it is more difficult to constantly be a filter, so instead you are likely to be a filter some of the time. You come to sesshin and become a filter; then as you leave, you say, "Oh, it's ridiculous, I can't do this in everyday life." So you forget and just go to work every day. That's okay, but if you become a priest you have to function constantly as a filter, and help other people function as a filter. You cannot have any particular pattern such as being stuck in a concept of "I am stupid" or "I am not stupid"; you cannot be like this; just be a filter, constantly. That's very hard. But there is no excuse. Priests are completely committed to functioning as a filter. This is the best way to help human beings; this is compassion. You can see the enormous scope of life, open to all sentient beings. We are not in a portion of the whole world, we are completely the world ourselves. At this very moment kind speech comes out. This whole body and mind are nothing but the whole world, because we have gone through this filter and become transparent. There is no partition, no border between trees and us or birds and us. This is called, temporarily, an enlightened person. Usually we like this state of becoming transparent, but this is not a final goal. We have to come back to the form of a human being.

In Gotō Egen, a Zen scripture, a story is told of an Indian saint who went to visit the famous Zen teacher in China, Zen Master Gyōzan. One morning Zen Master Gyōzan was standing on the porch in front of his temple, when the saint came down from the sky. Gyōzan said,

"Who are you?" The saint said, "I am a saint from India." Gyōzan said, "When did you leave?" The saint said, "I left this morning." Gyōzan said, "You are so late arriving! What did you do on the way?" Although the saint left India in the morning and arrived in China almost immediately the same morning, Gyōzan still asked what he did on the way that made him arrive so late. The saint said "Oh, I played a little bit." If, while going to a certain destination, you see something you are interested in and poke your head into it, forgetting to go towards your destination, that is playing with something on the way. That is why Zen Master Gyōzan finally said, "That's wonderful, but being a saint is not my business, so I leave that to you; but give Buddhism back to me."

Usually if we come through the filter we act like this saint, because there are lots of fantastic spiritual things to play with. You can talk with dead people, you can fly in the air, but it's not Buddhism. Buddhism just comes back to the form of a human being. This is very important. Returning to the form of a human being is compassion coming from a deep level.

In the Lotus Sūtra, Buddha gives advice to the bodhisattvas who are about to go out to teach, telling them that they have to sit on the seat of emptiness. This is to go through the filter. If we give Buddha's teaching with our body, with our words, however we teach the teachings it cannot be as a usual person. We must be something else; we must pass through the filter. Then we understand people who are interested in the teachings and those who are not. We accept all sentient beings as exactly one, regardless of whether we like them or dislike them. At that time compassion is always functioning under all circumstances.

My teacher, Yokoi Roshi, always looked down on me, whatever I did, but now I really appreciate his attitude toward me, because his use of rough language and his belittling whatever I did were based on compassion. Sometimes rough language is a great help, but don't use rough language recklessly, be careful. Don't imitate others. Rinzai teachers scream and shout, using the stick very hard, but don't imitate them. Imitation is a weakness of human beings. We always try to depend on somebody who is famous by imitating them. At that time, we completely lose our own subjectivity. Whatever happens, you shouldn't lose your own subjectivity. You must be alive.

Don't misunderstand kind speech, thinking it is working just for this moment. If somebody gives us kind, friendly, sympathetic words in order to help us, sometimes it doesn't work, because we are not ready to accept them. Even though we are not ready to accept kind speech at that moment, in the long run it is working. This is kind speech. For this we need compassion. If we use rough language and scold somebody, it is necessary that it be based on very deep compassion. If we forget, rough language really becomes rough language, hurting people. Be very cautious to reflect on whether we deserve to do so or not.

If you give quality to greetings and have compassion for all sentient beings as the basis of your life, good morning is a great opportunity to communicate, to give, to share kind speech with somebody. Usually we criticize someone we do not approve of it, but it is not the Buddha's way. Instead of criticizing, why don't we help them to improve, to grow. This is most important. Even though the world is not peaceful right now, day by day we can live in a peaceful way. If we practice in this way, that is great, because we are walking on the path of Buddha. It doesn't matter whether we reach the goal or not. Day by day, all we have to do is move toward it; this is our practice.

If we get angry, very naturally there is a feeling of vilification. So the important point is, if we see people who don't have virtuous qualities, instead of criticizing them, we should suffer finding a way to help them, in order to improve, grow, deepen and enrich all of our lives. Even if we don't see any progress after practicing kind speech with people who are not good, we are really helping them. Sometimes through a third person we may hear that someone has spoken kindly of us. At that time we are really touched. We are really moved by it and will never forget it. That's why, wherever we may go, we shouldn't speak ill of others. If we see somebody who is not good, even though he is not in front of us, we should see the good aspects of his life, and speak about it to others. This really helps. If such kind speech reaches the person indirectly from a third person, he is really touched by it. This is Buddha's practice.

Beneficial Action

The third of the methods of guidance, beneficial action, means to help others. There are two kinds of beneficial action: one is giving and the other is kind or loving speech. Without beneficial action, giving does not work. For instance to think of ourselves is to practice giving to ourselves, but it must be based on beneficial action. Sometimes, when we think of ourself, it is not in a beneficial way. We sometimes become nervous and confused. But even though it is difficult, we can't ignore thinking of ourself. Wherever we may go, whatever we do, we have to think of how to use ourself best, how to behave, how to take care of gassho and zazen, how to walk. We have to think about this but to do so too much is not beneficial. When thinking of ourself confuses us, it is not the real practice of giving. The practice of giving must be backed by beneficial action, which means to help others. We think of ourself in order to help others. Remember this point.

The practice of giving is exactly the same as loving speech. Loving speech is really to give something with your whole body and mind, and if you give something in that way, your whole body and mind really practice loving speech. People can understand and can listen to this sound of your speech. That is why beneficial action is based on two practices, giving and loving speech.

Beneficial action in Buddhism is to give thought constantly to how we can cause everybody, all sentient beings, including inanimate beings, to awaken to themselves, and beneficial action is to lead them to the Buddha Way—a peaceful, harmonious life—day by day. The Way means the practice we do with all sentient beings, not practice just for ourselves. The Way is the universal path. We have to actually pass along this universal path practically, day by day. This means to live our daily life with all sentient beings in peace and harmony. This is our hope, the target we have to aim at, whatever circumstances we are in.

When we see the human world today, it scares us. We feel fear just walking on the street. But even under such circumstances, there is no reason to stop living in peace and harmony. Under just such circumstances we have to live in peace, because there is still a chance to create our own beautiful world and to teach people too. We should not forget to give thought constantly, day by day, to how we can live in peace and harmony with all sentient beings. We have to do this. This is really beneficial. To awaken to oneself means to do something not only with one's head, but also with one's body, mind and words. In many ways we should do this. This is called beneficial action, helping others.

Beneficial action is to benefit all sentient beings skillfully, not only human beings but also inanimate beings. When we educate and help human beings, we cannot judge them quickly according to our understanding; we cannot educate people quickly. It is very difficult. So we must practice patience, generosity, compassion and kindness, thinking of others for the long-range and short-range course of their lives. Sometimes we can give words and suggestions, sometimes we cannot—we can just be present with them. Sometimes just doing something together is really important. These are ways of using skillful means to benefit all sentient beings, but this is very difficult for us to do, because skillful means do not come from a technique, but from the measure of our practice.

Buddha-dharma is the unity of Buddha and all sentient beings. This is the real portrait of our life. Thinking of ourself from our own viewpoint is not the real portrait of our existence. We have to see the total portrait of our life—the unity of Buddha and us. At that time majesty or dignity or imperturbability, whatever we call it, is coming from each pore. We don't know what it is, but immediately we can feel this. Majesty is a person's aliveness coming from the totality of a person's character and personality. No matter how long we study or how much we know, no matter how much information we can give to people from all the old Buddhist terms we have piled up like business cards in our drawer, this does not express the majesty of Buddha-dharma. Buddhist practice, human life is not like this.

Everybody has compassion. We are compassionate because we are alive. The reality of our existence is supported by many beings: air, rain, clouds, winter, spring. Winter and spring do not discriminate. They don't care where we come from or how much we complain about them; they have great compassion. Everybody, more or less, is protected by compassion, but we don't realize this. However, there are different degrees of protection by compassion. For instance, if we were members of a street gang, our situation would be different from those who are practicing here. If we practice here, we have more of a chance to be protected by compassion, because people around us help our life. We may think we grow by ourselves, and of course we should make effort, but this effort is just a speck of dust. By listening to Buddha's teaching we are protected by compassion even though we don't understand. All we have to do is just listen and sit down here and maybe we will understand in the future. This compassion extends into the future. If we were a member of a street gang, there would be less compassion there, because the people around us would not be interested in helping others so much. Still, compassion is open to everybody. We should realize this, awakening to this compassion. If we awaken to this compassion, we really appreciate others and can give something to others too. We can really help others: This is actual practice. The skillful means to educate, to lead people to a peaceful life, to nirvāna, come from the majesty of Buddha-dharma. It is not a technique.

There are two examples of beneficial action that come from old Chinese stories. As Ching-k'ang was walking in the street he saw a fisherman carrying a basket with a tortoise in it. He knew the tortoise would be sold in the fish market for food, and feeling very sorry for it, he bought it from the fisherman and let it go into the ocean. As the tortoise was going back into the ocean, it turned its head to the left three times and looked at Ching-k'ang; then the tortoise disappeared. Many years later, Ching-k'ang became the mayor of the small town where he had freed the tortoise. Traditionally in China and Japan, the mayor has his own seal carved in wood or stone. In those days, it was the custom to make the seal with gold and have the design of a tortoise head on the top of the seal. So Ching-k'ang asked a goldsmith to make the seal for him with the tortoise on the top. The seal was made with the tortoise head straight as usual, but when it was finished, the tortoise head was turned to the left. The goldsmith did not understand why the tortoise's head was turned to the left when he had made it straight; however he straightened it once more. Again it turned to the left. Three times he made a new seal; three times the tortoise's head turned to the left. Finally, the goldsmith told the mayor, "I did this design very carefully, but always the tortoise turns its head to the left. I don't know why. It's very strange." The major knew, however, that the tortoise he had freed many years ago had now appeared on the top of his seal. It is just a story, but there is truth in it because all sentient beings are connected with each other.

In another story, Yang-pao is said to have helped a sparrow that had been injured by a bird of prey. To express its gratitude, the sparrow later presented him with four silver rings. The sparrow and the tortoise appreciated the beneficial action of the people who helped them, because they did something without expecting any reward. They just did it. We can really communicate even with a tortoise and a bird, but if we expect something as a reward, it's very difficult to communicate with anyone or anything, no matter who or what it is.

Usually in our daily life, we want to benefit ourselves first, and then if we have spare time, we will help others. This is very common. But Buddha's way is completely the opposite. We practice together to benefit ourselves and others. In the monastery we eat pickles without making noise. According to common sense, it is ridiculous to eat pickles like this, or to use our metal spoon in a china bowl quietly. If our spoon touches the bottom of the bowl, very naturally it makes noise. So according to common sense this is ridiculous advice. The important point is to pay more careful attention to the china bowl and the metal spoon, giving to them with beneficial action. This really helps us and others simultaneously. Very naturally, however many people live and practice here, all can practice one thing. If we don't pay attention to the spoon, using it carelessly, very naturally this is messy practice and it interrupts others' lives. This is why practicing together is very important for us. If we eat a pickle, help the pickle first. If we use chopsticks, help the chopsticks first. This is our practice.

There was a lord in ancient China who was compassionate and helped others. On one occasion this lord stopped right in the middle of taking his bath, combed his hair, put on his clothes and helped visitors, three times. And then, while having dinner, this same lord left his dinner table three times to help people who had come to see him. This is a good example of the compassionate mind constantly helping all sentient beings.

Wherever we may be, whatever race we are, it doesn't matter. Whether in our own country or another country, whether the customs are Chinese, Japanese or American, it doesn't matter. If you are a human being, beneficial action is very natural, universal. This is what we can practice. This is most important. We can benefit a friendly person, but we usually cannot benefit a person we hate. My friend Yokoi Roshi always gave compassion to everybody. Every time he said goodbye to a person whom he did not like, he sent him off with gassho. He went to the railroad station and as the train was leaving, he did gassho. That gassho was an expression of his compassion. Even though he did not say anything, I was very impressed.

Once I was invited to a Catholic church to talk about Zen in their class on world religions. I talked about taking care of toilet paper, and they liked my talk because they had never heard of such a thing before. When I asked them how they used toilet paper they replied that they did not pay attention to how they used it. They pulled it off the roll and used just a small part of it and then threw it away. The next time you go to a public toilet, pay attention to the basket where paper towels have been thrown away. Almost always just a corner of the paper has been used and then it has been thrown away. This is not beneficial action. We cannot practice giving and we cannot practice loving speech to the paper with this kind of action. We should pay attention to how we use it, although I do not mean we must pay meticulous attention to it. If we are very busy, of course we should use the paper as quickly as possible; but still, there is a chance to pay attention to the existence of the paper. This is a wonderful communication.

When I was at the temple, my life was changing every day, because I had never experienced living in that way. There were just two people in the old, funny temple in the countryside of Japan: my old teacher and myself, a young monk. He taught me many things. One day I cut flowers and put them in a vase as an offering to Buddha. My teacher came to see the flowers and asked me why I had cut a particular flower. I hadn't given it any thought, so I said there was no reason, I just wanted to offer new flowers to Buddha. He pointed out a very young bud and said that if I cut a flower with a bud that was too young, that bud would have no chance to bloom. He suggested I leave it for a while until it grew more and then when I cut it, the bud would have a chance to bloom in the vase. This is an example of beneficial action. It is very important for us. When we cut flowers recklessly, carelessly, we are not paying attention to them. To pay attention is practicing giving and loving speech to that flower. This is beneficial to the flowers and simultaneously it is beneficial to us.

My teacher also taught me how to clean Japanese *tatami* with a special broom. Every day I used the broom to clean the room, but I used it without thinking, paying no attention to how I cleaned. My teacher taught me to pay attention to the tatami, cleaning with the direction of the grooves between the straw rows rather than against them, in order to get all the dust out. After that I practiced giving to the tatami and to the broom; I could express loving speech to them, and at the same time this action was beneficial to me also.

I was also taught to clean the temple grounds outside with bamboo brooms we made ourselves. At first when I cleaned the grounds the traces of the broom strokes went zigzag, this way and that way. My teacher taught me to pay attention to the broom's trace marks in order to understand how I had used the broom, and to clean in such a way that left the traces completely straight. Then the grounds looked very nice. It is not a matter of whether we have left beautiful traces or not. The important point is to pay attention to the broom, to the loving speech given by the broom. We should pay attention to the broom, the soil and the temple yard. The temple yard is not just for you, for me or for the teachers; it is for all sentient beings. Practicing giving and loving speech is beneficial to the yard, to the broom and to us.

When you clean your room, pay attention to the corners and under the table. There is lots of space that is easy to clean, but under the table or desk it is more difficult and sometimes we avoid what is difficult to reach or to see. But cleaning with attention to the whole room is an important practice for us. It is to practice giving and loving speech to the corners, to the room and to ourselves. It is beneficial for us. Then we can communicate with all sentient beings.

Identity Action

Identity action, the fourth method of guidance, means to practice something with complete, full devotion. This is a very important practice for us. Without this, we cannot master anything that we do, we cannot exist in this world. Identity action means there is no difference between the object of our devotion and us—we are completely one. If we want to become one with a baby, we have to jump into the baby's world; but it doesn't mean to lose sight of ourself. Mother is mother, but still there is total communication between mother and baby. In front of a baby, people make funny faces in order to please the baby, even though the baby doesn't understand. They completely become one with the baby but they don't lose sight of themselves. This is not so easy actually. It is a very difficult practice for us in everyday life. That is why we create problems in human society. The bodhisattvas practice again and again in order to master this point until it penetrates their skin, muscle and bone. It is very hard. Even though we understand Buddhism intellectually through scriptures, still it is difficult. We can explain it in words, but to actually practice it is very difficult.

Pai Lo-tien, a famous Chinese poet, asked a Zen master, "What is Buddha's teaching?" The Zen master said, "Buddha's teaching is to do something good, not to do something wrong." So Pai Lo-tien said, "That is pretty easy; even a three-year-old boy knows that." Then the Zen master said, "Even though a three-year-old boy knows this, an eighty-year-old man doesn't do it."

Buddha was born in this world as a human being, putting himself in the position of a human being to save, to teach all sentient beings, becoming one with the people and guiding them to a peaceful life. Since we have been born as human beings, the same applies to us. We are born in this world in the form of human beings—for what? In order to enjoy ourselves, to make lots of money and become rich, or to become a politician or a famous person? No, I don't think so. The main purpose of being born in this world is to live with people, because we cannot exist alone. However, we cannot just be present with people; we have to live with people in peace, in harmony, day by day. This is not a matter of discussion. We have to live in this way every day under all circumstances. For forty-five years, Shākyamuni Buddha taught in this way. This is why there is this most important practice called identity action. Buddha is a good example of why we have to practice like this.

"Action," in this case, means behavior that is characterized by courtesy and sharpness, that keeps people naturally in awe and that has a sort of majesty or dignity coming from the bottom of human life or existence. We don't know exactly where it comes from, but we notice when people exhibit it and we have complete respect for them. Action has a very broad meaning. It includes not only human action and attitudes, but also all circumstances, circumstances' actions, and attitudes' actions.

If we want to make a poem about a pine tree or about nature, we have to move, we have to act, we have to do something first, and become one with nature. If we come into nature, nature comes into us. However, if we don't act first, nature is nature and is far from us. If we want to know something about nature, we have to be in identity with nature first and then nature is in identity with us, teaching us something about nature.

The relationship of self and others is a big relationship. Relationship with people and with nature goes on and on, continuously, limitlessly. This relationship between nature and me involves not only the "I" we can see, but the huge "I" that is extending into the present, the past and the future, to heaven and hell, in all directions. So the relationship between nature and us is not only between nature and us, but is an endless relationship, constant and dynamic.

If we say the ocean consists of water, we are seeing the dualistic world. But water is the aliveness of being, constantly supporting the ocean without creating a gap between the ocean and water. Intellectually we know there are two beings, but the two beings are not always two. Within their activities the two completely become one, just like a spinning top. A top is decorated with stripes of separate colors, and when the top is spun into action, all the colors become one. They are not actually mixed up, because each color is still separate, but when the top is spinning, all the colors become one. The colors become blurred. Each color doesn't have its own egoistic sense; each extends into all the other colors.

When doing gassho, if gassho is seen from gassho, we do not appear. We are hidden in the gassho. If we become one with gassho, we simply cannot perceive who is doing gassho, but it doesn't mean we are excluded. We are there. If gassho is seen by us, we appear on the surface. Gassho does not appear; it is hidden in us. Nevertheless, we cannot say gassho is excluded. Gassho never excludes gassho itself. It is there. At that time, it is called gassho. This is identity action.

Wise leaders never hate people; they respect people. This is why people follow them. We have to be tolerant and make space where people can come to us. If we reject them, then there is no space for others to come in. Americans are not just Americans, Americans are the nation itself. We cannot say we are Americans without the existence of the nation. So Americans and the nation are exactly one, just like water and the ocean. If we say American, the nation is completely hidden behind the American, but it doesn't mean the American excludes the nation. The nation is there. If we say nation, at that time American is hidden behind nation, but it is not excluded; it is already there. Nation is not a material thing, it is not an imagined thing, it is not a concept; the nation is people, people are nations. This is also identity action. The leader is exactly the same as the people, a human being. He or she has to see all people in equality, but it doesn't mean there is no difference. The leader is the leader and the people are the people. The teacher is the teacher and the student is the student. We have to see equality, but not in the realm of equality; we have to see equality in the realm of differentiation. Differentiation must be formed not in differentiation, but in equality. Then, differentiation and equality are working in identity action.

Identity action does not function in a small area called ego, but in the vastness of existence. When we clean a room, we just clean the room. The room is not something different from us. We are the room, the room is us. Then we and the room communicate with each other in the rhythm of identity action. We have to take the best care of the room we can, because the room is not a material being apart from us. The room is a great being called Buddha-dharma. Buddha-dharma means the unity of buddha and us, buddha and the room. It is nothing but a great being, just a great being completely beyond our speculation. Cleaning the room is not something someone makes us do. This action comes up from us, from the unity of buddha and us and the room. To take the best care of the room means whether it is dirty or clean, take the best care of the room. If we take care of the room like this, the room can live a long time; if we don't, the room does not live long. This is very important for us to understand. If we clean recklessly, not paying attention to the room, its life will be cut short. But the room is a great being deserving to live the life that has been allotted to the room itself. So we should take the best care of the room that we can. It is not necessary to make its life long, but just to take care of it, because it already has its own life. Taking the best care of the life of each being and circumstance, we can practice giving, and then we can practice loving speech with our mind, words and body. This is beneficial action. In all these practices there is always identity action.

We are more or less ignorant and crazy, but it doesn't matter. We are already ignorant, so we must be right in the middle of ignorance and make the best of ignorance. That is all we have to do. But usually we add something extra to ignorance; we hate it and our life goes away from us. How can we be free from ignorance? How can we take care of ignorance? If we take care of our life according to our emotions, saying, "I hate my life," it is pretty easy for us to make our life short. My teacher always said his health was not strong. He said maybe he would die at sixty. He said he was weak, but he took the best care of his body and he lived to be eighty-six. The same applies to your room. If you rent your room from others you may think because you don't own it you don't have to take care of it. This is not the Buddhist way. Whether your room is rented or not, it doesn't matter. The room is a great being, our clothes are great beings, our boots and shoes are great beings, completely beyond our speculation. Day by day, we have to practice identity action, giving and loving speech, and then there is beneficial action.

If we see life as an object separate from us, it is easy for us to create fear and anxiety and confusion. When we see our life we feel many things. This is called experience. Of course it is okay, but it is not the total picture of the way to live. We must put it aside and be one with our life, that is all we have to do. This is most important. When we dance, we cannot look at the dance, at the stage, as something separate from us. We must be right in the middle of dancing. At that time we are one with the dance and are realizing the significance of the dance. Later, when we reflect on the significance of dance, we are separate from it, but our understanding is the result of dynamic identity action.

We are human beings, so we are always thinking in terms of others and us, a leader and the people, zazen and us, Buddha and ordinary beings. Even though we know Buddha's teaching pretty well, ignorance comes up very quickly in our daily life. So, day by day we have to do our best to practice identity action. Because they are aware of how ignorant everyone is, bodhisattvas take a vow to practice identity action continually.

With a gentle expression, with a kind, compassionate attitude, we have to take care of our life and other people's lives. If we practice identity action, the other three methods of guidance are included. Very naturally we can practice giving, we can practice loving speech, we can practice beneficial action, we can really help others. Then we can fulfill our duty in life.

Notes

Zen in Daily Life
Silence
1. Miazawa Kenji, "November 3rd," in *From the Country of the Eight Islands*, trans. and ed. Hiroaki Sato and Burton Watson (New York: Anchor Press, 1981), pp. 505–506.

Singsapa Leaves
1. The six pāramitās or perfections that the bodhisattva practices are generosity, moral conduct, patience, courage, meditation and wisdom.
2. The Eightfold Path consists of right views, right intention, right speech, right action, right livelihood, right effort, right mindfulness and right concentration.

Thirsting Desire
1. Buddha's teaching of the four holy truths, or the Four Noble Truths, is as follows: Life is suffering; suffering is caused by craving; suffering can cease; the cessation of suffering comes about by following the Eightfold Path. (See note 2, "Singsapa Leaves," above.)

Sanzen Is Zazen
1. Bunnō Katō et al., trans., *The Threefold Lotus Sutra* (Tokyo: John Weatherhill, 1975), p. 319.

Breeze in the Sumi Painting
1. Ikkyū, untitled, trans. Dainin Katagiri.
2. Shōkin Furuta, *Zen No Hyōgen Bi*, trans. Dainin Katagiri.

Entrance to the Buddha Way
All Beings Are Buddha
1. The Triple Treasure is:
   > I take refuge in the Buddha.
   > I take refuge in the Dharma.
   > I take refuge in the Sangha.

   The Three Collective Pure Precepts are:
   > Refrain from all evil.
   > Practice all that is good.
   > Purify the mind.

   The Ten Prohibitory Precepts are:
   > Refrain from taking life.
   > Refrain from stealing.

Refrain from committing adultery.
Refrain from telling lies.
Refrain from using intoxicants.
Refrain from misguided speech.
Refrain from extolling oneself while slandering others.
Refrain from being avaricious in the bestowal of the Dharma.
Refrain from being angry.
Refrain from abusing the Triple Treasure.

2. Irving Babbitt, trans., *The Dhammapada* (New York: New Directions, 1965), p. 36. Copyright 1936 by Edward S. Babbitt and Esther B. Howe. Reprinted by permission of New Directions Publishing Corporation.

Repentance

1. Jacques Prévert, *To Paint the Portrait of the Bird*, trans. Lawrence Ferlinghetti (Garden City, N.Y.: Doubleday, 1971). Copyright 1949 Editions Gallimard.
2. The six senses (a), six sense organs (b), six sense objects (c), and five skandhas (d) are:

   a. Color, sound, smell, taste, touch, thoughts;
   b. Eyes, ears, nose, mouth, body, mind;
   c. Visual object, auditory object, taste object, object of smell, tactile object, object of thought;
   d. Form, feelings, perceptions, impulses, consciousness.

Buddhist Faith and Practice

Right Zazen

1. Dōgen, "Bendōwa," in *Shōbōgenzō*, trans. Abe Masao and Norman Waddell, *The Eastern Buddhist* 4, no. 1 (May 1971), p. 129.
2. Dōgen, "Bendōwa," p. 138.

Right Faith

1. Dōgen, "The Thirty-seven Practices Contributing to the Bodhisattva's Enlightenment," in *Shōbōgenzō*, trans. Dainin Katagiri.
2. Dōgen, "Immo," in *Shōbōgenzō*, trans. Thomas Cleary (Honolulu: The University of Hawaii Press, 1986), p. 52.
3. Dōgen, "Bendōwa," p. 138.
4. Ibid., p. 138.
5. Kazuaki Tanahashi, ed., Reb Anderson and Kazuaki Tanahashi, trans., "The Bodhisattva's Four Methods of Guidance," in *The Moon in a Dewdrop: Writings of Zen Master Dōgen* (San Francisco: North Point Press, 1985), p. 44.
6. Dōgen, in "Bendōwa," p. 139.

Right Teacher

1. Dōgen, "Bendōwa," p. 139.

To Live Is Just to Live

1. Dōgen, "Bendōwa," p. 140.
2. Ibid., p. 140.

3. Dōgen, "The King of Samadhis Samadhi," in *Shōbōgenzō*, trans. Abe Masao and Norman Waddell, *The Eastern Buddhist* 7, no. 1 (May 1974), p. 119–120.

4. Dōgen, "Bendōwa," in *Shōbōgenzō*, p. 141.

5. Ibid., p. 141.

Understanding Life and Death

1. Yūhō Yokoi, trans., "The Meaning of Practice and Enlightenment," in *Zen Master Dōgen* (Tokyo: John Weatherhill, 1976), p. 58.

2. Yūhō Yokoi, trans., "Points to Watch in Buddhist Training," in *Zen Master Dōgen* (Tokyo: John Weatherhill, 1976), p. 57.

The Ten Steps of Faith

1. Dōgen, "The Thirty-seven Practices Contributing to the Bodhisattva's Enlightenment," in *Shōbōgenzō*, trans. Dainin Katagiri.

Glossary

ABHIDHARMA (Skt.)   One of the three divisions of the Buddhist canon, among the oldest recorded works on the Buddha's teaching; it is a philosophical and psychological commentary on his sermons.

ADHIMUKTI (Skt.)   Trust or confidence.

AKĀSHA (Skt.)   Ether or space in the sense of the vastness of the sky; primordial space beyond description.

AMITABHA BUDDHA   The Buddha of Infinite Light, the personification of compassion; the central figure in the Pure Land sect of Buddhism.

ANCESTORS   Successors of the Buddha who continue to transmit his teachings.

ARHAT (Skt.)   Literally, a "worthy one"; a follower of the Buddha who has overcome personal desire and difficulties. In the oldest extant writings, the Buddha was called an Arhat.

ASHOKA (270–230 B.C.E.)   An emperor of India and a great Buddhist ruler; he engraved the moral precepts of Buddhism on rocks and pillars throughout his empire.

AVALOKITESHVARA BODHISATTVA   A bodhisattva whose name means "one who hearkens to the cries of the world." Masculine in some traditions and feminine in others, this great being is the embodiment of compassion.

BODHI (Skt.)   Enlightenment; the supreme wisdom that a follower of Buddha seeks.

BODHI-MIND   The thought of bodhi or enlightenment.

BODHISATTVA (Skt.)   A heroic being or spiritual warrior who is committed to the path of compassion. The bodhisattva's vow is to relinquish one's personal enlightenment in order to work for the enlightenment of others.

BODY-MIND   As the body and mind are not two separate entities, the hyphen signifies the identity of the two.

BUDDHA   Title or appellation derived from the root *budh*, "to awaken." A buddha (with a lowercase *b*) is any being who has experienced complete enlightenment. There were seven major Buddhas before the historical founder of Buddhism, Shākyamuni Buddha. The next Buddha will be named Maitreya.

BUDDHA-DHARMA   The teaching of the Buddha.

BUDDHA-NATURE   Our original nature; universal nature.

BUDDHA'S EYE   Universal seeing; seeing as a buddha would see.

DAI-JI (Jap.)   One of the diagrams concerned with dharma transmission, or secret teachings passed on from master to disciple.

DAIOSHŌ (Jap.)   Honorific title meaning "great priest."

DHARMA (Skt.)   When written with an uppercase *D*, this term means the teachings of the Buddha, the Law or Truth; with a lowercase *d*, it refers to phenomena or the phenomenal world.

DHYĀNA (Skt.)   Meditation; concentration; stability; fixity of mind. In Chinese this term is rendered as *ch'an* and in Japanese as *zen*.

DIAMOND SŪTRA   One of the most famous scriptures of Mahāyāna Buddhism, composed in the fourth century.

DŌAN (Jap.)   The person who leads the chanting and does the instrumentation during a Buddhist service.

DŌGEN ZENJI (1200–1253)   The founder of Sōtō Zen Buddhism in Japan.

EIGHTFOLD PATH   Eight attitudes making up a path which, if practiced, leads to nirvana, or enlightenment. They are right view, right thought, right speech, right action, right livelihood, right effort, right mindfulness, and right concentration. The Noble Eightfold Path is the fourth of the Four Noble Truths taught by the Buddha.

EISAI (1141–1215)   Japanese Buddhist monk who brought Rinzai Zen Buddhism from China to Japan. He also brought tea plants from China and thus is known as the father of Japanese tea.

EKO (Jap.)   The practice of transferring one's merits to others.

FA YEN (885–958)   The founder of the Fa Yen sect of Buddhism in China, which lasted about one hundred years.

GASSHŌ (Jap.)   A gesture or greeting of respect in which the hands, joined palm to palm with fingers extended, are held level with the upper chest or the lower part of the face. It symbolizes unity of body and mind.

GAZAN   A Sōtō Zen monk who lived three generations after Dōgen Zenji and who was the successor of Keizan Jōkin.

GOTŌ EGEN   Well-known historical records of Chinese Zen masters, in twenty-two volumes.

GUTEI   Japanese name for the ninth-century Chinese Zen master Chuchih.

GYOZAN EJAKU (d. 890)   A famous Tang dynasty Zen master.

HARA (Jap.)   A central area in the lower abdomen from which the breath comes during meditation. The hara is a point of balance and source of *ki*, or life-force energy.

HEART SŪTRA (Skt. Mahāprajñāpāramitā Hridaya Sūtra)   One of the shortest and most popular scriptures in Buddhism, concerning "the wisdom which has gone beyond." As the heart of the Prajñāpāramitā Sūtras, it is considered one of the greatest scriptures in the world.

Hosso   A school of Japanese Buddhism, also called the Mere Ideation school. Its chief object was to investigate the qualities and nature of all existences.

HUI CH'AO   Successor of Fa Yen.

INTERDEPENDENT CO-ORIGINATION   Also called dependent origination (Skt. *pratītya-samutpāda*) or the twelvefold chain of causation. It describes the process of being coming into existence and continuing to exist in the mundane world.

JAKUJŌ (Jap.)   Complete tranquillity. *Jaku* means "there is no one with whom you want to talk," and *jo* means "serenity" or "imperturbability."

JAKU MOKU (Jap.)   A Japanese rendering of a Chinese word describing *muni* (Skt. for "sage"), the second part of the name Shākyamuni. The Japanese word connotes tranquillity and silence.

JIJUYŪ SAMĀDHI   The state of consciousness of a fully enlightened person. *Jijuyū* is a Japanese term for someone who has awakened to the truth and who uses the joy of this awakening for the benefit of others. *Samādhi* is a Sanskrit term for the highest state of concentration.

JU-CHING (1163–1228)   Dōgen Zenji's teacher in China, under whom he attained enlightenment. He is known as Tendō Nyojō in Japanese.

KALPA (Skt.)   In Hindu chronology, 4,320 million years, or an infinitely long period of time; the time it takes the universe to expand and contract.

KANNŌ DŌKŌ (Jap.)   Literally, "appeal and response crossing very quickly," or wholeheartedness.

KARMA (Skt.)   Action; result or effect of action. The doctrine that one's present experience is a product of previous actions and volitions, and that future conditions depend on what one does in the present.

KASANA (Skt).   A split-second; an Indian unit of time equaling one sixty-fifth of a second.

KEGON   A major school of Buddhism, known in China as Hua Yen. *Kegon* means "flower ornament." It is also the name of a major scripture

(Skt. Avatamsaka Sūtra) recounting the teachings of the Buddha soon after his enlightenment.

KEIZAN JŌKIN (1268–1325) A famous Japanese Zen master who became a monk under Dōgen Zenji's disciple Koun Ejo. He founded Sōji-ji, one of the two main monasteries of Sōtō Buddhism in Japan today.

KENDŌ (Jap.) Fencing performed with bamboo swords.

KINHIN (Jap.) Slow walking meditation done between periods of formal sitting meditation. Kinhin helps loosen up the legs while the practitioner maintains the meditative state of mind.

KŌAN (Jap.; Chin. *kung-an*) Literally, "public document." In Rinzai Buddhism a kōan is a statement or question that cannot be understood or resolved intellectually, e.g., "What is the sound of one hand clapping?" Meditation on a kōan leads one to transcend the intellect and experience the nondual nature of reality.

KOROMO (Jap.) Outer robe worn by Zen Buddhist monks, originally from China.

KOTI (Jap.) An astronomical number, sometimes meaning ten million, sometimes one hundred million.

LOTUS SŪTRA (Skt. Saddharma Pundarīka Sūtra) A scripture of the second century, one of the most important documents of Mahāyāna Buddhism; it teaches the attainability of enlightenment by everyone, the importance of faith, and the compassion of the bodhisattva way.

MAHĀYĀNA The School of the Great Vehicle; also known as the Northern School, as it spread to Tibet, Mongolia, Korea, and Japan. Mahāyāna emphasizes the inclusion of everyone (lay people and priests, men and women) as followers of the Buddha and as being able to realize perfect enlightenment.

MAITREYA The future Buddha; his name means "friendliness" or "loving-kindness."

MANTRA (Skt.) Mystical invocation used in some Buddhist schools, including the Shingon school in Japan and Tantric Buddhism in Tibet. The sounds of mantras, not the meanings, are the basis for their mystical power.

MIND With an uppercase *M*, the term refers to that Mind which is in complete accord with the truth of the universe; with a lowercase *m*, it means our ordinary mundane mind, which is not in accord with the vast universal quality of life. The Mind has transcended self; the mind clings tenaciously to the idea of self.

MONKEY MIND The mind that is always chasing after objects of desire, hopping about from one thing to another.

MUDRĀ (Skt.) A symbolic body posture or hand gesture. Its power lies in the actual posture itself as a means to communicate the quality of truth.

NAMO (Skt.) Full devotion, or the "throwing away" of body and mind.

NAMU; namu kie (Jap.) To take refuge.

NIRVĀNA (Skt.) The original meaning of this term is to "blow out or extinguish because of lack of fuel" (i.e., desire). Nirvana is the cessation of ignorance and union with the Truth or transcendence of duality. It is sometimes referred to as the state of enlightenment achieved by the Buddha.

NONEXISTENT Rather than referring to "no existence," this term means "beyond any conceptualization of existence."

NONTHINKING Condition in which there is no recognition of awareness of not-thinking. Even the experience of enlightenment has dropped away or been transcended. Nonthinking is true emptiness.

NO-PERSON Condition prior to conceptualization of self or the arising of "I" and "mine."

NO-SOUND Condition prior to conceptualization of sound or no-sound, i.e., prior to hearing either sound or silence. The term does not mean silence.

NOT-THINKING Experience of existence prior to conceptualization; however, mind still consciously recognizes or attaches to this experience.

ŌBAKU (d. 850) Japanese name for Chinese Buddhist monk Huang-po, the teacher of Rinzai (Lin-chi), founder of the Rinzai school.

ONE-POINTEDNESS The state of being precisely present in the moment; the ability to focus or hold attention on the task at hand without being distracted.

ONE VEHICLE The teaching of the Lotus Sūtra, which expounds that all beings—ordinary people and saints, men and women, laity and priests—can become enlightened. This was a revolutionary teaching in its time, as women and lay followers had been considered incapable of achieving buddhahood.

PARAMITA (Skt.) Highest condition; highest point; perfection. In Mahāyāna Buddhism, the six perfections practiced by bodhisattvas: generosity, moral conduct, patience, courage, meditation, and wisdom.

PRAJÑĀ (Skt.) Transcendental wisdom which transcends the duality of subject and object.

PRASĀDHA (Skt.) To grow clear and bright, or to become tranquil. The verb root is *sād*, "to sink down." Thus one becomes firmly settled in clarity and tranquillity.

PRATYEKA (Skt.) One who attains enlightenment by his or her own efforts (without the guidance of a master) and who does not wish to guide others to enlightenment.

RINZAI (d. 866/67) Known as Lin-chi in Chinese, he was a disciple of Huang Po and founded the Rinzai school of Zen Buddhism in Japan.

ROSHI Japanese title meaning "venerable old teacher." In America, *roshi* has come to be synonymous with "Zen master."

RYŪTAN SŌSHIN A great Zen master of the minth century, known in China as Lung-t'an.

SADDHARMA PUNDARĪKA *See* Lotus Sūtra; One Vehicle

SAMĀDHI (SKT.) The highest state of concentration or experience of unity or nonduality; the one-pointed state of mind.

SAMSĀRA (Skt.) Literally, "stream of becoming"; the world of change, of unsatisfactoriness. Samsāra is reflected in the condition of our usual daily life, in which the main focus is perpetuation of self (ego).

SANGHA (Skt.) During the time of the Buddha, the assembly of monks and nuns; today, according to Mahāyāna thought, the term refers to the community of all followers of the Buddha Way, whether lay or priest.

SANZEN (Jap.) In Rinzai Zen, the face-to-face encounter with the master concerning the depth of one's practice. In Sōto Zen, sanzen is zazen.

SAWAKI KODO ROSHI (1880–1965) A famous Sōtō Zen monk who shunned any form of institutionalization and who never had his own temple. He traveled extensively throughout Japan to teach zazen.

SELF-DELUSION Sense of self as separate from its object and fixed in nature. It is called delusion because in deep meditation the Buddha realized that there is no fixed entity whatsoever, that everything is in a state of constant change, and that self and other are therefore not separate things.

SESSHIN (Jap.) Literally, "to gather or collect the mind" (which is usually scattered). An intensive silent retreat, lasting for from two to seven days, in which most of the day, from early morning to late evening, is spent meditating.

SHĀKYA The clan or tribe from which Shākyamuni ("Sage of the Shākyas") came.

SHĀKYAMUNI BUDDHA The historical founder of Buddhism, Gautama Siddhārtha, who at the age of thirty-five experienced complete enlightenment and whose teachings for the next forty-five years were based on his experience of "I am enlightened simultaneously with all sentient beings."

SHĀRIPUTRA   One of the major disciples of the Buddha; also known as Upatissa.

SHIKAN TAZA (Jap.)   "Just sitting." *Shikan* is "wholeheartedness," *ta* means "hit," and *za* means "zazen." From moment to moment we have to hit the bull's-eye of zazen.

SHIN BUDDHISM   Also known as the Pure Land school; its founder in China (White Lotus sect, founded c. 400 C.E.) was Hui Yuan (334–416) and in Japan was Hōnen (1133–1211).

SHINGON   The Japanese Buddhist "School of the True Word," established in Japan c. 806 C.E. by Kōbō Daishi. Its practice involves extensive use of ritual, mantras, and hand mudrās. Ultimate reality is personified as Vairocana, the Cosmic Buddha.

SHINTO   The indigenous religion of Japan, known as the Way of the Gods. Its followers worship nature and their ancestors.

SHŌBŌGENZŌ   The masterwork of Dōgen Zenji; the title translates as "The Treasury of the True Dharma Eye." It consists of ninety-five fascicles or books composed between 1231 and 1253 C.E.

SHRADDĀ (Skt.)   Faith; remaining steadfast.

SHRĀVAKA (Skt.)   Originally, the name of a disciple of the Buddha who heard the Buddha's teaching directly. By extension the term in Mahāyāna Buddhism means a "listener" or "hearer," a follower of the Buddha Way who is unconcerned about the enlightenment of others.

SIDDHĀRTHA GAUTAMA   *See* Shākyamuni Buddha.

SILA (Skt.)   Moral precepts; virtue. Sometimes also referred to as discipline, sila is one of the original group of three practices in spiritual progress, along with wisdom and concentration.

SINGSAPA   A variety of tree growing in India.

SKANDHA (Skt.)   The five skandhas are the conditioned, ever-changing physical and mental forces that form a being or individual. They are classified as form, feeling, perception, impulse, and consciousness. According to the Buddha's deep insight, these transient groups make up one's sense of "I," and apart from them there is no fixed self.

SŌTŌ   One of the two main schools of Zen Buddhism, founded by Dōgen Zenji. Its main practice is shikana taza. The other major school is Rinzai.

SŌ TŌBA   A Chinese layman who was enlightened when he heard the sound of water flowing in a valley stream at night.

SUMI   Chinese and Japanese method of painting and calligraphy using a brush on rice paper or silk. Only dark brown or black ink is used.

SŪTRA (Skt.) Literally, "a thread on which jewels are strung." In the Theravādin tradition the sūtra is a text forming part of the Pali canon and containing the oral teachings of the Buddha. In Mahāyāna Buddhism, sūtras are not necessarily the actual transmitted words of the Buddha, but are his teachings.

SU TUNG P'O *See* Sō Tōba.

SUZUKI ROSHI (Suzuki Shunryū; 1905–1971) A Sōtō Zen priest who founded San Francisco Zen Center.

TAKUHATSU (Jap.) Ritual begging practiced by mendicant Buddhist monks in Japan, a tradition handed down by the Buddha.

TAN PAN KAN (Jap.) Literally, "a person carrying a board"; a metaphor for a person with a narrow view of life, able to see only one side.

TANTRA The Vajrayāna school of Buddhism. Tantric practice involves symbolic ritual, mantras, mudrās, and mandalas (symbolic diagrams). It spread from India to Tibet and China in the 6th century and then to Japan as the Shingon school.

TATAMI (Jap.) A thick straw mat used in Japan as a floor covering or in meditation halls on raised sitting platforms (tans). The usual size of a tatami is three by six feet.

TATHĀGATA (Skt.) A title for the Buddha, meaning "thus come" or "thus gone," which has the sense of "neither coming or going."

TENNŌ DŌGO (738/48–807) A famous Chinese Zen master, known in Chinese as T'ien-huang Tao-wu.

TEN PROHIBITORY PRECEPTS Precepts taken by lay or monk ordinands. They are abstaining from killing; telling falsehoods; committing unchaste sexual acts; harboring hatred, malice, or ill will; extolling the self while slandering others; dealing with intoxicants or drugs; taking what is not given; being avaricious in the bestowal of the Buddha's teachings; speaking ill of others; and denouncing the Triple Treasure.

TENRYŪ Ninth-century Chinese Zen master, known in China as Hang-chou T'ien-lung. He always held up one finger when asked about the teachings of the Buddha or about enlightenment. Zen Master Gutei asked him what the fundamental word of Zen was. Tenryu held up one finger, and Gutei was immediately enlightened.

THERAVĀDA Literally, "the Way of the Elders." Sometimes referred to as Hīnayāna (lesser vehicle), it is one of the three main divisions of Buddhism, Mahāyāna and Vajrayāna being the others.

THREE COLLECTIVE PURE PRECEPTS "With purity of heart, I vow to abstain from the unwholesome, with purity of heart I vow to do the wholesome, with purity of heart, I vow to benefit all beings."

TRIPLE TREASURE   Buddha, Dharma (the teachings or the Truth), and Sangha (followers of the Buddha Way).

VULTURE PEAK   A hill in northeastern India given to the Buddha as a retreat place for his followers.

THE WAY   The path or daily life of the buddhas and Buddhist practitioners. The way of enlightenment.

THE WAY-MIND   The mind that has returned to its original nature, that of serenity and tranquillity.

ZAZEN (Jap.)   Sitting meditation.

ZEN (Jap.)   A Chinese and Japanese school of Buddhism whose main emphasis is zazen or sitting meditation. *Zen* is the Japanese rendition of the Chinese word *ch'an*, which comes from the Sanskrit *dhyāna*, meaning "meditation" or "concentration."

ZENDŌ (Jap.)   A hall in a monastery used for sitting meditation. If practitioners also eat and sleep there, it is called a sōdō.

ZENJI (Jap.)   An honorific title, literally "Zen master" or "teacher." It is used only for the greatest Zen teachers.

Index

Abhidharma, 11, 97, 179
acceptance, 118, 135–136; of buddha, 69–71; of compassion, 73–75
action, and emptiness, 26; and experience, 64–65; and faith, 53, 106–107; forms of, 24–26, 64–65
action, beneficial, 164–170, 172–173; and compassion, 166–167; examples of, 167; and giving, 164–170; and kind speech, 164, 165–170; two kinds of, 164
action, identity, 170–174; and Buddha-dharma, 172–173; and existence, 171–174; gasshō as, 172; and ignorance, 173, 174; and oneness, 170–174
adhimukti, 138, 179
Adults' Day, 60
akāsha, 82, 179
aloneness, 130–131
Amitabha Buddha, 179
anger, 15, 17, 23–24
appeal, 82–83. See also response
Arhat, 179
arrogance, 15
Ashoka, King, 154, 179
aspiration, 140
attachment, 53, 73. See also desire
attitude, 156
Avalokiteshvara, 46–48, 58, 179
awakening, 98, 107. See also mindfulness

beneficial action. See action, beneficial
bodhi. See enlightenment
bodhi-mind, 89, 143, 179
bodhisattva, 20, 29, 86, 87, 130, 135, 179

"The Bodhisattva's Four Methods of Guidance," 145–174
body-mind, 148–149, 151, 155–156
bowing, 154
breathing, 123
buddha, 179–180; acceptance of, 67–71; as category of existence, 86–87; and experience, 62–63
Buddha, 9, 179–180; in daily life, 9; and ethical worth, 85–86; and intellectual worth, 84–85; refuge in, 79–80, 143; and spiritual worth, 86–87
Buddha Way, ritual for entering, 67–95
Buddha-dharma, 39, 180; and beneficial action, 166–167; and identity action, 172–173; and right faith, 100; and zazen, 97, 124
Buddha-life, 54–57
Buddha-nature, 180; and emptiness, 11–12; and impermanence, 9–13; precepts as, 78, 92; and Sangha, 80–81; and Truth, 93; and zazen, 12
Buddha's eye, 5–6, 7, 180
Buddhism, as a concept, 121; practice of, 115–129; and process of zazen, 121; as psychology, 98; purpose of, 95; as religion, 98; and right faith, 100–108. See also Zen Buddhism

causation, law of, 50–51, 89–90, 91, 149–150
cessation, 20; of suffering, 21–22
change. See impermanence
chanting, 120
Ching-k'ang, 167
clarity, 129–131

commitment, 68

communication, 124, 127

compassion, 70; acceptance of, 73–75; Avalokiteshvara, 46–48, 179; and beneficial action, 166–167; and faith, 104; and living, 3–4; and reality, 46–48; and repentance, 72–75; and ritual, 77; and suffering, 4; and wisdom, 6

conceptualization, and duality, 44–46; and faith, 102, 140; and reality, 46; and suffering, 47

consciousness, 31, 109–110, 119, 142; and serenity, 13–15; and unconsciousness, 13; and zazen, 55–56. *See also* ego-consciousness; self-consciousness

covetousness, 147–148

culture. *See* ritual

dai ji, 110, 180

death, 36–37; and Buddha-life, 56–57; and daily living, 37–39; and desire, 30; and emptiness, 25; impermanence of life, 133–137; and intimacy, 60–61; and life dualism, 19, 94, 132–137; and tathāgata, 34–35, 39, 186; and Ten Prohibitory Precepts, 92–93, 94; and wholeheartedness, 134; and zazen, 115. *See also* impermanence; life

desire, 15, 142; accepting into daily life, 33–34; and death, 30; as a holy truth, 33; kinds of, 32–33; suffering and, 30–34. *See also* attachment

devotion, 79, 183

Dhammapada, 69–70

Dharma, 30, 180; and actualized realization, 86; and art, 87; and daily life, 9; and ethical worth, 86; and faith, 138; and intellectual worth, 85; as law, 80; and mindfulness, 29–30; protection of, 142; refuge in, 79, 80, 143; and spiritual worth, 87; transmission, 108–109, 110–111

dhyāna, 98–99, 180. *See also* zazen

Diamond Sūtra, 115–116, 180

differentiation, 172

discipline, 61, 141–142

dispassion, 20

dōan, 72, 180

Dōgen Zenji, 180; on clarity and purity, 135; on flow process of human world, 44; on the four methods of guidance, 145–159; on knowledge, 58; on practice-enlightenment, 132, 133; on right faith, 100, 101, 104, 106, 107; on the right teacher, 108; on shikan taza, 126; on teaching, 127; on zazen, 97, 99, 116, 118–119, 124

dogmatism, 89

doubt, 15, 89–90

dualism, 64–65; of Buddhism, 55–57; and conceptualization, 44–46; life/death, 19, 94, 132–137; and repentance, 72; of self and nature, 171; and suffering, 146. *See also* oneness

effort, 61, 141; and selfishness, 9

ego-consciousness, 15; and judgment, 14; and nonthinking, 28; and Way-mind, 13–15; and zazen, 14. *See also* consciousness; self-consciousness; selfishness

egolessness, 74, 77, 90

Eightfold Path, 22, 175, 180

Eisai Zenji, 97, 181

eko, 142, 180

emptiness, 20, 49–57, 59, 163; and action, 26; and Buddha-nature, 11–12; and death, 25; and distractions, 52; and existence, 142; and law of causation, 50–51; and moments, 11–12; and reality, 48; and truth, 112; and zazen, 52–53

enlightenment (bodhi), 14, 58, 59, 107–108, 117–119, 161; and zazen, 128. *See also* knowing

equality, 57, 172

existence, and emptiness, 142; and experience, 173–174; and faith, 138–139; and identity action, 172; nature of, 160–161; and nonexis-

tence, 85–86; pure nature of, 54–57; purpose of, 114–115, 171; and silence, 39–44. *See also* reality
experience, and action, 64–65; and attachment, 73; and buddha, 62–63; and existence, 173–174; and form, 64–65

Fa Yen, 62, 63, 180
faith, and action, 53, 106–107; and clarity, 129–131; and compassion, 104; and conceptualization, 102, 140; and Dharma, 138; and existence, 138–139; meanings of, 138; and oneness, 100; and practice, 129; and purity, 131–132; and realization, 129; right, 100–108; ten steps of, 138–143; and tranquillity, 100–103; and Triple Treasure, 84; and trust, 43; and zazen, 43–44, 48
fearlessness, 145–147
feelings, 31, 35–36, 150–151
form, 31, and action, 24–26, 64–65; in daily life, 60; and experience, 64–65; and intimacy, 61
Four Noble Truths, 175

gasshō, 180; as identity action, 172
Gazan Zenji, 45–46, 180
Gensho Ogura, 70
genuineness, 41, 42, 43
giving, 61, 145–159; as beneficial action, 164–170; Dharma, 145, 147; fearlessness, 145–147; materials, 145, 155; to oneself, 156; three kinds of, 145; and zazen, 150–152, 155–157, 158
Gonmyo (Zen Master), 127
Gotō Egen, 162, 180
greediness, 147. *See also* desire; ego-consciousness; selfishness
guidance, beneficial action, 164–170; four methods of, 145–174; giving, 145–159; identity action, 170–174; kind speech, 159–164
Gutei (Zen Master), 35, 38–39, 180

Gyozan Ejaku (Zen Master), 162–163, 181

happiness, 4–5, 133, 136–137, 151
hara, 105, 180, 181
hatred, 17, 136
Hayashi Roshi, 49–50
health, 133
Heart Sūtra, 58, 181
helping, 67, 68–69, 71
Hesse, Hermann, 125
Hosso, 97, 181
Hui ch'ao, 62, 181
human nature, 114–115

identity action. *See* action, identity
ignorance, 15, 17, 18, 126; and identity action, 173–174; and radical suffering, 32
Ikkyu Zenji, 64
impermanence, 36–37, 89–90, 91; and Buddha-nature, 9–13; and the moment, 10–12; as truth, 68–69; and zazen, 14–15. *See also* death; life
Infinite Thought Bodhisattva, 47–48
interdependent co-origination, 181
intimacy, 59–62; and death, 60–61; and form, 61; and ritual, 60–61. *See also* oneness
iron man, 110–111, 114

jaku moku, 74, 181
jakujō, 100, 181
jijuyū samādhi, 108, 118–121, 181
Ju ching (Zen Master), 124, 181

kalpas, 115–116, 181
kannō dōkō (wholeheartedness), 75, 83, 181
Kapilavatthu, 16
karma, 181
karmic retribution, 50, 51
kasana, 181
Kegon, 97, 181
Keizan Jōkin, 45–46, 182
kendō, 124, 182
killing, 92–93, 94

"The King of Samādhis Samādhi," 124
kinhin, 182
Kishizawa Roshi, 110–111
knowing, 57–59. *See also* enlightenment
knowledge, 68, 69
kōan, 122, 124, 182
Komazawa University, 43, 105, 106
koromos, 119, 182
koti, 182
ksansas, 11

life, 36–37; clarity and purity in, 135;
   and daily living, 37–39; and death
   dualism, 19, 94, 132–137; impermanence of, 133–137; and tathāgata,
   34–35, 39, 186; and zazen, 115. *See
   also* death; impermanence
loneliness, 130
lotus posture, 27
Lotus Sūtra, 46–48, 103, 163, 182

Magadha, 16
Mahāyāna Buddhism, 28–30, 118
Maitreya, 130, 182
mantras, 119, 182
meditation, and appreciation, 4. *See
   also* zazen
Miazawa Kenji, 7–8
Middle Way, 28–30, 150
Mind, 13, 187; serenity and tranquillity, 13–15
mindfulness, 28–30, 79, 93, 140–141
monkey mind, 123, 126, 143, 182
morality, 88–89
mysticism, 130

namu kie, 79, 183
Nara, 49
nirvāna, 21, 22, 161, 183
Nishiari Roshi, 110
nonexistence, 183; and existence,
   85–86
no-nin, 74
nonthinking, 27–28, 60, 183
no-person, 183
no-sound, 39–40, 43, 183

nothingness, 114
nuclear weapons, 17, 18, 19, 22–24;
   freeze, 20, 21

Ōbaku (Zen Master), 153, 154, 183
occasion, 104–105
one finger, 34–39
One Vehicle, 103, 183
oneness, 59, 129; and faith, 100; and
   identity action, 170–174. *See also*
   dualism; intimacy
one-pointedness, 183
optimism, and pessimism, 1, 3–4, 5, 6

Pai Lo-tien, 170
pain, 5. *See also* silence; suffering
paramitas, 20, 61–62, 81–82, 175, 183
patience, 61
peace, 15–18, 22–24, 67, 70–71, 88;
   and anger, 23–24; and zazen, 16,
   17, 18
perception, 31
perfection, 131–132, 135, 146
pessimism, and optimism, 1, 3–4, 5, 6
politics, 20, 22–23
practice, and faith, 129; of faith, 138–
   143; of giving, 145–159; undefiled, 94
prajñā paramita, 58, 183
prasādha, 138, 183
pratyeka buddhas, 86, 87, 184
prayer, 82, 98–99
Prévert, Jacques, 75–78
psychology, 13, 98
purity, and faith, 131–132; and wholeheartedness, 134

reality, and clarity, 129–131; and compassion, 46–48; and conceptualization, 46; and emptiness, 48. *See also*
   existence
realization, actualized, 86; and faith,
   129; and knowledge, 69
religion, awakened, 98, 107; and communication, 127; revealed, 98, 107;
   stages of practice, 117–119
repentance, 67, 71–78

response, 82–83. *See also* appeal
Rinzai Zen Buddhism, 97, 184
Rinzai (Zen Master), 33, 34, 153
ritual, in action, 75–78; and attitude, 61; and compassion, 77; for entering Buddha Way, 67–95; and intimacy, 60–61; of repentance, 71–72, 75–78; and Zen practice, 25
Ryūtan Sōshin, 149, 184

samādhi, 29, 61, 74, 77, 184
samsāra, 184
Sangha, 54, 88, 184; and Buddha-nature, 80–81; and ethical worth, 86; and intellectual worth, 85; refuge in, 79, 80–81, 143; and spiritual worth, 87–88
sanzen, 45–48, 184
Sawaki Kodo Roshi, 43, 186
self, and happiness, 4–5
self-awakening, 107
self-consciousness, 125. *See also* consciousness; ego-consciousness
self-delusion, 15, 139, 184
selfishness, 13, 15, 89, 90. *See also* desire; ego-consciousness; greed
self-knowledge, 11–13, 58–59
Senri Uyeno, 1
senses, 76, 176
serenity, and consciousness, 13–15; and enlightenment, 14; and zazen, 15. *See also* tranquillity
Shākya, 184
Shākyamuni Buddha, 15–17, 30, 46–47, 63, 74–75, 79–80, 98, 99, 184; life of, 30, 170–171; teachings of, 40–41
Shāriputra, 103, 185
shikan taza, 53, 99, 116, 121–122, 123–124, 126, 128, 146, 185. *See also* zazen
Shin Buddhism, 185
Shingon, 116, 185
Shinto, 130, 185
Shōbōgenzō, 145, 185
shraddhā, 138, 185
shrāvaka buddhas, 86, 87, 184

"Shushogi," 132
sickness, 31. *See also* pain; suffering
Siddhārtha Gautama. *See* Shākyamuni Buddha
Siddhārtha (Hesse), 125
sila, 91, 185
silence, 1–9, 39–44; and Buddha's eye, 5–6; and existence, 39–44; flavors of, 1; mystical, 3, 5, 6; optimistic and pessimistic, 1, 3–4, 5, 6; and personality, 7; and zazen, 40. *See also* pain; suffering
simplicity, 44, 72–73
singsapa leaves, 19, 185
skandhas, 31, 76, 176, 185
Sō Tōba. *See* Su Tung p'o
Sōtō Zen, 24, 109, 111, 122, 124, 185
speech, kind, 159–164; and beneficial action, 164, 165–170; and compassion, 160, 162–164
stubbornness, 157
Su Tung p'o, 87, 185, 186
suffering, 8–9, 127–129; cause of, 21; cessation of, 21–22; and compassion, 4; and conceptualization, 47; conditions of, 21; and desire, 30–34; and dualism, 146; as a holy truth, 30–34; inception of, 83–84; mental, 31; physical, 31; radical, 31–32; and zazen, 32. *See also* pain; silence
Sumi painting, 63–65, 185
sūtras, 43, 44, 72, 186
Suzuki Roshi, 33, 137, 186

takuhatsu, 3, 186
tan pan kan, 28, 186
Tantric Buddhism, 97, 119–120, 186
tathāgatha, 34–35, 39, 140, 186
tea ceremony, Japanese, 134
teacher, teaching, 108–115, 124–129, 145
Ten Prohibitory Precepts, 67, 91–95, 175–176, 186
Tennō Dōgo, 149, 186
Tenryū (Zen Master), 38, 39, 186
Theravāda Buddhism, 29, 186
thinking, 27. *See also* nonthinking

Three Collective Pure Precepts, 67,
88–91, 175, 186
three refuges. *See* Triple Treasure
"To Paint the Portrait of the Bird"
(Prévert), 75–78
tranquillity, 13–15, 21; and enlightenment, 14; and faith, 100–103; and
sanzen, 44; and the unconditioned,
102. *See also* serenity
Triple Treasure, 67, 78–88, 90–91,
143, 175, 187; and ethical worth,
85–86; and faith, 84; and intellectual worth, 84–85; refuge in Buddha, 79–80, 90–91, 143; refuge in
Dharma, 79, 80, 90–91, 143; refuge
in Sangha, 79, 80–81, 90–91, 143;
and spiritual worth, 86–88. *See also*
Buddha; Dharma; Sangha
Truth, 59, 175; and Buddha-nature,
93; and emptiness, 112; four holy,
30–34; and precepts, 92; realization
of, 67–70; and right faith, 100

undefiled practice, 94
universal life, 3, 56, 160–161

vow, living in, 91–95, 142–143
Vulture Peak, 104, 187

war, 17. *See also* nuclear weapons
Way, 13, 97, 187; attaining the, 106–
107; life and death in the, 135
Way-mind, 13, 187; and ego-
consciousness, 13–15
wholeheartedness, 83, 99, 106; and
death, 134; and purity, 134. *See also*
kanno doko
wisdom, 61, 141; and compassion, 6;
and the Middle Way, 29; perfect, 21;
and zazen, 6
world, ten categories of the, 86–87

Yang-pao, 167
Yokoi Roshi, 163, 168

zazen, 6, 187; and body-mind, 155–
156; and Buddha-dharma, 39, 97,
180; and Buddha-life, 54–57; and
Buddha-nature, 12; and consciousness, 55–56; and ego-consciousness,
14; and emptiness, 52–53; as an end
in itself, 97, 98; and enlightenment,
128; and faith, 43–44, 48; and fearlessness, 146; form of, 56; as fourth
step of faith, 141; and genuineness,
42, 43; and giving, 150–152, 155–
157, 158; and impermanence, 14–
15; as jijuyū samādhi, 118–121; and
knowing, 59; and life and death,
115; and mindfulness, 29; misuse of,
41, 42, 43; nonthinking in, 27–28,
183; and occasion, 104–105; and
peace, 16, 17, 18; posture in, 27;
practicing, 99–100, 105, 121–122,
123–124, 137; results of, 52–53;
right, 97–100; sanzen as, 45–48;
and serenity, 15; and silence, 40;
sleeping in, 6; and suffering, 32; and
wisdom, 6; and Zen life, 25. *See also*
dhyana; meditation; shikan taza
Zen Buddhism, 97, 187; and daily
living, 109; truth and, 112. *See also*
Buddhism
Zen practice, in daily life, 24–26; and
ritual, 25
Zen teaching, and profit, 19–20
zendōs, 71, 187